THE
London Gardener
GUIDE AND SOURCEBOOK

THE London Gardener
GUIDE AND SOURCEBOOK

Elspeth Thompson

Drawings by Jean Sturgis

FRANCES LINCOLN

CONTENTS

For Clarkey and Simon –
my favourite London
gardeners – and all urban
gardeners everywhere

Frances Lincoln Ltd
4 Torriano Mews
Torriano Avenue
London NW5 2RZ
www.franceslincoln.com

The London Gardener
Copyright © Frances Lincoln Ltd, 2004
Text copyright © Elspeth Thompson, 2004
Drawings copyright © Jean Sturgis, 2004

Designed by Becky Clarke
Index by Valerie Chandler

First Frances Lincoln edition, 2004

A CIP catalogue record for this book is
available from the British Library.

ISBN 0 7112 2259 2

Printed and bound in Singapore

9 8 7 6 5 4 3 2 1

INTRODUCTION

When I first started gardening in London, just over twenty years ago, it seemed like a compromise. The window ledges, rooftops and balconies in Brixton, Finsbury Park and Bloomsbury where I cut my gardening teeth were initially a stopgap for when I would get my first 'proper' garden. I grew plants up walls when I ran out of space and raised seedlings in the back of my ancient VW camper van because I didn't have a greenhouse. And when, eight years ago, I finally became the owner of the tiny Brixton backyard that grew into the garden I still have today, I figured it would be good for a few years before I made my much-dreamed-of getaway to the country. But something had happened over the decades. Far from making do, I realized that I relished the challenges and rewards of gardening in the city. I love planting up an eccentric jumble of containers and shifting them about to create different effects throughout the year. I enjoy using mirrors to increase the feeling of light and space, and scavenging skip finds and junk shop treasures to give my gardens character. I am thrilled when ladybirds colonize my rose bushes and a blackbird chooses my window box in which to make her nest. And I love the way my narrow strip of front garden can give something back to the street. These small urban spaces are manageable: the weeding and pruning never get on top of me and I know where all the slugs and snails hide. They are sociable, too: at the two Dulwich allotments where I grow my own organic fruit and vegetables, I have learned much more from my fellow plot-holders than I ever would alone in the country, armed only with books.

My story is, I'm sure, echoed by many other London gardeners. Over the years we have become passionate about our small city spaces, our havens of green in the heart of the metropolis. Perhaps we *need* our gardens more than gardeners in the country, surrounded by wall-to-wall natural greenery, need theirs. Whatever the reason, we certainly treasure them – and we enjoy gleaning ideas and inspiration from other London gardens and gardeners. The queues that form whenever a new London back garden opens to the public through the National Gardens Scheme speak for themselves. Inspiration is all around us. We Londoners are lucky to have such a treasure-trove of historic parks and gardens, smart city squares, wildlife and community gardens on our doorstep. Sometimes we take them for granted, but it only takes a trip to another city – such as New York or Milan, where green space is at a premium – to remind us of our good fortune. More Londoners have their own gardens than in practically any other large city in the world. And when we step outside our front doors, what pleasures we have close to hand! We can marvel at the rare plants and Victorian palm houses at Kew, take a walk on the wild side in a nature reserve just a stone's throw from a busy railway terminus, walk through Hyde Park at midnight and smell the roses beneath a full moon. Looking up and around us on our busy way about town, we realize how small details such as window boxes outside hotels, bright seasonal bedding in central reservations – even the filigree patterns of bare plane trees against a winter sky – all add to our enjoyment of living in this great city. On top of all this, London is home to some of the best garden centres, specialist shops and suppliers, garden designers, training schools and horticultural societies in the country.

The idea of this book is to bring together all these different strands of gardening in the capital. The opening section deals with the particularities of gardening in London: the challenges of shade, polluted clay soil and lack of space, peace and privacy. It aims to provide ideas for overcoming the problems and creating the garden of your dreams, whether this is a haven for meditation, a living larder brimming with organic salad crops or an outdoor room for all the family that can accommodate children's games, *al fresco* eating and evening parties with equal ease and style. For those with really minimal space, there are tips on indoor gardening, window-ledge edibles and how to get involved in community gardening. At the end of most of the chapters are lists of places in London to look for inspiration on that particular subject – Knightsbridge and the Barbican for window boxes, for instance, or Mile End Park and the Water Gardens in Edgware Road for water features.

The second section takes the form of a tour through the different parts of the capital and the variety of parks, gardens, squares and other horticultural treats they have to offer, from Osterley Park to Canary Wharf and beyond. Community gardens and quirky hidden corners are often given as much space as the better-known parks and historical gardens – partly on the basis that many of the latter already have books and guidebooks devoted to them. And in the case of the famous parks such as Hyde Park and Regent's Park, I have veered away from historical detail to concentrate instead on the lesser-known areas and 'gardens within gardens' that remain undiscovered by many visitors. To keep to the gardening theme, I have excluded most of the wilder heaths, commons, churchyards and cemeteries, unless they contain cultivated areas of specific horticultural interest.

The final section comprises a directory of garden centres, markets, specialist shops and suppliers, garden designers and maintenance people, gardening courses and societies. The intention is that, whether you are looking for a supplier of lead-look planters, a good tree surgeon, a source of organic horse manure or your local RHS-affiliated gardening society, you'll find what you want within these pages. Though I have endeavoured to cover most areas, and have included many people and places that come personally recommended, a book of this size cannot claim to be fully comprehensive. So if you are disappointed not to find your favourite local park, garden centre or specialist supplier listed, don't hesitate to send in the details, and we will do our best to include them in a future edition.

The aim has been to produce a book that will be useful both to Londoners who live and garden here *and* to visitors from other cities and parts of the world, who will be able to adapt parts of section one to their own circumstances, and benefit from the first London guide specifically geared to the needs and interests of gardeners. The decision was made not to include maps, so arm yourself with the miniature copy of the London A–Z (adequate for all but the gardens on the outskirts), a stout pair of walking shoes and – most vital – curiosity. Many of the gardens and other places featured were found through one trail leading to another, or tracing a tantalizing snippet of memory from a friend. Keep your eyes and ears open, and don't be afraid of what looks like a blind alley – it was just one such seeming dead end that led me to the enchanting gardens of St John's Lodge in Regent's Park.

Many people have helped me in the compiling of this book – by suggesting places to visit and people to include and, in many cases, accompanying me on a most pleasant summer of garden and nursery visits. They are, in alphabetical order, Ros Badger, Tracey Bloom, Roger Bowdler, Declan Buckley, Alice Bulman, Michael Clark, Dara Dhanowa, Rebecca

Edwards, Joanna Goodrich, Chris Hough, Jane Hymas, Frances Lindgren, Mary Mathieson, Chiara Menage, Christina Moore, Simon Steele, Alec and Margaret Thompson, Sarah Thompson, Magda Truszowska, Teresa Watkins and Mopsa Wolff. Apologies to anyone else I may have inadvertently forgotten. The staff of the garden centres and other shops have also been extremely patient and helpful, as were those at the RHS and other organizations. I'd like to make special mention of Todd Longstaffe-Gowan, friend, garden designer and historian, who was good-humoured about the title of this book replicating that of his own much more erudite publication, the annual journal of the London Parks and Gardens Trust (an excellent organization much mentioned on the following pages) and well worth getting hold of. Thanks also to Jean Sturgis for her spirited illustrations, and to all those at Frances Lincoln, especially John Nicoll and Jo Christian, who encouraged this book's metamorphosis from a throwaway idea mentioned over lunch to the finished publication you now hold in your hand, and Michael Brunström and Becky Clarke. My agent, Jane Turnbull, has been wonderfully efficient and enthusiastic. And my husband, Frank Wilson, has been a huge support as ever, and patient when I took the scale and scope of the book beyond its original remit. Finally, I'd like to thank my sister Sarah Thompson, whose careful checking, wise suggestions and proof reading have made this a better book.

In the year since *The London Gardener* was begun, the irony is that I have finally become the owner of a weekend house and garden by the sea. So it has been a schizophrenic twelve months, my time and energies split between seeking out London's hidden gardens and making a start on the country garden of my dreams. Initially, I worried about the timing of it all. Would trawling around London for the book become a chore? Would my taste for urban gardening suffer once I'd sunk my hands in rural soil? No longer a full-time Londoner, would I be able to put my heart and soul into the writing and research? I needn't have worried. Working on this book has made me fall in love with London all over again. As for my Brixton garden, it is currently in the throes of an ambitious overhaul: the front bed given over to bearded irises, the back garden de-cluttered and streamlined with two smart custom-built troughs replacing the jumble of pots, and a modern-day grotto in the basement area, dripping with water and ferns. I couldn't live in London – even part-time – without it. And if I should ever leave London for good, I know that I shall take all the pleasures and ideas gleaned from gardening in the capital with me. Once a London gardener, in my case, always a London gardener . . .

Brixton, December 2003

Part One

GARDENING IN
LONDON

STREETSCAPES

Trees

What would London be without its trees? There are some ancient specimens in our parks: Richmond Park, Brockwell Park and Kew Gardens have oaks that may be at least six hundred years old, while the enormous weeping willow that overhangs the Serpentine in Hyde Park bathes the café tables in dappled lime-green light all summer long. But it's the street trees that really make a difference to our everyday lives. Imagine the capital without the London plane – planted in prime streets and squares from the seventeenth century onwards for its shade potential and ability to withstand pollution. The colossal planes in Holland Park or Bloomsbury provide pleasure all the year round, making a delicate filigree web against the winter sky even after their lush green leaves have fallen – and there's a majestic plane outside the Dorchester on Park Lane that is so popular with visitors that many request a room looking out on to its branches. Come spring, London is a-froth with pink and white cherry blossom; the sight of it, from the Outer Circle of Regent's Park to smaller residential streets and squares, works like a spell on flagging spirits. And clever lighting can continue the enchantment even after dark: the twinkling fairy lights that have become a permanent fixture in the trees outside Sadler's Wells Theatre in Islington make even the rush hour traffic magical. Be thankful if the street where you live is lined with trees. And take time to look up at the trees as you walk about town.

Trees not only soften the relentless straight lines of the urban landscape, they also provide welcome shade in summer and shelter from harsh winds, and reduce the risk of flash flooding by intercepting rainfall. Even more important, with our traffic-choked streets, is their ability to improve air quality by filtering pollution, absorbing carbon monoxide and other toxic gases and giving out oxygen for us to breathe. Streets with trees in them not only look better, they feel better too. Thankfully, the number of street trees in London is now on the rise, thanks to mass street planting initiatives by local councils and organizations such as Trees for London.

Trees for London is one of the capital's most dynamic young charities, founded back in 1989 by a group of friends who used to go out clubbing all over London. Walking back home in the early hours, they were struck by the fact that the streets in wealthier areas such as Hampstead and Holland Park were lined with beautiful mature trees, whereas in Brixton or Bow you could walk for miles without seeing so much as a sapling. They started holding rave parties and planting trees with the profits – with the active co-operation of council tree officers in various boroughs. Now a registered charity with a full-time director, Trees for London doesn't just stop at street trees: it has transformed neglected land around council flats, created orchards in school playgrounds and planted a thick band of indigenous trees to form a noise and pollution barrier on the Blackwall Tunnel approach road. True to the organization's nightclubbing roots, Trees for London's planting days are like big outdoor parties, with a good club DJ and a barbecue; encouraging young people to get involved in this way has proved to be effective in cutting down on damage from vandalism. Their current pledge, supported by the *Evening Standard*, to plant a million trees by 2010 is already making good progress. For further information about how to sponsor a tree or become a Trees for London volunteer, see page 264.

Some of the most exciting new work with trees in the capital is being carried out by Gavin Jones, an artist and environmentalist who helped create the wonderful Cameron Community Gardens in the East End and also ploughed a patch of wasteland near Beckton gasworks – using carthorses – and sowed it with poppies (▶ 178). At the community gardens, he experimented with training a row of young fruit trees into a living screen by twisting and looping the trunks in and out of one another – 'like knitting only extremely slow'. He has since devised a more compact upright version, where the trees are planted in a circle and woven together into a tall spire. Jones passionately believes these 'eco-spires' could transform London. They could fit in awkward places unsuited to the spreading canopy of a conventional tree, and the light and airy structures would make valuable feeding, nesting and roosting spots for birds and other wildlife. An avenue of them could, he says, 'enchant any town or city'. (Check out his website www.ecospires.com.)

Unfortunately, not everyone appreciates London's street trees. Up to 25 per cent of new council plantings are lost to vandals, while larger established trees are prone to damage by trenching gangs working on behalf of the public utilities companies or cable TV. Often, streets are dug up time and time again in the course of a single year, and the trees cannot cope with the repeated disturbance to their roots. We lost an old maple in our street this way a few years ago. Look out for signs of stress or damage and report them to your local council. In dry summers, street trees can suffer from drought, so get out with a bucket and give a tree a drink. You can even train to be a volunteer tree officer to help look after the trees in your area. Just ask your local council for details.

Places to go for inspiration:

Berkeley Square Gardens (▶ 115)

City of London Cemetery (▶ 184)

Fulham Palace Park (▶ 214)

Holland Park (▶ 212)

Hyde Park (▶ 143)

Syon House and Park (▶ 226)

West Ham Park (▶ 181)

Community Gardening

London is full of community gardens – urban oases that have been created, often on derelict or under-used land, with the involvement of local people. Some, such as the Cameron Community Gardens in Bow (▶ 178) or the Culpeper Community Garden in Islington (▶ 189), have been featured on the television and in glossy magazines. Others – and there may well be one hidden around a street corner near you – just carry on quietly, unnoticed by many but a real lifeline for those who use them or help to maintain them. For many Londoners without a garden, involvement with a local community garden not only gives them a space in which to garden; it can also provide them with opportunities to learn skills and to meet like-minded friends. Most community gardens will welcome new volunteers with open arms.

When I first went to New York ten years ago, I was fascinated and inspired by the community gardens of the Lower East Side, where Manhattanites, starved even of the tiny terrace gardens we take for granted in the UK, started gardening on derelict lots in the 1970s and early 1980s. Among the scruffy Spanish churches and graffiti-scrawled shop-fronts there are now leafy havens planted with birch and eucalyptus trees, flowering shrubs and ferns. Some have wildlife ponds, or wooden pergolas grown over with ivy and clematis. Others are divided up into miniscule allotment plots the size of a kitchen table top. One had a surreal forty-foot sculpture made from birdhouses, old rocking horses, plastic snakes and flags of fabric; another had a blue-painted shrine to the Madonna. I was impressed by the community composting schemes, and stages used for poetry readings and musical performances – even residents' weddings. Why didn't we have this sort of thing in London? I wondered.

But on my return, I found out that we did; I just hadn't been looking hard enough. I've since discovered the joys of the Chumleigh Multicultural Gardens in Southwark (▶ 206), and the beautifully designed little garden at Bonnington Square in Vauxhall (▶ 157). Most inspiring of all for me is the Cameron Community Garden, where Gavin Jones helped his fellow residents, many of whom have Bengali roots, to transform a boring lawn hugged in on three sides by high council flats into a vibrant and productive garden (▶ 178). Gavin got this plan going by applying (with his partner Sally Cameron, who has since died) for the £1800 a year that the housing estate allotted for lawn cutting. He has put years of work into the garden, and has since set up as a consultant in designing urban community gardens and what he calls 'bell jar ecology'.

Inspired by Jones and his fellow community gardeners, I tried to get a community garden off the ground myself, on the site of an old warehouse at the back of our house in Brixton. Two years of form-filling and meetings later and nothing had come of it; the site has since been converted into an artist's studio. The trouble was, the land was privately owned, and many of the grants available would only support schemes on land owned by the local authority, or land that had been donated or allowed to be used for that purpose. If you are interested in creating a community garden in a seemingly disused patch of land, the first thing to do is to try to find out who owns it, and apply to them for permission. If it belongs to your local authority, you may be lucky enough to gain their support and funding. The British Trust for Conservation Volunteers (BTCV) is very positive about community gardens and offers advice for free, even when the idea is still in its early stages. If a group of friends or neighbours is involved, it is easy to register yourselves as a BTCV-affiliated group – the registration fee entitles you to a small start-up grant, together with professional help and support in running your group and applying for funding, insurance cover, loan of tools and resources and the right to use the BTCV name and logo on grant applications. For further information ring BTCV head office (▶ 265). Get ready for a lot of form-filling – it will fast become a way of life! But the rewards, if all goes well, will most definitely be worth it.

Easier than starting from scratch may be to apply for community involvement in an existing local square or corner of a council-owned park. The now-disbanded organization Green Adventure helped secure lottery money for the derelict greenhouses in Brockwell Park, south London, to be transformed into a lively community project, where local residents of all ages and abilities can come and help raise herbs, flowers and vegetables that are sold at the project entrance or through local organic box schemes. And in Islington, some friends of mine banded together with others in their street to breathe some life into their local square, which had become a dull and under-used space. Being Islington, they had a lawyer, an accountant, a garden designer and any number of keen gardeners in their midst, and plans for community clearing days and planting weekends were soon under way. The square is now a much more pleasant place, and is therefore more used and more safe. Strength in numbers seems to be the answer, so try to gather some good support before you start. The new Living Spaces scheme set up by the government in 2003 enables local residents to apply for grants ranging from £1000 to £100,000 and get help from a trained 'enabler' who will draw up an action plan and encourage a start-up group (call 0845 600 3190 for an application pack and see page 276). English Heritage (▶ 266) may have grants available (but only for Grade I and II listed properties), while the London Parks and Green Spaces Forum (▶ 261) may also be of assistance. CABE (the Commission for Architecture and the Built Environment) may be able to help with their 'Wasted Space' campaign aimed at shaming councils and developers into using pockets of abandoned land (▶ 266).

Whatever and wherever your plans for a community garden, begin with a brainstorming session to work out what your aims are. Who will be using the garden, primarily, and how can their needs be met in its design? Will you be able to employ a garden designer, or can you rely on the talents within your team? Think about seating and lighting as well as the planting. What sort of wildlife do you want to encourage? Consider also how you might reflect the history and character of the area in the garden's name and in its design. The arts and environmental charity Common Ground (▶ 266) publishes excellent booklets on what they call 'Local Distinctiveness', including one for just £2.50 entitled *The Art of Gentle Gardening*, which is full of ideas on how to use aspects of local history and plants that have a longstanding association with the area. And what about involving local artists? Mosaic paths and murals stay colourful right the way through winter when most of the flowers will be over. Endeavour to get even the roughest, toughest kids and teenagers involved in making the garden; Trees for London have found that actively involving residents in planting days means lower levels of vandalism. People seem less likely to damage something they have had a hand in themselves. A community garden should be for *all* the community.

Places to go for inspiration:

Bonnington Square (▶ 157)

Bromley-by-Bow Centre Gardens (▶ 178)

The Calthorpe Project (▶ 185)

Cameron Community Gardens (▶ 178)

Culpeper Community Garden (▶ 189)

Phoenix Community Garden (▶ 119)

Guerilla Gardening

If setting up a community garden sounds a bit too much like hard work, or you don't have a taste for red tape, you may want to try your hand at a bit of guerilla gardening. By this I don't mean adding turf 'Mohican' haircuts to London statues as demonstrators did during the anti-capitalism marches (fun though that was). I mean urban gardening according to the principles espoused by Liz Christy, founder of the Green Guerillas in New York City and a great gardening heroine of mine. Back in the 1970s, Ms Christy, a painter who lived in Greenwich Village, got fed up with seeing so many vacant lots all over Manhattan. Together with like-minded friends, she started lobbing 'seed bombs' (paper balloons filled with seeds, soil and water) over the high fences that enclosed these patches of derelict land, and a revolutionary gardening movement was born. They also sowed sunflowers along central traffic reservations, and in 1974 planted the city's first community garden (now named the Liz Christy Garden in her memory and protected as a permanent park on the corner of Bowery and Houston Street). That same spirit lives on in many cities around the world, in all sorts of different ways.

In London, you can see it in south London's bohemian Bonnington Square (▶ 157), where every spare scrap of verge and even the bare patches of earth around street trees have been adorned with plants. But guerilla gardening isn't confined to the wilder fringes of town. Up in highly respectable Primrose Hill, someone has seen fit to transform a former triangle of turf on the corner of Regent's Park Road and Gloucester Avenue into a truly stunning piece of planting worthy of any of the posh gardens in the streets near by. A friend who lives there has seen a man tending it sometimes, and says he looks like a local resident, so whether he has sought permission for his kerbside garden I don't know. I do know how much pleasure it brings to pedestrians, who all smile at it as they go past.

Technically, this sort of gardening is illegal, and you could get into trouble, as I found out when I endeavoured to replace a dead tree outside my house (planted a few years beforehand by the council). There was no further budget for tree planting, I was told – but my offer to plant one myself at my own expense was met only with a lecture on insurance culpability. But surely a few seeds wouldn't do anyone any harm? Look around you for potential guerilla sites: a boring turf verge, the bare earth around a tree, a trough or large planter whose contents the council has allowed to die. A few packets of nasturtium or sunflower seeds, a quiet clear night and perhaps a trusty assistant or two is all you need to make a real difference. . . . Some people have even been known to throw paper 'seed bombs' on to weedy embankments from the windows of trains. I'm not saying this is a great idea. I wouldn't like to encourage anyone to go breaking the law. . . . But the world is definitely the brighter for such acts of horticultural heroism.

A Walk on the Wild Side

In some parts of London, Nature has just been left to get on with things herself, and a beautiful job she has done of it, too. The wilder reaches of Hampstead Heath, Highgate and Dulwich Woods and Barnes, Tooting Bec, Wandsworth and Wimbledon Commons are among the expanses of open land where you can almost (but for the distant drone of traffic) make believe you are in the countryside, and where the beauty of majestic trees, wildflowers in spring and bleached long grass in high summer owes more to the year's natural cycles than to human intervention. Some of London's cemeteries are havens for wild nature, too – the less manicured the better. Highgate is the supreme example, but the compulsory guided tours do not penetrate the mysterious wilder reaches. Head for Abney Park Cemetery in Stoke Newington, with its drunken angel tombstones leaning this way and that, Norwood Cemetery with its great stone mausoleums, and Nunhead in south London for a wildlife trail with a dose of local history and the odd touch of the macabre thrown in. As a schoolgirl, I had a friend whose garden backed on to Nunhead Cemetery (long before the Friends' Society neatened it up) and we used to steal over the wall and sit on the crumbling, ivy-clad tombs telling ghost stories while foxes, squirrels and woodpeckers carried on their business all around us, undisturbed.

Canal towpaths are also good places for a walk on the wild side. You can stroll from Limehouse to Little Venice and beyond and see a huge variety of wildflowers and plants, all buzzing with insects in summer – not to mention the more animate wildlife swimming in or on the water.

There are often some great views into gardens that lead down to the waterside – the Angel end of the Regent's Canal in Islington is good for this. (I would hesitate to walk such paths alone, however.) Canal towpaths, along with railway sidings and motorway verges, can also act as migration corridors up which various species of plants, insects and birds can travel. And when their traditional countryside habitats are being threatened by modern farming practices, many of them are relocating to the wilder fringes of the city – or even into our own back gardens if they find the conditions they require. Next time you are on a train heading out of London, put down your newspaper and look out of the window – it is not only the rural landscapes further out of town that are interesting. On the overground train from Vauxhall to Hampton Court I lost count of the different species of wildflower I saw growing beside the tracks – alongside a sprinkling of more ornamental blooms that may have leapt the fences of the back gardens to 'go native'. Even the bracken and nettles provide important breeding and feeding grounds for wildlife. And on the Gatwick Express, I am always intrigued by the strange juxtaposition of graffiti (some of it of the rather more expert and artistic type) with sprays of dog roses and buddleia and spires of rosebay willowherb.

There are places in London where the exuberance of wild nature takes you unawares. It might be the sight of a sturdy burdock thrusting its way through layers of tarmac in spring, sprays of buddleia waving from a brick chimney stack against a blue sky, or the pretty purple flowers of ivy-leaved toadflax that have managed to colonize the cracks in a seemingly inhospitable wall. Many of these plants would be dismissed as weeds in our own back gardens, and yet the sight of them in the thick of the city, doing their own thing, against the odds, and often against a backdrop of unremitting grey, is cheering. These wild city plants tend to live fast – like a lot of city-dwelling people, in fact; groundsel, for instance, with its tufty yellow flowers, can grow from nothing to set its own seed in just four to five weeks. They have developed their own strategies for urban survival. Some produce huge quantities of seed as an insurance policy (the average chickweed plant puts out two thousand). Others take up temporary accommodation inside birds or animals, to aid seed dispersal (up to thirty species of plant have been germinated from sparrow droppings) or hitch a ride, with the help of the Velcro-like seed cases of goose grass, forget-me-not and burdock, on a passing dog, cat or human. (One botanist claims to have raised three hundred plants of twenty different varieties from seed trapped in his trouser turn-ups.) And some plants are exotic immigrants from abroad: stowaways on ships or in the stomachs of migrating birds, runaways from Victorian gardens (such as Japanese knotweed and giant hogweed from Russia), or sprouted from packets of bird seed. Look carefully next time you pass your local dump or some derelict and seemingly barren patch of land. You never know what you might find.

There are wonderfully wild patches all over London, but it is hard to be specific about their whereabouts, as change is built into their very existence: as fast as one unlikely cloud of wildflowers is concreted over by a developer, another springs up somewhere else. I have been particularly thrilled, however, by the profusion of plants making a Piranesi-like fringe along the tops of the railway arches around Borough Market, and by the intriguing mixture of wild and urban that greets train passengers coming into Royal Oak station, just outside Paddington. Normally hardly the most prepossessing part of west London, Royal Oak station is transformed in late summer and early autumn by the pink and purple buddleia that sprouts forth from every possible nook and cranny around the platforms. This is the point where the Hammersmith & City tube line emerges above ground to join the trains heading west to Oxford, Bristol and beyond. It's a supremely urban landscape, arranged in a series of parallel horizontals from the railway tracks to the platforms and graffiti-ridden retaining walls to the concrete sweep of the Westway overhead. Catch it at the right time and you can see tubes and trains sliding out in opposite directions while cars, buses and lorries zoom past in a blur overhead. A clever artist could paint an abstract of it.

What always strikes me, however, is how well the place suits its mad urban fringe of purple flowers. Buddleia is renowned for its capacity to take root wherever it can find a crevice and a little water. At Royal Oak, it has managed to find footholds in cracks in the paving, along the tops of walls, in angles of the openwork metal bridges that span the different platforms, and even down among the tracks. Further out of the station itself, it is joined by that other lovely colonizer of urban decay, rosebay willowherb. Even the graffiti looks better when glimpsed through this glorious pink and purple haze. Buddleia and rosebay are pioneer plants, among the first to put in a bid to reclaim derelict land for nature (as they did so famously on bomb sites in the capital during the Second World War). Left to their own devices, other plants would follow in the soil slowly formed by their decaying leaves: scrubby young birch in ten or twenty years, and then saplings of the oak, after which the station was once named. It wouldn't take *that* long for London to become forest again. As post-apocalyptic visions go, it's really quite appealing.

CHALLENGES

Shade

There are far worse things to have than a shady garden. In the city, where the streets can be hot and noisy and full of hassle in summer, a shady garden can provide a cool, calm refuge. What could be more restful, at the end of a hard day, than to walk through the house and out the back door into a lush leafy space where sunlight is filtered by the textures and patterns of foliage, throwing dappled shadows on the ground?

Shade from surrounding buildings, walls and fences means that few Londoners are going to get day-long sunshine in their gardens anyway. Even the coveted south-facing plots will have a north-facing area that gets very little light when the sun is low in winter, and most of us have to make do with a few sunny patches in which to sit with a cup of coffee in the mornings, or catch the last rays in the early evening. So we might as well be positive about shade.

The first thing to do with shade is admit that you've got it. It's surprising the number of people who buy a house or flat not knowing which way it faces – and even the most careful can come a cropper. I was pleased that our little garden faced south-west, but had not bargained for the fact that its high brick walls and tall neighbouring buildings would throw most of it into total shade for much of the year. Carrying on regardless, planting sun-lovers like lavender and cistus which are never going to thrive, is not a good way to have a healthy garden, and I soon learned to choose plants that would thrive, rather than just survive, in my shady north border. There are degrees of shade, of course. The most challenging is the dense, dry shade beneath evergreen trees or in the rain shadow of a high wall. But there is always something that will grow in even the most unpromising of places: different types of cyclamen are great under trees, their variegated heart-shaped foliage as pretty as the flowers, and of course there are those old stand-bys, ivies, ferns and moss. Box, yew, pulmonarias, Solomon's seal, euonymus, cordylines, hydrangeas and hostas are among the plants that can cope with the shade at the base of a wall or fence. Many of the architectural foliage plants not only enjoy a fair degree of shade, they also benefit from the largely frost-free microclimate in an enclosed urban garden. The graceful gold-stemmed bamboo, *Phyllostachys aurea*, is a good choice for small gardens as it is a slow-growing clumper rather than a spreader, and tree ferns make a feathery umbrella in a dull corner. (For more ideas, see pages 63–5.) And, to my mind, shade is the one circumstance in which variegated plants come into their own: the pale markings on their leaves which can look like disease in some settings create the effect of dappled light. In my darkest corner (made darker now by the canopy of the bamboo above it), I have the variegated ivy *Hedera canariensis* 'Gloire de Marengo' climbing up the white trellised walls, with a ground cover of silver-variegated lamiums, golden and silver ivies and the stunning marbled leaves of *Arum italicum* 'Marmoratum' filling the gaps between a few prized ferns. Variegated shrubs might have a similar effect in a larger area, or pots of white-flowering plants.

There are surprising numbers of plants that flower in shade – among them Japanese anemones, winter and summer jasmine, nicotianas, including the stately 4-foot *N. sylvestris*, and even roses, such as the creamy, pink-flushed 'Madame Alfred Carrière', soft pink 'Gloire de Dijon', creamy 'Mermaid' and shocking-pink-and-white-striped 'Honorine de Brabant'. White flowers are always welcome in dark corners, and Diana Yakeley's (▶ 274) elegant Islington garden (often open through the National Gardens Scheme) uses only white flowers (many in pots, so that different kinds can be substituted throughout the year) to complement the foliage shapes and textures in different shades of green. There are even some silver-leaved plants (normally associated with sunny Mediterranean-style gardens) that are happy in shade, provided the soil is free-draining. Artemisias and santolinas can be clipped into silver globes, while pretty *Convolvulus cneorum* continues to put out its pink-tinged bell-shaped flowers in or out of the sun. I have also had success with the grey-green-leaved, slightly tender *Melianthus major*, against the advice of all the books, which say it needs sun. I can hardly bear to cut it down each spring, but it can become leggy in shade, and soon puts forth fans of new leaves, notched around the edges as if they had been cut out with pinking shears.

If you still yearn for more light, you can work wonders with a lick of paint and a mirror. Painting the walls white can make an enormous difference, and if you train some climbers in co-ordinated colours, you can create an attractive wallpaper effect. Mirrors not only reflect more

light, they can also create a convincing illusion of more space, and make the plants in front of them appear twice as abundant. They can totally transform a small shady garden, reflecting sunlight into previously gloomy corners while looking like a doorway or window into a different world. Just after I placed a 6-foot-square mirror in a recess in my rear garden wall, a new visitor pointed to it and asked 'Is that your garden through there, as well?' I've often wondered about attaching a mirror on hinges to the sunny rear wall of the house so I could send sunlight wherever I wanted.

Frame your mirror in wood or, better still, use a salvaged door or window frame to reinforce the effect of an opening, and use yachting varnish on the back and sides to protect the fragile mirrored surface from damp. Try it out in different positions, shifting it and tilting the angle until you arrive at the exact effect you are after. And remember not to place the mirror immediately opposite the main view from the house; the illusion will be shattered if you see your own reflection too soon. Mirrors are one way of coping with the gloomy basement well that is the lot of many ground floor flats. If the whole house is yours, the best option here (though an expensive one) is to excavate the area and unite it with the rest of the garden via wide, shallow steps; this works particularly well where the kitchen/dining area is in the basement and you want access and views to the garden from here as well as from the sitting room on the raised ground floor above. If the basement area has to remain intact, there is often a mere yard or so of space between the windows and the retaining wall, so mirrors in strategic places, white paint and fairy lights are all ways to bring a bit of cheer. The architect Dale Loth has made a stunning water garden outside his basement study, by clothing the retaining wall in ridged stainless steel, down which water trickles into a narrow canal planted with bamboos and arum lilies. Or, like me, you could go for a grotto effect with lots of ferns, dripping water and shells. If all else fails, why not commission a mural? Ruth Collier of Couture Gardens (▶ 270) transformed the dingy L-shaped area behind a tall terraced house in King's Cross by asking artist David Thomas to paint an enormous arum lily up a white-painted wall. Create your own sunshine with palm trees along a beach or cacti in the Arizona desert – the only way to ensure sunshine in a London garden all the year round.

Soil

Dig down a foot or so in many London gardens and you'll hit a layer of clay that gives the bricks known as 'London stocks' their characteristic yellowy colour. The topsoil is likely to be sticky and stodgy in texture, rather than rich and crumbly. Gardeners moan about clay soil as it can bake as hard as rock in a hot summer and become puddled with water in winter. It is slow to warm up and dry out in spring; slugs like it; and digging can be back-breaking work. But clay soil has its good points, too. It is naturally very fertile, and its structure can be easily improved. Giving open ground a rough dig over in the autumn will help; the action of wind, rain and frost over winter should break down the large dense clods into smaller, more manageable lumps, as will a sprinkling of hydrated lime, gypsum or (the preferred organic option) calcified seaweed. The addition of grit will improve drainage no end – it's worth digging horticultural grit (a couple of spadefuls per square yard) into new borders or allotment beds as you prepare them for planting and, in established areas, adding a large handful into the hole whenever you plant something new. Working in large amounts of organic matter such as well-rotted horse manure, garden compost or spent mushroom compost is the other key to improving clay. You'll then have the makings of the 'friable loam' which is the holy grail cited by all the books – though you'll have to keep up the good work with annual mulches.

The most common problem in the average London garden isn't the clay itself, however; it's that the soil has grown exhausted and lifeless after long periods of neglect. Unless you're lucky enough to inherit soil that's been improved by a previous occupant, the chances are that the beds will be filled with dusty, dense, compacted soil that's devoid of any 'body', and lacking in earthworms and beneficial soil organisms as well as basic nutrients. The soil in new developments can be even worse. Developers often remove and sell the good topsoil before work starts, and what's left is compacted by boots and heavy machinery and strewn with rubble, other rubbish and plasterer's slops. It's not unheard of for this mess to be covered with a thin layer of turf or bark on the day that the builders leave. Try to prevent such a scenario by ensuring your contract includes a clause stating that you will be left with a proper garden and good topsoil. Otherwise, there will be nothing for it but to buy back a ton or two of topsoil once you've moved in – and it doesn't come cheap.

Adding organic matter is by far the best way to improve clay-rich, compacted and lifeless soil. It is also the best defence against the effects of environmental toxins (see pages 73–6). Just as good food improves our general health and builds up the body's resistance to disease, stress and pollution, so a diet of compost or well-rotted manure restores the soil. As the organic matter is drawn down into the soil by worms and broken down by beneficial bacteria and fungi, it works its way between the fine particles of a clay soil to create air spaces through which water can drain and roots can grow. It also holds moisture in dry weather, and is rich in nutrients that can be used both by plants and by soil-dwelling insects, animals and micro-organisms.

The poorest clay soils may need a wheelbarrow load of organic matter per 2–3 square yards of soil. This can be very expensive, and will definitely be exhausting to dig in. But the rewards will be great: healthy, well-drained and nutrient-packed soil that is the basis of all good gardening. It was the belief that 'the health of plant, animal and man depends on a *living* soil' that led to the formation of the Soil Association in 1946 (▶ 267). Feed the soil, it says, and the plants will pretty much look after themselves. In fact, there are many cheap sources of organic matter to be found in London, if you know where to look. Some of the city farms allow you to take away a certain number of bags of manure for free, if you fill them yourself. Riding stables and police stables are another good source: a friend's allotment in Wimbledon gets sweepings from the stables at Buckingham Palace delivered every month. (See page 248 for other ideas.) Or you could make your own leaf mould from fallen leaves. The crucial thing is to ensure the organic matter is well-rotted down before adding it to the soil. Concentrated nitrogen and other nutrients in fresh manure not only harm plants, they will also rob the soil of goodness as they break down. If fresh or partly rotted organic matter is all you can find, add it to your compost heap in layers, or leave it in the plastic sacks for six months or so to decompose further.

Incorporating organic matter is even more important if you are thinking of growing food crops – both to improve your yields and to counteract the effects of toxins in the environment. 'You're not going to grow food up there are you?' friends asked, when I had a flat with a roof terrace on a busy road in Finsbury Park. I, too, was worried that lead and other toxic emissions from car and lorry exhausts would pollute the soil and poison my produce. But a little research helped put my mind at rest enough to risk a few tubs of beans and tomatoes. The toxic 'heavy metals' present in traffic fumes as tiny particles are actually heavier than the air, and only travel at a low level for around 70–165 feet on average across open ground. My first-floor roof terrace was fine, as would be the average back garden, where the house would provide a barrier from the road. Now that lead has been phased out in petrol, its danger is much reduced – though toxins can persist in the soil for many years. I would still hesitate to grow edibles at ground level on a busy street where a constant stream of vehicles, often stuck in traffic jams, spews out fumes near by. You can get around the soil problem by growing in shop-bought compost in containers, and adding large quantities of compost and manure, but I would still wash all produce thoroughly before use. The only other real problem areas for food crops are on and around sites that have been used for industry. Land near gasworks, asbestos works, kilns, ceramic and cement manufacturing works is often polluted with chemicals that can remain in the soil for a surprising length of time and be taken up by plants. If you're worried, check with your local council's environmental department, who may be able to arrange to have the soil tested for you. You may still be able to grow crops in containers, or improve the soil quality over time so toxicity is no longer a problem.

Light and Noise Pollution

There is no doubt that London is a polluted place. Driving back along the motorway after a day out in the country, you can often see the toxic air hanging like a dirty yellowy-grey cloud over the city. And, via rainfall and other means, this soon makes its way into the soil. Pollution in the soil – and how to counteract it by means of a 'detox' diet of compost and nutrients – has already been mentioned in the section on soil (see pages 22–5). But what about the other forms of pollution that plague us in the Big Smoke? Light and noise pollution are also serious problems and can have almost as detrimental an effect on our enjoyment of our gardens.

It's all very well living in a city that never sleeps, but, like it or not, our ceaseless 24/7 lifestyle has sucked in the natural world. Nature needs her rest as much as we do. And if, as I have, you've heard blackbirds singing repeatedly in the dead of night, and noticed that trees next to lamp posts form their spring leaves earlier on the side nearest the light, you'll know that she isn't getting her full eight hours. The means used by commercial growers to get chrysanthemums and other flowers to bloom outside their normal flowering time are based on artificially altering their exposure to light. The implications for urban plants are clearly worrying. The problem of artificially light skies has begun to spread far beyond cities –

new photographs from space show most of Great Britain bathed in an eerie glow at night – but the sources of the problem tend, of course, to be concentrated in built-up areas. Street lights, floodlighting of sports centres, and security lights in supermarket car parks and private gardens are among the worst culprits, turning birds into insomniacs and confusing those that migrate at night. Churches have recently been added to the list of offenders, since the Millennium Commission allocated funds to floodlight churches throughout the country; though it undoubtedly looks dramatic, this sort of lighting is particularly detrimental, as it shoots straight up into the sky. Of course, the security argument gets pushed to the fore in a city like London – but recent findings by the police suggest that light does not necessarily put off criminals. Studies show that break-ins and vandal attacks are often higher in well-lit areas, and that cars parked under street lights are more likely to be broken into than those further away. Thieves need to see, too. We may want our parks, and footpaths through heaths and commons to be safe at night. But isn't it just as important to preserve areas where proper darkness can penetrate – the sort of darkness that bats, fish and moths need in order to feed and mate and procreate?

Do what you can to combat this plague of brightness by questioning how much after-dark lighting you need around your house. If you are not using the garden after dark, don't always have the lights on as a matter of course, and ask yourself if you really need one of those Colditz-like security lamps at the front gate. If you do decide to keep one, ensure that the movement sensors will not be triggered by every prowling cat or passer-by. Make sure that all bright lights are mounted so that the light is directed downwards and away from neighbours. Go for lower wattage bulbs than the blinding 300–500 watts that many shops will encourage you to buy, and avoid leaving any outdoor light on all night long. Get active. If your local sports centre or supermarket is lit unnecessarily, band up with some other concerned neighbours and see if you can get the wattage or the hours of illumination reduced. The Campaign for Dark Skies (▶ 265) may be able to help and advise you.

Noise pollution is another threat to city gardening, and can come in many forms, including traffic, aircraft and rowdy neighbours. The last thing you want, having created a beautiful leafy haven, is to have your tranquillity disturbed by any or all of the above. If you have tried all feasible routes and failed to get the noise reduced, your best bet is to try to re-focus your awareness of noise to *inside* the garden. It's amazing what the trickling of water or the swishing of a bamboo hedge can do. You're not necessarily attempting

to mask the offending sounds. You'd need a water feature with the power of Niagara Falls to drown out low-flying aircraft, and no amount of carefully chosen foliage is going to shield you from the teenagers playing techno music next door. But if the noise level is manageable – and thankfully it usually is – such measures will help to distract and soothe your mind. If all else fails, invest in a pair of good headphones and play tapes of simulated birdsong or jungle sounds until things quieten down.

Raising Your Own

I only began to feel like a 'real gardener' once I started raising my own plants. You might imagine you need a big greenhouse and complicated equipment to do this – and indeed, a large, light, frost-free space and/or an electric propagator definitely make life a lot easier – but there is nothing to stop you raising perfectly good plants from seeds and cuttings inside your house. A warm, light windowsill is ideal – Penelope Bennett, who wrote the excellent *Windowbox Allotment* (Ebury), constructed a special frame with shelves that could be fixed to the inside of her bedroom window so that she could keep a multi-storey seed tray production line going. In Holland, I've also seen miniature greenhouses that can be attached to the *outside* of your window, but I don't know of anyone who manufactures them here. Think creatively. For years, when I lived in a tiny flat in Gray's Inn Road, I raised plenty of plants from seed in the back of my old VW camper van; windows in the roof made it more than light enough, and I used to try to park where the plants would get more sun, trundling round the corner in the afternoon if necessary. The tomatoes I raised in my van were always excellent. The only trouble was, I had to remember never to brake suddenly and to take it easy going round corners.

Start off with something easy, like sunflowers, nasturtiums, courgettes or runner beans. These germinate fast and reliably, and can easily be sown outside, once the weather is warm. But sowing under cover means you can get a head start on nature. And by the time you transplant your seedlings outside, they should be large enough to withstand the almost inevitable damage by slugs and snails. It is heartbreaking to find a newly germinated row of seedlings nibbled down to bare stalks. Sometimes, no evidence remains at all, and you are left waiting in vain for the fruits of your labours to appear. The other advantage of sowing in pots or trays is that you know what to look out for. In my early days of gardening, I would succumb to the temptation to scatter a packet of seed in a border, only to be baffled by which of the rash of

tiny green plantlets that soon appeared were seedlings and which were weedlings. Often the first leaves of a plant bear no resemblance to the mature form; once you are familiar with what plants look like when young, you can broadcast seeds such as love-in-a-mist, opium poppies and the Californian poppy (*Eschscholzia californica*) and look out for other self-seeders in the border to nurture or transplant elsewhere. The latter, to me, is one of the true joys of gardening.

You can sow seed in seed trays or pots, or in plastic 'plug trays' with individual compartments, or in 'root trainers', which are similar only with more root room and hinge devices so they can be opened up like a book in order to remove the seedling without damaging the roots. Although I started out using seed trays, I now favour pots, plug trays or root trainers, as they mean less root disturbance. Many seedlings will suffer a check in growth if their young roots are disturbed, and may even die. A great device from Grassroots Gardening (▶ 254) enables you to make large numbers of your own individual plugs from newspaper – much greener and cheaper than buying plastic trays or peat plugs. If you sow two seeds per plug or individual compartment, you can be pretty sure at least one will germinate, and if both do, you can thin out the weaker of the two later.

Whatever receptacle you use should have drainage (you can use supermarket veg trays as seed trays if you pierce some holes in the base) and be at least an inch and a half high (deeper for plants such as runner beans, sweet peas, dill and parsley, which form long tap roots). Fill with good-quality seed compost, sieving out any lumps to make it fine and friable and comfortable for seedlings to grow in. Tamp (pat) the soil down flat with your fingers or a ruler, before soaking it in water. The easiest way of doing this is to plunge the pots or trays up to their necks in a sink of water until you're sure they have drunk their fill (peat or coir plugs will need to be soaked till they swell up ready for sowing). Remove and allow to drain. If you water before sowing you will avoid the risk of washing the seeds out of place; you shouldn't need to water again until the seedlings are established. Follow the instructions on the packet (or in reference books) for sowing depths and distances. Some seeds, such as Virginia stock, like to be sown on the surface of the compost and left uncovered; others require a thin covering of sieved soil. At this point, most seeds will benefit from being placed in the dark. Some will also need the warmth of an airing cupboard or heated propagator; again, check the packet or books for instructions. Cover the sown seeds with something like a polystyrene tile or folded newspaper: as well as aiding germination this cuts down on water loss, preserves warmth and (if you are using a propagator) conserves the bottom heat from heated cables. (Seeds not requiring dark can be covered in clear polythene.) Check every day for signs of germination and, as soon as there are any signs of life, remove the cover and move your young plants to a sunny window-sill, or somewhere where they will enjoy maximum light and not suffer a huge temperature drop at night.

As the plantlets grow larger, resist the temptation to over-water. Damping-off disease is a threat in over-moist soil and causes the young stems to rot. When one or two sets of 'true' leaves have appeared (after the first set of often atypical leaves), seedlings in trays or very small plugs can be carefully 'pricked out' (holding them ever so gently by the leaves and never by the stem) into larger pots. As the weather outside gets warmer, plants destined for outdoors must be acclimatized gently to their new conditions – this is called 'hardening off'. Leave the plants outside on warm days and bring them in again at night; start leaving them out at night only when all danger of frost has passed, and remember to protect them from slugs and snails (see pages 79–82). I used to rush this process and the plants quite literally went on strike, refusing to grow for weeks afterwards. Respect and nurture your seedlings, and they will give of their best!

CITY SPACES

Window Boxes

Well-planted window boxes make a real difference to the look and feel of any house or flat, from both inside and out. From indoors, even grey buildings and greyer skies look better when glimpsed through a fringe of green – it's especially nice to have a window box that you can see in the morning when you wake up, or can gaze out on from the desk where you work. And from the street, window boxes not only make your home look beautiful and well cared for, they also provide a lot of pleasure for passers-by. Some may be so high up they can only be glimpsed from the top of a double decker or by craning your neck. But I love those tiny potted gardens in improbable places. Primrose Hill, Chelsea and the Barbican are good areas to go window box spotting, but there is inspiration everywhere. Few daffodils have ever looked more beautiful than those I remember seeing along the window ledges of a concrete council block off the Old Kent Road.

Most London buildings have window ledges deep enough for a window box to sit on. Measure the space before you make or buy your planter –

and go for the biggest dimensions possible, as this will increase the variety of things you can grow and reduce the need for watering. Some of the troughs in the shops are terribly small, and will require a lot of attention if they are not to dry out. If your window ledge is narrow, it would be better to make or commission a taller box, which will provide more room for soil and roots – but not so high as to cut out too much light from the house. You may need a safety bracket to fix the box in place, particularly if the box is high up.

Terracotta, wood and plastic are the most common choices for planters, but galvanized metal is great for a more modern look, and there are some convincing imitation lead troughs from shops and mail order catalogues – as seen adorning the smartest Georgian façades from Islington to Chelsea. Commissioning your own isn't as expensive as you might think. A good metalworker (see 'Hard Landscaping Supplies', page 249) could make you a galvanized trough for well under £100, and a carpenter knock up a nice wooden one for less. For our wide front bay window, a friend made me a lovely big box that measures 4 feet 6 inches long x 12 inches wide x 14 inches deep and is painted a sludgy grey-green that complements the different types of lavender that grow in it and the dark purple paintwork on the rest of the house.

If you're going for a large box, check that your window ledge is strong enough to bear the combined weight of the box, plants and soil, especially when wet. You should also make sure your planter has adequate drainage. Before planting, cover the holes with broken crocks and fill the bottom inch or two with gravel or lightweight aggregate so the plants won't sit in water. To improve matters further, sit your box on 'chocks' – small pieces of wood or little terracotta legs that are sold for the purpose.

There are two basic options when planting window boxes: permanent plantings that will remain in place year-in, year-out, and seasonal displays that will be changed two or three times a year. If you're clever, you can combine the two by leaving spaces in between the permanent plants for spring bulbs and summer bedding plants, but this can be tricky as the roots of the larger plants spread. A few years ago Guy Cooper and Gordon Taylor (more commonly known as the 'Curious Gardeners' from the television series of the same name) devised an ingenious window box system that involved planting each plant in individual containers that could be kept in place or removed as required. Avant garde gardeners that they are, Cooper and Taylor had the workings of their scheme on show, using clear plastic picnic drinks holders inserted into a shiny metal wine rack. But you could use the same principles with any old containers – even sawn-off plastic drink bottles – that would remain hidden within the body of a normal box.

All over London, from barristers' chambers in Bloomsbury to smart Pimlico townhouses, you'll see versions of the traditional window box with a central conifer or cordyline, small shrub or box ball on either side and fringe of trailing ivy, with infills of cyclamen, solanums or bright red salvias, according to the season. These are often planted and tended by maintenance companies, which may explain their sometimes stiff and regimented look. But a bold display of just one thing can look wonderful. I chose lavenders for my big front window box for both beauty and ease of maintenance. They are kept in shape by a good annual prune after flowering; I occasionally pop a few leftover nasturtium seeds in the corners for a bit of extra late-summer colour. I soon gave up on daffodils when I discovered that the dying foliage ruins the display. If you're clever, you can plant bulbs in layers, to come up in succession through a ground cover of ivy or mind-your-own-business – snowdrops and dwarf iris followed by daffodils and then tulips (whose floppy leaves should hide the dying daffodils) and even lilies. Low-growing ornamental grasses can be used to great effect in window boxes – they are easy to care for and the swishing sound and movement provide another element of interest. For a charity window box auction I was involved with, the garden designer Penelope Hobhouse came up with the stunning idea of planting her galvanized trough with just one plant, the wild rye grass *Elymus hispidus*, whose subtle metallic sheen complemented the planter perfectly. Diversify your grass species and you could even have a miniature meadow outside your window, buzzing with bees and butterflies: John Chambers (▸ 252) sells a wildflower seed mixture specially selected for containers.

The possibilities are endless – and the best place to look for inspiration is other gardeners' windows. One house near me has three terracotta troughs, one on each side of a big bay window, and in each there is just one plant of the mad corkscrew grass, *Juncus effusus* f. *spiralis*, sprouting from a mulch of purplish slate chippings. Another I pass on my bike on my ride into town has a froth of white pelargoniums cascading over shiny zinc planters – simplicity itself, but it couldn't be prettier. And sometimes more is more – anyone who ever saw it will never forget the eccentric window display in Percy Circus in King's Cross, where a window box spilling over with nasturtiums, French marigolds, salvias and other colourful bedding plants used to extend itself, via wall-mounted pots, wires and brackets, to stretch right around the window in a gaudy floral frame.

Places to go for inspiration:

The Barbican Centre (▶ 159)   Neal's Yard (▶ 120)
Ennismore Garden Mews (▶ 147)   Portman Square (▶ 135)
Manchester Square (▶ 135)   South Audley Street (▶ 115)

Balconies and Roof Terraces

It must be every Londoner's dream to have a roof terrace high above the hubbub – mine's to have two: one facing east, for quiet early morning breakfasts while the city kick-starts itself into action below, and one facing west, in which to raise a glass to the sunset after a hard day's work. For the increasing number of loft-owners in areas like Clerkenwell and King's Cross this dream is now a reality, but it's often possible to tuck a small terrace on to the roof of the kitchen or bathroom extensions at the back of a Victorian terrace, or to gain access to the flat roofs of tenement buildings. It will be well worth the effort and expense. In a city crammed with tall buildings, where back gardens are often small and shady, making space for even smallest balcony a few floors up will reward you with better light for longer, as well as big skies and – important in busy areas – distance from the traffic.

If you want to make a roof terrace or balcony from scratch, it is advisable to talk to your local council first. Anything that alters the profile of the building or your neighbours' view may need planning permission, and there are safety issues such as fire escapes and boundary walls or fences to consider. The law requires safety barriers at least 1.1m high for all balconies and terraces. And, before you keenly cover your terrace or balcony with colourful pots and climbers, consider the weight capacity of the roof. You don't want your rooftop garden falling through into the bedroom below. An engineer or architect can calculate the weight-loading of your roof, based on the number and size of beams holding it up. For all but the strongest, rock-solid structures, it is often best to concentrate your pots and planters around the edges of the balcony or terrace, or to spread their weight via the use of decking or other devices.

Asphalt, which has been used on many flat roofs in London, is useless for a roof garden, as it is flexible, particularly in the heat of summer, when anything heavy is likely to sink into and then through it. A sand-and-cement screed can be laid on top of it; or decking, or paving stones with sheets of polystyrene and plastic membranes underneath.

Remember that most surfaces will get very hot in day-long sunshine. Lawns are tricky on rooftops, and the roof needs to be prepared with a waterproof membrane, insulating layer and drainage mat before any soil is

put in place, but there are sedges and little succulents that can be coaxed into covering a thin layer of topsoil and shingle. The great turf roof at the Centre for Wildlife Gardening (▶ 205) may inspire you, and you can contact CAT for more details (▶ 265). All else failing, my friends Clarkey and Simon made a small 'mobile lawn' from turfs laid on an old wooden platform on castors so that their dog had somewhere cool to sit on hot summer days. And don't forget Astroturf: kitsch it may be, but it's soft underfoot and can be kept clean with the occasional pressure wash.

The most hospitable roof terraces are tucked into corners between surrounding buildings, away from the prevailing winds. If yours is at all exposed, you'll need to consider a windbreak. The higher you go, the blowier it gets; even in midsummer, lunch outside can be an all-hands-ontablecloth affair, while the icy winds of winter may be strong and cold enough to ruin all your hard work. So you need some sort of protection for both plants and people. The best wind protection is something that filters the wind, rather than blocking or re-directing it. Trellis is one option, with a wind-resistant climber growing up it; you can also buy rolls of screening made from bamboo canes or French heather, which can be attached to strong uprights. A hedge planted in sturdy troughs is an organic solution: glossy-leaved *Elaeagnus x ebbingei* is highly wind-resistant, as are bamboos, whose rustling leaves may also screen out traffic noise. On the roof terrace of his former home in Vauxhall the designer Dan Pearson had clouds of lavender, rosemary and thyme in wooden boxes bracketed along the top of the retaining brick walls. For a more modern look, fine metal mesh is very smart, and has the added advantage of not blocking the view. Or you could get creative with a mobile screen stitched from industrial weatherproof textiles.

When it comes to plants, it's impossible to generalize. A sheltered balcony may create a favoured microclimate where tender semi-tropical plants may thrive, but for an exposed roof terrace, think windswept desert. Mediterranean plants and some of the ornamental grasses may be your best bet – try plants with silver or succulent leaves such as lavenders, thrift, the tufty blue-grey grass *Festuca glauca* and the beautiful pink-tinged white bells and metallic leaves of *Convolvulus cneorum*. No matter what plants you choose, they will certainly need *some* watering, and it's surprising how many people make a roof garden without installing a tap. The ideal, of course, is to have an irrigation system, but you'll still need another tap for hand-watering. If you're serious about roof-gardening, it is definitely worth the expense (see 'Other Gardening Mail Order', page 254), and you'll appreciate features such as automatic timers which can be programmed to water while you're away on holiday. Otherwise, water-retaining granules (sold as Swell Gel) can be added to the soil when planting, or poured into holes in the compost of established pots to keep the soil moist for longer.

The best balconies and roof gardens provide privacy and sunshine *and* great views of the city. I know Londoners who sunbathe naked on them, do their yoga on them, even sun-dry tomatoes on them. If Richard Rogers and other eco-architects had their way, London's rooftops would all be glazed over and we'd be growing all our own food up there. The garden designers Helen Tindale and Karena Batstone designed a roof terrace for a client in Clapham that featured a state-of-the-art hot tub screened by grasses and bamboo. And think of Stella McCartney's controversial rooftop shower. When it comes to ideas for rooftop gardens, the sky really is your limit.

Places to go for inspiration:

Aveda Institute Roof Terrace (▶ 120)   RIBA Roof Terrace (▶ 135)
Bonnington Square (▶ 157)   Kensington Roof Gardens (▶ 147)
No. 1 Poultry Roof Garden (▶ 165)

Front Gardens

London front gardens come in all sizes. Large villas and detached houses from St John's Wood to Wandsworth are set back behind gardens that are twice the size of the average rear plot, while smaller flat-fronted terraces may have nothing at all, their front doors opening straight on to the street. There are rows of pretty Georgian cottages – Willow Road in Hampstead (▶ 192) and Malvern Terrace in Barnsbury (▶ 192), for example – where the long narrow front gardens with picket fences and a froth of perennials look like one of Helen Allingham's country watercolours. The average London householder, however, will have a narrow strip of land just a few feet deep, separated from the pavement by a fence, wall or hedge. Most London houses would originally have had iron railings, but since the Second World War, when railings were seized and melted down to make armaments, railings remain the preserve of the more expensive areas – whether this is because poorer houses were targeted first, or that the rich were more able to replace them, I don't know. But it certainly accounts for the curious patchwork effect along the average urban street: a low brick wall here, a privet hedge there, or those strange painted breezeblocks with flower-shaped openings.

Sometimes the walls or hedges are so high as to prevent any view of the garden behind, and this seems a pity. Not only will plants grow more happily where there is a more open aspect, a lower boundary allows the garden to give something back to the street.

Front gardens are sociable places. Many of the people I now call friends are those who stopped to chat while I was out watering the pots in our front garden when we first moved in, and since its major redesign a couple of years ago, passers-by have even said they make a diversion on their journey to the tube in the mornings to see what's going on. It's nothing special – we just lowered the front wall to make space for a picket fence on top (partly to stop local lads from sitting on the wall and throwing drink cans into the garden), painted the fence purple to match the front door and filled the new brick bed behind with glaucous grey or purple-tinged plants. People seem to like all the tall plants in such a confined space – there are cardoons with their electric-blue thistles and scrolling silver leaves; the black hollyhock *Alcea rosea* 'Nigra', towering dark red sunflowers ('Claret' and 'Prado Red'), feathery fronds of bronze fennel and even an echium (*Echium pininana*) that I hope will send out a 10-foot spire of blue blooms this year. I like them, too, as they provide some privacy from inside the house – a similar effect, but so much more fun than a high hedge.

It seems a shame to me that many Londoners use their front gardens just as a space to store their rubbish and recycling bins. This wasn't so bad when the bins were old-style galvanized metal, but the arrival of the ubiquitous plastic wheelie bin has done nothing for the look of our streets. There can be few more depressing sites than an ugly (and possibly smelly) plastic rubbish bin as you walk in and out of your front door. When we were lowering the wall in our front garden, I moved the gate a little to the right to make space for a retained bed on the left, and made an opening at the far right-hand end of the wall to slot in the wheelie bin, recycling box and wormery. True, we have a little further to walk with our bags of rubbish, but at least the bin is not the first thing I see. And access for the bin men is easier.

You don't have to do much to make a difference to your front garden – but do something, and your efforts will be rewarded. It could be just a couple of large pots of scented shrubs by the door that will release their scent as you brush past, planting a flowering tree in an old dustbin, or painting that wall or fence a colour that co-ordinates with the planting. The best inspiration comes from other London gardeners. Take time to look at the examples in the streets around your home or workplace – it's not being nosy, it's looking for ideas. Many of the private gardens open to the public through the National Gardens Scheme (▶ 263) will have innovative front gardens – some may be worth a quick snoop if you're in the area, even if you've missed the date to see the back garden. Here are just a few of the best ideas I've seen on my travels:

- Picket fences or railings look great with bushy plants such as lavender, silvery senecio, hebes or rosemary poking through the gaps – especially if the colours have been chosen to harmonize.
- Convert your front wall into a raised bed by building another wall parallel to it and filling the gap between them with soil. (Remember that

walls need concrete footings, and make sure there is adequate drainage. If the ground is covered in concrete, smash through it in a few places to reach the soil below.)

- Slate chippings look good as a low-maintenance ground cover, and come in a variety of colours including a subtle greyish purple. But make sure you have a retaining wall or ledge or they'll scatter all over the pavement. Avoid in areas of heavy bike or pushchair traffic, and provide a protective buffer zone if you have polished wood floors inside.

- Minimalism works well with the right façade. I've seen a lovely hedge of the feathery bamboo *Fargesia nitida* with just plain concrete paving slabs behind; a low white wall with a hedge of lavender behind and slate chippings underfoot; and a minimalist parterre – a simple pattern of low box hedging with pots of seasonal bulbs or other plants in the 'compartments'.

- Keeping to one colour scheme in a small space can look smart, and will help concentrate your mind when buying plants. There's a front garden in Notting Hill that's filled with nothing but pale blue bearded iris. A bit boring for the rest of the year, perhaps, but for a few weeks in late May and early June it's sheer heaven.

One last word about front gardens. Someone once asked me if I wasn't scared that people would take my flowers or steal my pots. She said she had done nothing in her own front garden for that reason. Quite apart from the fact that I've only once been prey to a plant burglar, it struck me as terribly sad that the fear of having nothing should keep someone with nothing. I prefer to believe that beauty is contagious. When one house starts, another will follow. If you need further inspiration, head for Choumert Square in Peckham, where the string of minuscule front gardens – many of them created on a shoe-string budget – are the pride and joy of all the owners.

Places to go for inspiration:

Containers

Gardening in pots or containers is often considered a compromise – something you do if you haven't enough space or time to garden 'properly'. Yet for many Londoners, container gardening is not only a lifeline, it has become a whole new approach that brings spontaneity and seasonal change to gardens of all sizes, shapes and styles. From a few pots of spring bulbs on a front doorstep to a collection of favourite plants grouped on a terrace, potted gardens can be as instant or as permanent as you wish. You can have trees in galvanized dustbins, a tepee of sweet peas, or organic herbs and tomatoes in smart glazed pots. The containers can be built into the structure of your garden, or moved around at will to provide shade, privacy, or seasonal scent and colour as certain plants come into their own. Snowdrops and *Iris reticulata* near your windows in winter bring cheer and beauty when it's too cold to go out; replace them in summer with fragrant stocks and lilies that will waft their scent inside. And when your vegetables are over in the autumn, plant tulips or sow bright hardy annuals – the promise of next summer.

Before I had a garden of my own, I grew things in pots, buckets, old tin baths and laundry tubs – in fact, anything that had a drainage hole in the bottom and would accommodate a plant or two. I gardened on window ledges, in tiny balconies, along the small strips of space around side-returns and rooftops. I loved it, but I thought that when I got a garden my potted gardening would stop. It didn't. Seven years on, my tiny Brixton garden is crowded with containers of various shapes and sizes. While I've relished the chance to plant trees in open ground, and give my grapevines and clematis the root run they need, I have not turned my back on my pots. In fact, they are the fun part of the garden – the element I most enjoy.

There is the satisfaction of matching the right plant to the right pot – the colours and textures of flowers and foliage, as well as the size and shape of plant and planter come into play. There is the artistry of arranging the pots to their best advantage, and ringing the changes at certain times of year when different plants come into their own. And there's the joy and ease of looking after them: though watering can be more demanding, it's often easier to care for plants in pots. Fussy plants can be given their exact requirements in terms of soil, water, feed and so on, and as they are nearer eye level, it's easier to spot pests and diseases and nip these in the bud. Far from being makeshift, make-do players in the garden, container plants can be the stars of the show, acting out a year-long drama against a more permanent backdrop.

You can buy new containers in wood, metal or glazed terracotta, or scavenge for discarded dustbins, enamel bread bins, old olive oil tins or anything else that takes your fancy. The crucial thing is to check for drainage holes, making new ones if necessary, and to go for the largest size feasible, unless you want to be watering twice a day in summer. Placing some fragments of broken crock in the bottom, over the hole, will prevent all the moisture from seeping straight out, while adding an inch or two of gravel (or low-weight clay pellets or polystyrene) ensures that the roots won't sit in water. Use a good-quality potting compost such as John Innes No. 2 (with garden soil you run the risk of introducing pests) and mix it with well-rotted horse manure, garden compost and a liberal sprinkling of bonemeal, leaving at least an inch free at the top to make watering easier. With smaller pots, it's advisable to mix water-retaining granules (available from garden centres) in with the soil when you're planting, but don't overdo it or they will ooze up and lie in a jelly-like mass on the surface. Using a mulch will help keep water in and weeds down – pebbles, spent oyster shells and coloured aquarium gravel look attractive and may even help deter slugs and snails.

Most plants will grow happily in containers – in fact some, like fig trees and agapanthus, positively prefer to have their roots restrained. Others simply look better in pots. For years now, I've grown a collection of hellebores in old fluted metal laundry tubs, and it is such a treat to be able to see their heavenly speckled faces without stooping to the ground. Container-grown plants tend to need more feeding than those in the border, however, and you will probably need to re-pot every two to three years – or at least to replace the top six inches of soil. Yellowing leaves and stunted growth are a sign that a plant is unhappy – if it gets really pot-bound it may even crack its container. The other main thing to look out for is vine weevil – the scourge of container gardeners everywhere and particularly in London. The beastly grey-black beetles can be found on the plants in summer, when they bite notches into the outer edges of leaves. But it's the pale, creamy curved grubs that cause the real damage, feasting on the roots of your favourite plants – camellias, heucheras, sedums and fuchsias are among those that are particularly vulnerable. Unless you're vigilant, the first you'll know of it will be when you go to touch a plant that looks sick and the top growth comes clean away in your hand. There are various chemical remedies on the market, but if your neighbour has vine weevils more will march back over the wall. (For details of biological controls, see page 79.)

If you like moving your pots around the garden, how about moving them into the house as well? A potted rose or datura can fill a whole room with its scent, while a bay pyramid or box spiral can be adorned with fairy lights as an alternative Christmas tree. (See 'Inside Out Gardening', page 110, for more ideas.) Fixing wheels to larger planters makes scooting them about much easier – or keep a skateboard or low trolley on casters for the purpose. Container gardening really does make gardening a moveable feast. And, with so many Londoners moving house every few years, there's the added advantage that you can take your garden with you when you go.

Places to go for inspiration:

Bonnington Square (▶ 157)
The Chelsea Gardener (▶ 232)
Claridge's Hotel (▶ 116)
Clifton Nurseries (▶ 232)

The Dorchester Hotel (▶ 116)
Grosvenor House (▶ 116)
Little Venice (▶ 140)
Neal's Yard (▶ 120)

DESIGNING
BACK GARDENS

Small is Beautiful

We can't all have the hundred-foot, south-west-facing garden with the perfect lawn and old roses that never get blackspot. In London, as in most cities, space is at a premium, and most of us have to make do with an average plot of forty feet or so. Many Londoners not only make do, but make a miracle of much smaller plots hemmed in on all sides by surrounding buildings. It is always inspiring to see what Londoners do with their back gardens, whatever the size. When I was a child, and my family moved from the countryside to the suburbs of London, my favourite pastime was to wander unseen along the edges of the golf course at the end of our garden and look at all the other back gardens. Unfortunately, there are few places in London where this is possible – though, like Virginia Woolf, who described it so well in *A Room of One's Own*, I love the glimpses of back gardens stretching into infinity that you get from the top windows of high terraced houses. Happily, the National Gardens Scheme enables us to be nosy/seek inspiration while helping good causes. The annual NGS Yellow Book of private gardens in England and Wales that open to the public in aid of charity on specified dates is available from good bookshops, and there is a smaller leaflet on London gardens (▶ 263). Some of the gardens are open for just one day a year, so it's worth noting down the ones in your area, or that you think sound most interesting, so you don't miss them. It's fun visiting other people's gardens anywhere, but seeing them in the city where you live provides insight into how other Londoners cope with the challenges of shade, lack of space, clay soil and overlooking buildings that beset us all.

Lack of space can actually end up being a blessing. If you have a busy job or like to go away a lot at weekends, the last thing you want is a huge high-maintenance garden. It's relatively easy to keep on top of a small garden – and you get to know the places where the slugs and snails hide. A small space needn't be boring: you can ring the changes with containers on wheels and other moveable features and by dressing it up for parties. Put some thought into the initial design, and you'll be amazed at what you can achieve. In fact, a classic solution to the problem of the long thin London garden – the width of the house but a hundred feet or so in length – is to divide the large area up into a number of smaller, inter-linking gardens.

Good design is even more crucial when you are pressed for space. Sit down with a pen and paper and make a list of the ways in which you might want to use your garden, and the people who will be its main users. This will prove extremely instructive and, even if you do end up working with a garden designer, it'll give you a useful starting point for discussions. You should also track the light at different times of the year, making a note of how, where and when it falls. In a small garden, the shade from surrounding buildings may mean you get a lot less light than you might like, and you may have some difficult decisions to make. Do you devote the sunny areas to sun-loving plants or sun-loving people? My back garden, for instance, gets no direct sunshine till the sun hauls itself over the roof at around eleven o'clock, but then about half of it enjoys full sun until evening right through the summer months. Because I like to sit in the sunshine, my sunniest area

is mainly taken up by the deck, with a line of tomato plants in pots along the south-facing wall, and morning glory, wisteria and other sun-loving climbers growing up the south-west-facing rear wall of the house. The big open border opposite is devoted to a variety of shade-loving foliage plants. As most of these are evergreen, they provide an interesting view through the French windows all winter when it's too cold to sit out, and a glossy green backdrop for the pots of early flowering bulbs in the foreground.

Views from the house are important in a climate where the garden will be admired from inside for quite a few months of the year. The designer David Hicks, whose most lasting legacy was in garden design, used to begin all his exterior schemes from indoors, and take the axes and proportions for his 'garden rooms' from the lines of the house. In some London houses you'll be lucky to have a view out from the main rooms; the layout of the average Victorian terrace, with its kitchen/diner and bathroom tacked on to the back, leaves the rear reception room looking out on to the 'side-return' – that dark, dreary dog-leg in which nothing will grow and whose main purpose seems to be to bump up the overall dimensions of the garden in estate agents' details. In the original layout, the only access to the garden was often through a kitchen door, also to the side; this can also be the case in otherwise rather grand Georgian houses. If you don't have proper access and views to the garden, it's worth taking the plunge and opening some up. I've seen side-returns glazed over and incorporated into stunning, state-of-the-art kitchens, and the entire rear wall taken up by glass doors that fold or slide back to create a seamless indoor/outdoor space in summer. Even if your budget doesn't run to major building works, you might be able to move one doorway or create a new window that brings a view of the garden into the house.

Most designers will tell you it's desirable not to be able to see all of the garden from the house, and a sense of 'something beyond' does add to the experience of exploring a garden. Even in the smallest gardens it's usually possible to create a 'secret garden' within the garden – whether it is used for vegetable growing, a children's playground or quiet meditation is up to you. One view you won't want from the house is that of tools and bags of compost and pots of old bulbs that are dying down. Sometimes there's room for a work area behind a summerhouse or shed. If you've no room for a shed, put some trellis up to make a screen for a work area behind; or find a settle bench with plenty of storage in the base. I've commandeered the basement area beneath our deck as my potting shed, with plenty of shelves and a table that can be folded flat against the wall when not in use. We all need somewhere to hide.

Ground Control

The garden writer Mirabel Osler has written passionately about 'freeing oneself from the tyranny of the lawn', and in a small to average-sized London garden, I am inclined to agree. On the plus side, lawns are lovely to sit out on in summer, kind to the knees of crawling children and past-their-prime weeders, and just, somehow, the done thing in a garden, like candles on a birthday cake, or hats at a wedding. They are also relatively cheap – turf costs from £2.50 per square yard and, if you've the patience, a sown one is a good deal cheaper. You could even intersperse some plants of chamomile or creeping thyme, or turn a section of it over to a wildflower meadow (see page 69). For those with the room and enough sunshine, it would be hard to let go of the lawn. Greenacres (▸ 248) are a good source of products such as rapid, ready-sprouted grass seed for re-sowing bald patches that can help you get the best out of urban lawns.

But in smaller city gardens, are they really worth the bother? Lawns are hard work, and mowing the lawn constitutes one of those perpetual 'jobs to be done' – no sooner has it been completed than the next ordeal already looms. Remember that you'll need not only a lawnmower but also a shed to keep it in which, in small gardens, can prove problematic. As many London gardeners have found to their cost, a lawn never looks better than in the couple of months immediately after laying it (indeed, some bite the bullet and lay a new one each spring). The main trouble is shade from surrounding buildings (lawns love sun), coupled with our erratic climate. A few days of solid rain followed by energetic bike use by young children is enough to turn any lawn into a soggy, muddy mess. And in a dry summer, water bans or no, it seems impossible to prevent your sward turning into a depressing patchy brown expanse that rustles wherever you walk. When I visited that ultimate urban garden, the Queen's own at Buckingham Palace, on a press trip one August, I was shocked to see that, in spite of throngs of gardeners and more sprinklers than the Water Board would allow at Wimbledon, the royal lawns were a uniform shade of straw. She would no doubt blame the sifting, shuffling feet of all those garden-party goers, but if even the Queen can't cope with a lawn in the city, what hope is there for the rest of us?

Other alternatives include decking and gravel, both of which are quite rightly suffering from backlash at the moment. As anyone (like me) who has installed a deck in their garden will know by now, these are not the maintenance-free zones they are made out to be. Indeed, as I sweep my deck of dead leaves in the autumn, and get down on hands and knees each spring to scrub off the layer of slippery green algae that has accumulated over the winter, I contemplate the fact that, the more we try to turn our gardens into outdoor rooms, the more gardening comes to resemble housework. As for gravel, the weeds will shoot through unless you lay a permeable under-layer, and you'll have to contend with leaves and debris accumulating in it, children and pets dislodging it, toddlers trying to eat it, and cats mistaking it for a litter tray.

A terrace of some sort of stone, tiles or bricks is a stylish and timeless option. Pale limestone is pricey but beautiful, and the perfect complement to streamlined modern designs; while old bricks laid in a herringbone pattern will look as if they have always been there just a few weeks later. If you can leave some spaces for planting in between the pavers to soften larger expanses of paving, so much the better. One East End gardener I visited had made the most of his shady north-facing garden by covering the main area with a pebble mosaic. It took him and his partner many months to lay, but looks great all the year round (from upstairs as well), and requires only the odd session with a pressure-hose to keep it in tip-top condition. Balancing garden furniture on the bumpy surface might be a problem, though.

Decide whether you want your seating area in the morning or evening sun, or in the shade (you can have more than one if you have the space), and take your pick of the flooring options available. Take your time. Like flooring in a house, the right (or wrong) material underfoot has more impact than any other single part of the garden – choose the outdoor equivalent of a naff swirly carpet and you'll have a hard time covering it up. While you're making your decision, bring a heap of old rugs and blankets and cushions outside and turn your garden into a Moroccan souk for the summer. You may find you like it that way instead.

Some gardeners get round the problem of what to lay underfoot by planting up every inch of the garden. A sea of flowers and foliage certainly looks lovely, and if dense enough, will keep the weeds down and water in, but the eye (not to mention the feet) needs a resting space. Gardens that just lead you down endless pathways and back again are tiring, both mentally and physically.

The Outdoor Room

These days, Londoners see their gardens more and more as an extension of the house, an outdoor space into which many of the activities enjoyed inside – eating, entertaining, cooking, playing, relaxing, even sleeping or studying – can spill over in good weather. Flats with gardens are always easier to sell, and even the smallest backyard or balcony has the potential for outdoor living. There's nothing nicer than heading outside on a sunny summer morning for breakfast and seeing how the day unfolds – an *al fresco* lunch

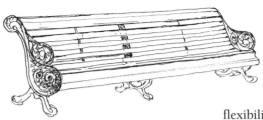

with friends and their children, perhaps, or a barbecue party that carries on late into the evening.

The key to designing for outdoor living in a restricted space is flexibility. See if some of the main elements can be employed to do two jobs at once. Steps can double up as extra seating, for instance, as can the surrounds of raised beds and water features, if they are made wide enough – this will avoid cluttering up your garden with excess furniture. The designer and TV presenter Joe Swift (▶ 273) likes to build wood or cast concrete corner seats into his urban gardens so that a table placed in that corner already has seating on two sides. The backs of these seats, in turn, can provide retaining walls for raised beds in which lavender, herbs or other pleasantly aromatic plants can be grown. Sometimes Swift paints the seats in colours that blend or contrast with the garden's planting scheme.

A place to sit and eat or hang out with friends is pretty central to what most Londoners want from their garden. It makes sense to create this near the house, on a deck or terrace where you can carry drinks and food in and out with ease – though sometimes part of the fun is to make a pilgrimage to a more secluded corner. If your garden is very sunny, you may want to provide some shade in the form of a pergola up which vines or other climbers can be grown, or a simple awning made from tough canvas with rope slung through metal eyelets in the corners. No one likes eating in the glare of the midday sun. Pergolas can be extremely simple affairs fashioned from lengths of timber – the Traditional Garden Supply Company (▶ 257) currently does one for under £200. A simple but stylish pergola I saw at the garden designer Sue Berger's house in Bristol was made from the rusty metal reinforcing bars, twisted like barley sugar, which are used in the construction of buildings. At night, fairy lights and tin lanterns can be strung among the supports and foliage. The furniture you choose should be in keeping with the general style of your outdoor room – the latest Italian designs in slick steel or plastic, raw hunks of wood or slate, or a cheerful mismatch of old metal tables and painted cricket chairs.

If you like to cook outside, why not design the perfect built-in barbecue, with room to warm plates and chop vegetables alongside? Or, for a real luxury everyone will love, follow domestic goddess Nigella Lawson's example and have a pizza oven built into a wall. If you are really pushed for space, buy one of those stylish free-standing shiny steel drum barbecues, or a Mexican 'chimera' which can double up as an attractive outdoor heater once the food is cooked and eaten. Once glamorous and rare, and reminiscent of Paris cafés, the gas-fired patio heater has now become rather commonplace, but they are easy and effective, so I'm not going to knock them. In a simpler style of garden where such an appliance might look out of place, why not build a fire in a sturdy metal brazier or sink a metal or earth-lined 'fire pit' into a stone terrace? There is something eternally elemental and romantic about warming oneself around real flames. Keep an eye on the safety aspect, however, and avoid overhanging branches.

Outdoor rooms don't only need tables and chairs; just as inside the house, they can be furnished with smaller occasional tables for drinks and half-finished books, potted plants and pieces of art. Going back to the 'doubling up' principle, you could get hold of some rough-hewn blocks of wood that can function as low stools or tables but also look splendidly sculptural just standing around. In a small urban garden, sculpture is best confined to just a few elements, or the space will begin to resemble a craft shop or gallery. Again, think of things that can 'double up' – the New Art Centre at Roche Court near Salisbury (▶ 247) has sculptural marble bowls that also work as bird baths, and a 'wing' structure that provides shade or shelter. One of the simplest and most atmospheric ideas is to incorporate inscriptions into your garden. Follow the Scottish artist Ian Hamilton Finlay's lead and hang a fragment of poetry, inscribed in slate, from a wall or the branches of a tree, or just add a word ('PEACE', 'LOVE', 'SILENCE') on a single boulder to the plants in your border. Wolseley Fine Arts in Notting Hill (▶ 247) is a good source for garden art – they have a small sculpture garden at the rear of the gallery and hold an annual garden sculpture show in June. John Pitt (▶ 246), who is represented there, can also create inscriptions to order. (For other ideas, see 'Urban Inspiration', pages 70–73.)

If you're having a party, you can dress up your garden, just as you dress up yourself. Awnings and lots of rugs and cushions strewn about the place are a must by day (stick to a colour scheme such as plain white or different shades of one colour such as pink), while dramatic lighting will jazz up the atmosphere by night. Flares on bamboo poles create an exciting welcome, especially in winter, or follow the Italian example and line steps and paths with rows of containerized candles. In a minimalist white garden, slides projected around the walls would be the ultimate in outdoor entertainment. (See pages 55–7 for more lighting ideas.)

But outdoor living isn't all lunches and parties. Some lucky self-employed people work in their gardens, making the commute to their job a mere amble across the lawn. You may not have room for a huge state-of-the-art studio, but why not consider a customized summerhouse or shed? The artist Kevin Wilson, whose Dulwich garden is open through the National Gardens Scheme, added a Louisiana-style deck and veranda to a standard kit shed to create the perfect outdoor hangout, complete with rocking chairs and wood-burning stove, while landscape architect Jonathan Bell (▶ 268) made himself an enviable minimalist office in the form of a simple glass and timber cube in his tiny garden in Hammersmith. At the end of the day, you may just love your outdoor room so much that you don't want to come inside to sleep. And you'd be in excellent company. Multiple Chelsea gold medal winner Tom Stuart-Smith (▶ 274) and his family spend hot summer nights in an ornate little marquee that's a left-over from one of his show gardens, while Declan Buckley (▶ 269) was asked by one London client to incorporate an outdoor bed into his design. He obliged – with a timber surround and canopy and a springy turf 'mattress'. How heavenly to snuggle beneath the covers and look up and see the stars through a tracery of trees overhead.

Trees in Your Garden

Why not do your bit for London's oxygen supply and plant a tree in your own front or back garden? Unless you have a huge garden, choose a small or slow-growing tree that won't take over the space. Eucalyptus, for example, look wonderful, and the soothing soft rattle of their leaves in the wind can help mask traffic noise, but they can quickly get out of hand. And if you want to avoid heavy shade in summer, it's best to go for a type of tree with a light, open canopy. Some of my favourite trees that are suitable for front or back gardens include:

- *Prunus* x *subhirtella* 'Autumnalis', the lovely winter-flowering cherry, whose pink-tinged white blossom appears on the bare black branches from November till the first leaves form in spring. A row of them bordering the street in a front garden in Hampstead is decorated with fairy lights at Christmas.
- *Amelanchier canadensis*, with its starry white flowers and stunning autumn colour; this rarely grows above 15 feet and is a great front garden tree.
- *Magnolia stellata* is more delicate and compact than most magnolias and it has pure white star-shaped flowers that stand out against a dark backdrop.
- Crab apples are great for year-round appeal, with clouds of white or pink-tinged spring blossom, and cracking autumn foliage followed by

a fine crop of brightly coloured fruit suspended on bare branches like party decorations. They rarely grow higher than 30 feet so are unlikely to get you into trouble.

- Silver birches, particularly the Himalayan birch, *Betula utilis* var. *jacquemontii*, which has bark that is cleaner and whiter than most. Birches look prettiest when young, but can reach 60–90 feet, depending on the variety and situation. One way around this, though it might sound drastic, is to cut the tree down almost to the ground when it begins to get too big. The trunk should re-sprout with several smaller stems – the multi-stemmed birch beloved of modernist architects. There's no doubt that birches do complement modern architecture; even the grimmest 1960s office block looks better when glimpsed through a grove of graceful birch trees.

- Fruit trees look great when they are in blossom, and have the added advantage of producing something edible, too. I think I would choose a Comice pear for its blossom, as well as the delicious fruit, which never travels well, and a damson or Victoria plum. Buy or order fruit trees from a reputable nursery, where you can get advice on pollinators. They can be bought and trained in a variety of different shapes and sizes – those really short on space should consider 'columnar' or 'stepover' apples.

- *Cercis siliquastrum*, otherwise known as the Judas tree, is a picture in spring, when tiny pea-like flowers in shades of magenta and mauve cluster all along the bare branches. It makes a stunning street tree in the Mediterranean, but needs a sunny corner here.

- *Sorbus cashmiriana* is, for me, the most beautiful of all the sorbuses, with soft green leaves lined in grey-green, pale pink flowers in May and clusters of pearly white berries which persist long after leaf-fall. It can survive a fair amount of shade.

The crucial thing to remember when planting a tree is to make the hole large enough. You've probably heard the saying that it's better to have a dime plant in a dollar hole than the other way around, and there's a lot of truth in it, especially when it comes to trees. A whippy sapling will soon catch up with a larger, more expensive specimen, given the right position and treatment. The planting hole should be at least twice as deep and wide as the root ball of the tree (or, if it's bare-rooted, the reach of the roots). The soil in the bottom should be forked a little loose and mixed with a good couple of spadefuls of well-rotted manure or garden compost and a handful of bonemeal. If you're staking the tree (and you should ask for advice on this when you buy your tree, as different trees need different treatment), this is the time to add the stake, so it will be anchored firmly in the ground. Pour a large bucket of water into the hole (the tree itself should have been soaking in water for about an hour or so). The next part of the procedure is, ideally, a two-person job: one holds the tree erect so its roots stand loosely in the centre of the hole, with the stake a couple of inches away from the trunk, while the other packs the excavated soil back in and around it. When you have finished, stamp the soil down firmly around the trunk and attach the stake loosely with a rubber tree tie. Water frequently for the first few months, particularly if the weather is dry.

Trees can also be planted in large containers, of course. I have several in old galvanized dustbins in my front garden, underplanted with spring bulbs and mind-your-own-business. One day, I tell them, when I have enough room in the country, they may be liberated into open ground. But till then, they seem happy. At the hairdressers Fourth Floor in Northington Street WC1, the owner Richard Stepney has several small apple trees in terracotta pots, underplanted with creeping thymes, on the narrow roof terrace that runs round two sides of the 1930s building. It's a wonderful thing to sit out there, way above the city, and watch the bees buzzing from flower to flower – judging by the healthy crop of apples, they do a good job. If you have bags of patience, you can even raise your own trees, from acorns or beechnuts. The popular Trees of Time and Place project encouraged people to collect seed from their favourite trees – that billowing poplar from the local park, or one with childhood memories – raise them in pots and plant the seedlings out in community woodlands.

When planting a tree in open ground, do take care not to plant it too close to your house. Insurance companies can be famously suspicious about any tree that is less than 30 feet from the house; indeed, I sometimes think they'd be happier if all the trees in London were dug up and replaced by plastic ones. But trees are often blamed for problems caused by something else entirely. One of the most unusual private houses in the capital is that designed and lived in by Richard Burton, the architect whose National Gallery proposal had Prince Charles complaining about 'monstrous carbuncles' many years ago. Burton built his Kentish Town home around a huge London plane tree that rises up through the roof of the entrance hall and forms a stunning canopy above the glass-roofed kitchen. His erstwhile neighbours once complained that the tree's roots had weakened their house wall, but after lengthy investigations the culprit was found to be the clematis in their own backyard.

Water

'Just as a room without a mirror is dead, so a garden without water is never quite alive,' asserted Beverley Nichols in his 1950s classic, *Merry Hall* (recently republished by the Timber Press). Though I am not in accord with the archly misogynous Mr Nichols about everything (he devotes an entire acerbic chapter to 'Women and Flowers'), I heartily agree with him here. Water seems to add another dimension to any garden – whether it be the shifting reflections on the surface of a still pool, the soothing sound of a gentle fountain or the energizing effect of a waterfall. But creating a water feature needs thought and planning, particularly in the average small London garden. Crammed into a corner like an extra piece of furniture, the bubble-jet fountain springing from an overturned urn or surrounded by a sack of pebbles has become the cliché launched by a thousand makeover shows. In order truly to enhance a garden, water must be carefully integrated into the overall design – and ideally from the start.

Decide what you want the water in your garden to do. Water can work as a mirror, a coolant, a humidifier, or to give added impact to a piece of sculpture. It can be the means to indulge a love of water plants such as water lilies or flag iris, or to provide a home for frogs, fish and dragonflies. In the city it also has other, vital uses. Its sound can mask noise from neighbours, road or air traffic, or provide a focus for meditation after a busy day at work. Then decide how you want it to look. Water is often associated with natural-looking gardens, but in all but the largest plots or in wildlife gardens, there seems little point in feigning naturalness: reed-fringed ponds and rocky cascades may work well in rural acres, but in a small urban setting they will fool nobody. Bold graphic shapes such as squares, circles and rectangles sit well in an outdoor room, and their proportions can be chosen to harmonize with those of the house. They also fit well into the regular unit sizes of stone paving or decking – and if you're clever with the surround, you can avoid the common problem of the lining showing when the level drops in summer. All sorts of stylish modern materials, including pale limestone, galvanized metal and colour-rendered concrete can be employed to make a strong contemporary statement.

If the water is to be moving, you will need to install a pump; take details of the scheme you have in mind to a good garden centre or water garden specialist for advice. Ask to hear the pump running – although it will obviously be buried out of sight, some pumps can be incredibly loud, and will undermine the aura of peace you are aiming to achieve. Solar pumps are an option for the ecologically minded, but most will only work when the sun is shining. Ask the folk at CAT (▶ 265) about pumps that can store solar-generated power for use on dull days and in the evenings.

London is full of stylish water gardens. Those at Mile End Park (▶ 175) and the Barbican Centre (▶ 159) spring to mind, but the most stunning and innovative by far are the Water Gardens on the Hyde Park Estate, Edgware Road (▶ 142). Here, artist Tony Heywood has transformed a dreary 1960s tower block complex into a series of exciting water gardens complete with mobile islands, modern sculpture and ambitious, atmospheric planting.

When it comes to inspiration in private gardens, a clever solution to the shady basement well was created by the architect Dale Loth in Islington. By excavating out a little into the garden, he transformed the area into a Japanese-inspired water garden with a rectangular pool (with underwater lighting) fed by water trickling down a wall of rippled stainless steel, with clumps of arum lilies and bamboo, and metal grille steps up to the rest of the garden. A touch of drama was commissioned by the hairdresser Charles Worthington, who wanted a sculptural water feature to provide a focus for the high rear wall of his small London garden. Stephen Woodhams (▶ 274) designed for him a wall-mounted fountain dripping down a sheet of sandblasted glass into a white concrete tank, the edges of which double up as extra seating. As is often the case, they had to experiment to get the flow just right – the first attempt was so loud it drowned out conversation.

Some of the most effective urban water features are simple shallow pools that reflect the changing patterns of clouds and foliage overhead. A galvanized metal rill just a couple of inches deep was enough to bring a softer, sensual dimension to a minimalist roof terrace in Clerkenwell. You could even add a geometric-shaped island, with sculptural elements in among the planting. Still pools need more maintenance to keep clean than moving water features, but they may have room for a few oxygenating plants, which will help do the job, or even a water lily or two. If you don't have the depth for a water lily, don't despair. The interior designer Tricia Guild floats rose heads and petals on the surface of her small square pond when she is having a party – a practice of which even the testy Beverley Nichols (who used to do exactly the same thing) would have to approve.

Plants for water gardens can be divided into three groups: oxygenators, marginals and aquatics.

- **Oxygenators** live beneath the surface and work hard to keep the water clear. Canadian pondweed (*Lagarosiphon major*) and *Ceratophyllum demersum* are two of the most reliable and fast-working, and are generally sold with weights to sink them to the base of the pond, where they should multiply.
- **Marginal plants** like to be planted in 1–6 inches of water around the edges of a pond, and good ones for contemporary water gardens include the stately arum lily (*Zantedeschia aethiopica*), the lovely blue water iris (*Iris laevigata*), the dwarf bulrush (*Typha minima*) and *Equisetum* x *trachyodon* with its striking sectioned stems – though it may be wise to contain its roots within a pot.
- **Aquatics**, most of which need a depth of 10–26 inches, include the water hawthorn (*Aponogeton distachyos*), with its long oval leaves and vanilla-scented flower spikes and, of course, the much-loved water lily (*Nymphaea*). There is one to suit almost every pond size – but remember that they need some sun in order to flower. (Water garden suppliers are listed on page 241.)

Places to go for inspiration:

The Barbican Centre (▶ 159)   London Wetlands Centre (▶ 216)
Cutler Street Gardens (▶ 169)   Mile End Park (▶ 175)
Diana, Princess of Wales Fountain (▶ 144)   The Sanderson Hotel (▶ 121)
Jubilee Park (▶ 179)   The Water Gardens (▶ 142)
Kensington Roof Gardens (▶ 147)

Lighting

As evening is the time when many Londoners can enjoy their gardens, lighting is vital to extend the life of your outdoor room late into the night. It can also be useful for safety and security reasons. You want enough light to see and eat by, and to outline potential hazards such as steps or water features. Beyond that, the function of outdoor lighting is to provide atmosphere. Too often, the only lighting in a garden is an ugly spotlight on the back of the house which throws its Colditz-like glare all over the garden – or, worse, comes on whenever anyone moves. (See pages 25–6 for the adverse effects of over-lighting.)

You'll have to decide whether to install an electronic system or rely on impromptu effects using candles and so on. Candles are the cheapest and easiest way of lighting the garden, and can also create magical effects, but must be treated with care, for safety reasons. On all but the stillest nights, you'll need to protect the flame against wind as well as causing a fire, so enclose the candles in punched tin or glass lanterns – Habitat, Heal's and other shops usually have a good supply in all shapes and sizes (▶ 244). Even plain night lights in empty jam jars can look great dotted around the garden – ring the changes with small coloured tumblers or Moroccan tea glasses to look pretty on a dining table. Or make up your own effects: for summer parties, I often mass twenty or more night lights in the base of a huge punched tin bowl from Mexico – the sides of the bowl reflect the light all around the garden. For a touch of true romance, try suspending an old-fashioned candelabrum from the branch of a tree – but make sure hot wax doesn't drip on people's heads.

If you opt for electrical lighting, this can range from a string of fairy lights plugged into an outdoor socket (which an electrician will have to install) or a cheap low-voltage set bought from a garden centre with change from £50, to an elaborate circuit system installed by a professional. Smaller gardens may be fine with a self-installed system featuring smaller low-voltage fittings, shorter cable runs and a transformer to lower the voltage. Shops such as B&Q and Homebase (▶ 249) usually stock systems which include lamps on spikes that can be sunk into the ground and angled up through foliage or the branches of trees. Be sure to conceal the wires in an area where spades and forks won't penetrate. In larger London gardens where outdoor entertaining will be a frequent event, the latter may well be worth the investment. Though expensive, the lighting system can be easily and efficiently controlled by the flick of a switch (or, more likely, a portable control panel of keypads and dimmers) and, if well installed, should be safe and problem-free. It will probably use the mains voltage system, and should have special outdoor sockets and plastic-coated armoured cable buried at least 18 inches deep in the soil. A master switch in the house can control different circuits for different purposes and different parts of the garden, and the subtler effects can be monitored by remote control. A good garden designer should be able to advise on lighting systems – or, ideally, contact a specialist such as John Cullen Lighting (▶ 250).

Focus different types of electric lighting in different areas of the garden. Downlighters can be employed to highlight features such as trees and sculpture from above, and create soft pools of light where you are eating. If placed high in a tree, a downlighter can create the effect of the full moon shining through the branches and casting delicate shadows on grass or paving. Trendy Los Angeles garden designer Judy Kameon rigged up a simple Japanese round paper lantern in the large tree above her dining table and the effect was pure, subtle magic. Uplighters work in the opposite way, of course. Bury them at the bases of plants to throw them into silhouette and cast dramatic shadows up and around the walls. They can be recessed behind glass around the edges of decks or paving, or hidden beneath the treads of stairs. For a more bohemian look that is easy to create, stud starry outdoor fairy lights among the branches of trees or wind them around the posts of a pergola – stick to plain white bulbs to prevent the place looking like Santa's Grotto. One summer I strung fairy lights back and forth in a long zigzag from the back of our house to the rear garden wall. My fears at having created a Greek taverna scenario receded once scented and flowering climbers began to entwine themselves along the wires. In a more minimalist garden, a square 'net' panel of fairy lights hung from a white wall would look simply stunning.

For formal entrances and longer driveways there are electric lights on posts, while wall-mounted lights are useful around front doors, if only to help you find your keys. Solar-powered fittings which store up the sunshine all day and come on after dark are available for these purposes – some of the mail order companies stock them as well as larger garden centres, but do check first that they will be powerful enough for your requirements.

Waterproofing is vital for garden lighting, so if you can't find what you want in a garden centre or DIY store, you might come up with something striking or unusual in a ship's chandler or bathroom store. And how about experimenting with neon? Done cleverly, this can give your garden the surreal edge of a modern art installation. Stephen Woodhams (▶ 274) has used strips of blue neon lighting to bring out the sheen of the galvanized metal in many of his London roof gardens and terraces, while in his own south London garden the bases of a row of large concrete aggregate planters were ringed with pink neon hoops.

Water features combine well with lighting: a ghostly green gleam from the base of a pond or rill can bathe the entire garden in an otherworldly glow, and maybe send shadows of fish swimming around the walls. And a still pond, however tiny, can be transformed into something really glamorous with a flotilla of floating candles – citronella scented ones will also help keep mosquitoes at bay.

Places to go for inspiration:

Kensington Roof Gardens (▶ 147)   Tate Modern (▶ 153)
The Sanderson Hotel Courtyard (▶ 121)

STYLES OF GARDENING

Minimalist

There are many reasons for choosing a minimalist style of garden – one of which is watching too many makeover programmes on the television. In fact, most of the 'instant gardens' on the box are too busy and fussy to be truly minimalist – filled with far too many 'features' and contrasting materials. A real minimalist garden has a quiet, uncluttered atmosphere that relaxes the mind; it is worth remembering that some of the earliest minimalist gardens were created by Zen Buddhists for contemplation. This air of quiet is one good reason why some people go for a minimalist style for their London garden. After a hectic day at work or battling with the tube or traffic, it is a wonderful feeling to step outside into a clear and uncomplicated space, with just a few key design elements and plants to focus the eye and perhaps the trickle of water to help still the mind.

Minimalism also makes for flexible spaces that connect in a satisfactory way with the architecture of the house. If you have spent a lot of time and trouble (not to say money) making the inside of your home reflect a penchant for clean lines and contemporary design, the chances are you will not want traditional herbaceous borders, ornate terracotta pots and cherub statues outside. It is relatively easy to link the interior and exterior spaces by continuing the same materials outside. This looks particularly effective if the spaces are allowed physically to flow into one another by the means of large windows or sliding doors. At the minimalist architect John Pawson's house in Notting Hill, the pale limestone paving of the ground floor living space continued seamlessly out into the garden – as did a simple stonework top that stretched along one wall of the house. The 'walls' of this outside room were chunky wooden trellis, and among the very few plants were some young fig trees and an ancient wisteria, which threw dramatic dappled shadows on the stone floor. The sparseness of the minimalist garden makes room for such beautiful and fleeting natural effects that might easily be lost in a more complex scheme. The shadows of gently flexing bamboos against a plain white wall are often just as beautiful as the plants themselves, and the annual pink snowfall of petals from an ornamental cherry tree can turn a simple courtyard into a magical, almost surreal space for a few days each year[A relatively empty space can also be charged most dramatically by just one piece of modern sculpture, or an unusual means of lighting. Think about incorporating neon, as Stephen Woodhams has done to great effect – used well it can have all the power of a contemporary art installation.

To create a successful minimalist garden, whether in a long back garden or small balcony, it is crucial not to mix too many different materials. Concrete, glass, steel and plastic are all very well, but perhaps not all at once – and you don't have to shy away from natural materials. Carefully selected wood, slate and stone are wonderful in minimalist schemes, and their inherent earthiness can counter the coldness of a garden made from mostly artificial ingredients. And don't forget colour: paint one wall a beautiful deep blue or pink in the style of the Mexican architect Luis Barragan, or bring in some discreet colour in the form of furnishings, pots or – shock horror – flowers.

While it is generally true that minimalist gardens have a greater ratio of hard landscaping to plants, I don't think anyone buying this book would want to take the minimalist theme to its most extreme and make a Zen garden with just rocks and gravel and no plants at all. Architectural plants such as some of those listed below provide year-round sculptural interest, and also make great shadows. They can be planted out into a border or kept in large simple pots in keeping with the garden's style. Just one last word, though. Many people choose a minimalist garden because they think that it will be easy to look after. While it is true that cutting out the lawn and complicated borders will keep the work down, be aware that for this style of gardening good grooming is absolutely essential. Surfaces must be clear and clean, stone terraces free of moss and algae, leaves must be swept up and plants kept looking healthy. Less may be more, but only if it's pristine.

Key plants:
- **Black bamboo (*Phyllostachys nigra*)**
  This is a must for the minimalist garden, even if at one time it had become so fashionable it was almost a cliché. Whether planted as a specimen in a large pot or *en masse* as a swishing screen, its graphic form and graceful movement bring a dramatic presence to a modern garden. Keep well fed and watered, and give it enough sun, or its much-prized black stems will turn green.

- **Cloud-pruned box**
  This brings some man-made wavy lines in among the straight lines of most modern architecture. Particularly suited to schemes with a Zen or Japanese influence, the specimen trees look great in concrete or metal pots. Larger box hedges can also be cloud-pruned, in the style of the Belgian designer Jacques Wirtz, to make wonderful undulating forms.
- *Magnolia grandiflora*
  Just one tree – provided it is the right one – can bring real presence and drama to a modern urban garden. *Magnolia grandiflora* is evergreen, and the foliage, with its felty, cinnamon-coloured underside, is attractive in itself. But the huge creamy cup-shaped flowers are what you wait for, from summer through to early autumn. (See 'Trees in Your Garden', pages 50–52, for further ideas.)
- **Phormiums**
  The strappy sword-shaped leaves of phormiums work as a strong 'punctuation mark' in a border. Their dramatic height can also help in screening or to create privacy. There are striped and variegated phormiums available, but one of the most commonly found, and one of the best, is the bronzy *Phormium tenax* Purpureum Group.
- *Ophiopogon planiscapus* 'Nigrescens'
  The strappy black leaves of this low-growing grass are a real eye-catcher and sit well alongside the grey of slate or stone or the fresh lime green of grass or bamboo. The shiny black berries are also attractive.
- **Alliums**
  The perfect bulb for the minimalist, low-maintenance garden, alliums have a strong graphic form and come up reliably year after year. Go for the large spherical heads of 'Globemaster' for the greatest impact, but don't forget the drumstick allium, *A. sphaerocephalon*, which comes out later, in June.
- *Festuca glauca*
  Many grasses are useful in the minimalist garden, but the low, blue-grey tufts of *Festuca glauca*, whether used *en masse* or planted in pots, sit particularly well in pared-down planting schemes.

Places to go for inspiration:

Aveda Institute Roof Terrace (▶ 120)   RIBA Roof Terrace (▶ 135)
Jubilee Park and Canada Square (▶ 179)   The Sanderson Hotel Courtyard (▶ 121)
London Wetlands Centre (▶ 216)   Tate Modern (▶ 153)
Pirelli Garden (▶ 149)   Thames Barrier Park (▶ 183)
No. 1 Poultry Roof Garden (▶ 165)   Tower Place (▶ 171)

Formal

This category ranges from traditional neo-classicism, with its symmetrically placed pots or urns of clipped box or bay, to a softer, more feminine version that one might call 'Kensington Chic'. Its barest mode employs large expensive expanses of York stone that will need pressure-cleaning to keep them pristine; the frillier incarnations may include an immaculate handkerchief of lawn (invariably laid new every year) and a froth of white flowers among the glossy greenery. Good grooming – as no doubt practised personally by the gardens' owners – is essential to this style of gardening.

A formal style works with many types of building, from Georgian town houses to modern office blocks. The geometric framework – usually of low box hedges and some sort of paving or gravel – can be given a more modern edge by using pale limestone or slate chippings. Pots containing topiary standards or seasonal plantings can be used to punctuate the design – these may range from traditional terracotta or lookalike lead to bold contemporary designs in glazed clay, concrete or galvanized metal. Ring the changes by shunting the pots around or bringing new ones into play when plants are at their peak. Position trees, water features or ornaments such as urns or stone sculpture, to create focus for views on side axes as well as the main vista from the house. Symmetry works best with this style, unless you are going for a more minimal, Japanese-inspired formality, in which case you may find more ideas in the section above.

George Carter (▶ 270) is one of the masters of what might be termed 'neo-classicism with a twist'. He has many neat and elegant London gardens to his name – often for central *pieds-à-terre* where largely absentee owners want a simple, smart, minimum-maintenance solution. A touch of whimsy is sometimes added in the form of two-dimensional cut-outs of classical urns or other decorative schemes that can be used to screen sheds, bins or other eyesores, and his schemes are often dramatically lit at night to provide an interesting view from the house. At the more decorative end of the scale, Anthony Noel (▶ 272) is famous for working magic on even the smallest, most unprepossessing spaces. His former back garden in Fulham, where a tiny lawn and York stone terrace were surrounded by oversized stone urns, a gurgling water feature and pots of standard fuchsias and mop-head marguerites, became almost legendary. Though his colour scheme is usually confined to green and white, with a touch of pink in the form of 'Stargazer' lilies and 'Lord Bute' pelargoniums, Noel enjoys giving pots, plant supports and garden furniture a lick of unorthodox colour – bright turquoise blue one year, Schiaparelli pink and black the next. Visited in June when the greenery is at its freshest and the flowers at their frothiest, his gardens have a joyous air of being *en fête*, just waiting for the party to begin.

Key plants:

- **Clipped box**

  And lots of it, of course. Low box hedges and topiary provide the basic structure. Start with small box bushes planted a foot apart in good soil or, to save money, plant cuttings *in situ* and wait. If you're low on patience, instant, ready-grown box hedging and completed topiary shapes are available from specialist nurseries.

- **Tulips**

  The classic varieties for a formal urban garden have to be the viridiflora tulip 'Spring Green' (cream streaked with pale green), purple-black 'Queen of Night' and the jolly crimson-and-white-striped 'Carneval de Nice'. Pointy 'White Triumphator' and the plain or striped parrot varieties also look good, either ranged in pots or as infill for a parterre.

- **Regale lilies**

  Planted in pots that can be brought into prime position when the lilies are coming into full dark pink bud, these not only look timelessly elegant, their scent is to die for. In the border they will multiply if left undisturbed, but mark their place to avoid damaging the young shoots in spring.

- ***Jasminum officinale***

  Choose it for its heavenly fragrance and starry white flowers. Grow it up trellis or arches or along strong supporting wires; it can even be trained around a wire globe on a stick to make a standard lollipop shape. The pointed pink buds are part of the appeal in spring.

- **Camellias**

  Camellias are glamorous enough to turn a dingy dark basement area into something more grand. When their neat pom-pom flowers have faded (go for the whites, pale pinks and stripes rather than screaming pinks and reds) the dark glossy foliage is a good foil for pale summer flowers. Need acid soil and will thrive in containers.

- **Bay**
  Potted bay trees pruned as lollipop standards or obelisks look smart flanking a front door or gateway to the garden. The soil around their bases can always be covered with white or mauve violas to soften the symmetry. And the aromatic prunings will be useful in the kitchen.
- **White petunias**
  Not normally thought of as 'posh plants', petunias come into their own in plain white (or perhaps even some of the striped varieties if judiciously used). Their pretty ruffled blooms will flower away merrily beneath standard trees in pots, or provide a simple and long-lasting solution for a window box. Busy lizzies (again, in *white* only) can do a similar job in shade.

Places to go for inspiration:

The Cherry Orchard, Ham House (▶ 225)   Hall Place (▶ 209)
Christchurch, Greyfriars (▶ 166)   St John's Lodge, Regent's Park (▶ 138)
Clifton Nurseries (▶ 232)   Museum of Garden History (▶ 155)
The Dorchester Hotel (▶ 116)   St Mary Aldermanbury (▶ 164)
Grosvenor House (▶ 116)

Urban Jungle

One of the edges London gardeners have over their rural counterparts (except those in particularly protected areas such as Cornwall) is that the urban microclimate allows us to get away with a variety of exotic-looking plants that would probably require winter protection elsewhere. The temperature in a sheltered London garden is usually a good few degrees higher than in a similar garden anywhere else in the country, and this can be the source of great fun and drama, as garden designers such as Myles Challis (▶ 270), who pioneered the 'new exotic' look back in the 1980s, began to discover. The baton has since been taken up by a younger band of designers including Declan Buckley (▶ 269), James Fraser (▶ 268) and Jason de Grellier Payne (▶ 271), all of whom have their own distinctive way of using these striking plants.

Many of the 'new exotic' plants have bold architectural leaf shapes that suit pared-down, modernistic design schemes. But they can equally well be used in profusion, to create a latter-day living Rousseau painting in the heart of the city. Many of the palms and great bamboos tower high above you, as in a tropical greenhouse without a roof, and others can be used for effective screening. A trip around this type of garden, no matter how small, tends to be a voyage of exploration, full of surprises. At Declan Buckley's garden in Islington – sometimes open through the NGS (▶ 263) – stone Buddha heads and a Sri Lankan monk's gilded parasol are hidden among the greenery, while some of Jason de Grellier Payne's gardens terminate in secret pools surrounded by mossy rocks and ferns and swishing bamboos.

Many of the 'new exotic' plants are evergreen, making it relatively easy to create a tropical-style garden that looks good all year round. By building up a collection of contrasting leaf shapes and textures, you can create a green tapestry that will be fascinating in all weathers. In the summer months, the dahlias and canna lilies that are often found in municipal bedding schemes can provide a splash of colour in among the green – the striped leaves of canna varieties such as 'Durban' look particularly good with the low sun shining through them. Exotic gardening is by no means confined to tender or tropical plants: it can also include hardier species that originate from more temperate areas such as Kenya and the hillier parts of Chile and Mexico. James Fraser in particular uses some extremely striking plants from his native New Zealand – such as the spear-like *Pseudopanax* – that really take to the British climate.

New exotic gardening can take people by stealth. They buy a tree fern, then a chusan palm, then a couple of bamboos and a banana and they are hooked. If you are starting from scratch, it's a good idea to consult one of the designers listed above, or to ask the advice of specialist nurseries such as the Palm Centre (▶ 236), who can make sure you are buying the right plants for your conditions. Even within London, conditions can vary from garden to garden, and if your soil is heavy clay it may need loosening up to improve the drainage (see page 23). If there is one thing most of these plants hate, it is having their roots stand in cold wet soil over winter. If all else fails, you can keep the most tender treasures in pots and wrap them in fleece like Christo sculptures over winter, or bring them inside when frosts threaten.

Key plants:
- **Tree ferns**
  The leafy umbrellas of *Dicksonia antarctica* will lend an instant jungly air to your garden, even if it is more of a shady backyard than a tropical sun-trap. Their main requirement is shelter from the worst frosts, and to be kept damp in dry weather. The great fibrous trunks are actually part of the root system. The taller they are the more expensive.
- *Pseudopanax*
  Natives of New Zealand and China, these curious-looking plants are spear-shaped when young, with narrow, jagged-edged down-turned

leaves. The ferocious leaves are, in fact, a ploy to protect the young plants from predators; once they are out of reach of danger the leaves become larger and wider.

- **Canna lilies**
These are instantly exotic, especially those with bronze or striped leaves, which should be planted where the low late-summer sun can shine right through them. The lily-like flowers come in fiery shades from yellow through bright orange to scarlet. Cannas are tender, so are often kept in pots to be brought under cover in winter.

- ***Astelia chathamica***
Like a huge silver phormium, the strappy foliage makes a fountain of light in a semi-shaded spot. The sword-shaped leaves are elegantly arched, gleaming silver on one side and white on the reverse. Every so often the plants produce a strange frothy yellow flower.

- **Japanese banana**
For sheer hardiness, the evergreen banana *Musa basjoo* is the one to start with in a London garden. In very cold weather or more exposed spots it is advisable to protect the long stems in winter, to ensure that the plants grow to their full height (20 feet) – to sit beneath one in high summer, with the sun shining through the ribbed leaves, is heaven.

> **Places to go for inspiration:**
> The Barbican Centre (▶ 159)
> Chumleigh Multicultural Gardens (▶ 206)
> Declan Buckley's gardens (▶ 269)
> Golders Hill Park (▶ 194)
> Horniman Gardens (▶ 206)
> James Fraser's gardens (▶ 268)
> Jason de Grellier Payne's gardens (▶ 271)
> Lincoln's Inn Fields (▶ 132)
> The Palm Centre (▶ 236)
> Royal Botanic Gardens, Kew (▶ 222)

Family

Family gardens don't have to mean a lawn strewn with bikes and striped with skidmarks, and hideous plastic scattered everywhere you look. The obvious option is to screen off an area where the children can play, but a) there might not be room for this in a small-to-average urban garden; b) you might want to be able to keep an eye on the kids from the house; and

c) the chances are they won't stick to their restricted area anyway. Much more clever and creative to integrate the children's needs and fantasies into the overall design of the garden. It's back to the principle of 'doubling up' – making various garden elements perform more than one job at a time (see page 48). The design team Helen Tindale and Karena Batstone (▶ 274), who have designed some stunning contemporary London gardens, have made this something of a speciality. If the clients are keen to retain a lawn, they design a decking boardwalk all around it, which looks great and has the other huge advantage of being better to ride a bike on than grass. In one garden, the boardwalk led to a larger area of decking where a trapdoor concealed a sandpit when it was not in use. Just to one side, hidden behind a swishing screen of bamboo, was a 'jungle gym' of rope swings and trapezes slung from the branch of a tree, with a springy bark floor beneath to cushion any falls. Joe Swift (▶ 273) likes to make retaining walls for raised beds and other features wide and low enough for children to run along (or even ride bikes on) safely – he even designs an extra step or ramp if necessary to give them the extra 'leg-up'. And Jinny Blom (▶ 269), most famous for her collaboration with Prince Charles at the Chelsea Flower Show 2002, had the brainwave of using the 'dead space' beneath a huge horse chestnut tree, in which it is hard to get anything including grass to grow, as a decked 'stage' for performances. Think laterally. Rather than import a hideous brightly coloured swing, why not make a simple DIY version from wood and rope and sling it from a tree or the cross-beam of a pergola? If you need a shed, could half of it double up as a wendy house? Or how about a living willow bower? They look beautiful, provide shade in summer, and the kids could take part in the construction.

Of course, gardens for children need to be safe. For some people, this would rule out water features – but, though it is true that a baby can drown in less than two inches of water, there are still ways of incorporating water that needn't be a worry. One is to keep the depth as shallow as possible – a chic modernist rill in galvanized metal, just an inch or so deep, is still perfect for sailing toy boats on. Or you can cover the surface of a pond with galvanized metal grid – children will love the sensation of walking on the water. Some plants, of course, are deadly poisonous, and it is worth equipping yourself with a list of the worst offenders. Joe Swift's book *The Plant Room* (BBC) contains a long list of poisonous plants, including monkshood, datura, ivy, privet and solanums, alongside the more commonly known foxglove, laburnum and yew. Skin irritants such as euphorbias, which can leave skin that comes into contact with its milky sap burned and blistered, or echiums, contact with which provokes the sensation that lots of tiny needles are pricking the skin, are also best avoided. Spiky plants may hold some danger, particularly if the offending spikes are at a child's eye level.

Lastly, why not encourage your children to share your own love of gardens and nature? If they should show interest in taking over a tiny part of the garden for their own purposes, give them a patch and a packet or two of seeds. Sunflowers, nasturtiums, radishes and other things that are fast and easy to grow will help satisfy a child's natural impatience: for adults, the timespan and changing seasons involved in gardening are part and parcel of its appeal, but children will just get bored. Bulbs are also fun – planting them in a pot and inspecting the surface for signs of life as winter turns to spring. Or how about a tomato plant for each child with a prize for the one who produces the most fruit? Even if there is space for nothing else, that old trick of writing the child's name in mustard and cress seed on damp blotting paper on a windowsill never fails to delight. After all, planting a seed and watching it grow is the closest thing to magic I've ever found. It's to be hoped that children who grow up with a close relationship with the natural world will be moved to take care of it in later life. In the words of one of my heroines, Rachel Carson, who wrote the anti-pesticide classic *Silent Spring* as well as the lesser-known *The Sense of Wonder*, about introducing children to nature: 'A child's world is fresh and new and beautiful, full of wonder and excitement. . . . If I had influence with the good fairy who is supposed to preside over the christening of all children, I should ask that her gift be a sense of wonder so indestructible that it would last throughout life, as an unfailing antidote against the boredom and disenchantments of later years, the sterile preoccupations with things that are artificial, the alienation from the sources of our strength.'

Places to go for inspiration:
The Calthorpe Project (▶ 185)
The Centre for Wildlife Gardening (▶ 205)
Coram's Fields (▶ 130)
Diana, Princess of Wales Memorial Playground (▶ 145)
Emslie Horniman Pleasance Park (▶ 213)

The Eco Garden

Wildlife gardening has become fashionable in recent years, which is good news for the many species of birds, butterflies and insects that have made their way into London following the destruction of their natural habitats in the surrounding countryside by harmful farming practices. Just creating a garden of any type will attract more wildlife – when we planted up our previously bare concrete courtyard in Brixton it didn't take long for the birds and insects to arrive. But by choosing the right plants and garden features you can do a lot more to attract specific types of wildlife, many of which, like worms and lacewings and ladybirds, will be beneficial to your garden. There are many wildlife and community gardens throughout the capital that offer advice and inspiration if you are thinking about developing your garden in this way – first stop should be the Centre for Wildlife Gardening in Peckham, run by the London Wildlife Trust, which offers courses on wildlife gardening in its splendid green-roofed eco-resource centre and has a wonderfully picturesque display garden that is full of ideas to adapt at home. (See page 262 and ring for a free information pack on wildlife gardening.)

By far the greatest gift to wildlife you can create in your garden is a pond. Within weeks you may have clumps of frogspawn, toads and newts and skitting water boatmen, and dragonflies and damsel flies flitting above the surface. Provide some rocky shelters for frogs and toads on the banks and they should help keep your slug population down. A pond should be made in the sunniest spot possible, away from overhanging trees that may shade and clog up the water. Make it as large as you reasonably can – the minimum depth for a small pond is two feet – and step the sides so that frogs and toads and other creatures can hop out easily. The Centre for Wildlife Gardening information pack offers advice on pond construction and planting. Keep levels topped up in hot weather and aim to have the pond about three-quarters full of plants as this helps to keep the water clear.

When it comes to the rest of the garden, certain plants are great for birds and other forms of wildlife while still playing an attractive part in your design. Climbers such as ivy, honeysuckle, hop and wisteria provide nesting cover for birds, nectar for bees and butterflies and (sometimes) berries for birds. Covering a bare brick wall with climbers not only looks better, it provides valuable breeding and feeding grounds for a variety of wild creatures. Plants that bear berries in winter are, of course, a great boon for the birds, but don't forget to provide bird food, too – there are some well-designed feeders around that will look as good to your eyes as they do to the birds'. Placing nesting boxes well out of the reach of cats is also a great way to encourage more birds to your garden, but be patient. It took two years for blue tits to set up home in the little birdhouse my father made me, but now we have a brood every year.

It goes without saying that if you are creating an eco-garden you should not be using any chemical fertilizers or pesticides. But you will probably find that gardening naturally means that you have less need of them. A well-manured, chemical-free soil should be teeming with worms and micro-organisms that will help your plants grow so strongly that they are more resistant to pests and diseases. In addition, many of the visiting birds and insects will play a beneficial role – blue tits, for instance, love feeding on aphids, as do ladybirds and lacewings and their larvae. The aim is to create a harmonious balance between plants and animals that does not allow one species to dominate at the expense of another (this is called biodiversity). There can be some confusion about the relationship between wildlife gardening and controlling problem wildlife, but there is usually a natural solution that will save you reaching for the pesticide gun – or worse. (See pages 79–84 for ideas and alternatives.)

For some people, creating a wildlife garden provides a good excuse for not doing the gardening. While it is true that most creatures thrive best where they are left undisturbed, there is no need to turn your backyard into an untended wilderness. Good design and eco-principles can go hand in hand, as in Pam Lewis's beautiful wildlife garden in Dorset – Sticky Wicket – where a series of concentric circles planted with alliums, geraniums, small sedums and self-seeded cloud grass creates one of the most stylish butterfly gardens around. The London Wetlands Centre (▶ 216) is a more local source of inspiration for this fusion of environmental principles with strong contemporary design.

Turning your lawn into a wildflower meadow is by no means as easy as the vendors of those 'instant meadow' seed packets would have you believe, and it would be worth seeking specialist advice before you try. But if you decide to go down that road, or are simply leaving some grass in a certain area to grow long, consider mowing a path – or series of radial paths – through it, or try surrounding the area of naturalistic planting with a neatly clipped hedge, as in the Wilderness Garden at Ham House (▶ 225). This not only looks good, it sends out the message that you have not merely forgotten to do the mowing. Another area you might not have thought of greening is your roof. Turf or sedum roofs are attractive and create havens for plant and insect life; they also provide valuable insulation, saving on your heating bills. They need careful construction, however, and it would be a good idea to send for CAT's useful tip sheet on the subject (▶ 265) before you get the ladder out and lay turfs on your garage roof. When choosing hard landscaping materials for your garden, try to select those from sustainable or recycled sources. (See 'Green Gardening', pages 77–8, for many examples.)

Finally, an eco-garden needs to address water usage. In a climate that is considered by many to be getting hotter and drier by the year, it is important not to waste water. Consider installing an irrigation system that works by the 'leaky hose' rather than sprinkler principle – this will direct water right at the plants' roots where it is needed (see page 254 for suppliers). Better still, think about using plants that don't require much watering. Take inspiration from Beth Chatto's Gravel Garden (see the book of that name published by Frances Lincoln) in Essex or the Mediterranean-style plantings in Dulwich Park (▶ 200), where beautiful year-round effects are created using plants that can survive drought conditions. (Of course, knowing our weather, the chances are that you may plant such a garden only to become waterlogged the next year.) In wet weather, a water butt that collects rainwater from the gutters (or is even plumbed up to receive the 'grey water' from your bath) will conserve this water until it is needed. HDRA, CAT and the Centre for Wildlife Gardening all publish tip sheets on water-wise gardening and other aspects of ecological gardening. (See the Directory for contact details.)

Places to go for inspiration:
Camley Street Nature Park (▶ 187)
Centre for Wildlife Gardening (▶ 205)
Dulwich Park (▶ 200)
Garden Barge Square (▶ 152)
Holland Park (▶ 212)
London Wetlands Centre (▶ 216)
Roots & Shoots (▶ 207)
St John's Wood Church Grounds (▶ 138)

Urban Inspiration

This may be a personal prejudice, but I think that gardens in the city should look as if they are *of* the city. The *rus in urbe* thing just doesn't do it for me: rustic wicker plant supports and too much traditional trellis and terracotta in a London backyard are the gardening equivalent of a surfeit of country pine and dried flowers in an urban kitchen. Instead of creating an illusion of the countryside they somehow make you miss it more. Much better – and more honest – to make at least some reference to the city environment in the design of an urban garden. This doesn't mean your plot has to bristle with old scaffolding and have graffiti scrawled up the walls. But you might want to look at some of the alternative options before you run to the garden centre for standard items and materials that have homogenized our gardens up and down the country, whether in the country or in town.

- If you're laying a terrace, could you use old London stocks or stone salvaged from a local building instead of imitation York stone or ersatz cobbles? If making a mosaic, could you incorporate stones, china fragments, old keys or other items that have some relevance to the site?
- For decking, try to avoid the ready-grooved timber on sale in garden centres. In our backyard we used old scaffolding planks. Not only are they sturdier, they also have an attractive metal trim on each end that picks up on the metal we have used elsewhere (galvanized grid for a 'bridge' out over the basement area; metal pots and plant supports) and reinforces the urban inspiration behind the garden. Be sure to prime them properly first.
- I've already mentioned old metal dustbins as stylish urban containers – big enough for small trees. My friends Simon and Clarkey made a container on wheels using an old trolley and offcuts of timber. Weathered a beautiful silvery grey by the sun, it made a great home for a young silver birch tree, which could be trundled about their Brixton roof terrace to provide shade where required. They also used the baskets discarded by the traders in the market below, in which fruit was transported to the UK from the Caribbean. Lined with black plastic, they made great containers for low-growing herbs and flowers, and linked the garden with the local area.
- Metal – old or new – is a good material for urban gardens. A smart modern roof garden can gleam with grey and silver foliage plants in shiny galvanized planters, or have one wall lined with zinc sheeting to reflect the planting, and bring interesting light and shadow effects into the garden. In a different style of garden, old painted fire buckets might overflow with tumbler tomatoes or chilli peppers, or a builders' bath (from building supply shops) make a water garden with flag irises and one (non-spreading) water lily. And before you buy flimsy timber trellis or archways, consider the metal alternative. Getting such things custom-made for your space is not hard. We had a local metalworker knock us up a galvanized arch around the French windows, with a

built-in trough and handrail at one side. Be careful siting metal in full sun, where the heat may damage plants.

- If you go for wood, choose chunky designs that show off the sculptural shape and grain of the wood. Blocks of wood make great seating and also look good grouped in the garden when unused. A plank of reclaimed timber (you can sometimes buy it with the bark attached, which in a contemporary setting looks sculptural rather than rustic) on supports makes a simply stylish bench. Other wooden elements can be given a contemporary urban spin with a lick of the right colour paint. Even suburban picket fencing gets a groovy new makeover when painted an unusual colour such as charcoal grey or aubergine. Instead of cottagey diamond trellis, make your own chunky urban version out of 1 x 1 timber. I even managed this myself with a little help, and painted it white against the white brick walls of our garden, and planted lots of climbers to scramble up it. But you could use other colours, chosen to contrast or co-ordinate with the wall or/and the planting.

- Look around you for inspiration. Eighteenth-century garden designers used to 'borrow' elements from the surrounding landscape to enhance the gardens they were designing (for instance, framing a view to a distant church spire) and you can do the same. Look at the surrounding colours, shapes and plants and see if they will provide a springboard for your design. For instance, if your neighbour has a golden locust tree (*Robinia pseudoacacia*) in his or her garden, pick up on its golden chartreuse foliage in the plants you include in your own borders – euphorbias, *Alchemilla mollis* and Bowles' golden grass, to name but three. This will have the effect of unifying the space and making it appear much larger.

- If you're after a piece of sculpture as a focal point, why not consider making something yourself using found materials, or commissioning a local artist to create something for you? London is full of artists who would relish such work. Check out the Crafts Council's slide library for ideas and contacts (▶ 246) or visit Wolseley Fine Art's annual Art in the Garden show (▶ 247). Ever since visiting Little Sparta, the garden created by the Scottish poet and artist Ian Hamilton Finlay twenty-five years ago, I have been enchanted by the idea of inscriptions in the garden. Just a few words or a fragment of a poem can be all it takes to bring a whole new dimension into your garden. Choose the words to reflect your garden, its surroundings and your feelings for them.

When all's said and done, urban inspiration is more of a mind-set than anything else. Some people have that knack of finding inspiration in even the most unprepossessing of places or materials. The artist Jo Self, a neighbour of mine, has made an intriguing contemporary garden in a former builder's yard and filled it with all manner of plants and trees, hanging baskets made from old post office sacks, and a 'high-rise' greenhouse made from scaffolding and plastic insulation boards that lights up inside at night to create a visual echo of the tall block of flats next door.

Places to go for inspiration:

The Calthorpe Project (▶ 185)

Emslie Horniman Pleasance Park (▶ 213)

James Fraser's gardens (▶ 268)

Meanwhile Community Gardens (▶ 213)

Mile End Park (▶ 175)

Phoenix Community Garden (▶ 119)

The Water Gardens (▶ 142)

 # GREEN GARDENING

Composting

Composting – otherwise known as creating your own soil from recycled kitchen, garden and paper waste – is one of those activities one can get surprisingly evangelical about. Ever since I installed my first wormery (see pages 75–6) on a tiny central London balcony, I have found myself slightly shocked when people throw compostable waste away – particularly when they have big gardens. I've even been known to gather up the compostable remains of a dinner party and bring them home to my allotment rather than let them hit the rubbish bin (a mountain of globe artichoke sheddings, packed into a pair of carrier bags, once made it home via a stop at a night club – let's hope the coat-check girls didn't peek inside the bags). Once you've started composting, you may acquire the zeal of the convert, too. The environmental benefits are immeasurable: not only are you reducing the amount of rubbish that is sent to landfill sites (which produce methane gas – twenty times more effective than carbon dioxide in causing global warming), you are also creating the best soil conditioner that money can buy – and for absolutely free. If you need further convincing, proposed tough new environmental laws that may charge householders per bag for rubbish removal will be an extra incentive to get composting.

There's a whole lot of mystique about compost-making, which is one of the things that puts people off. But in practice it works as a great big experiment every time – and if it goes wrong (usually either too dry and inactive or too smelly and slimy) there are simple remedies to rectify the situation. The important thing is to start. At an allotment site or in a large garden there may be space to create the dream composting factory: three adjacent bays (about a yard square and open at one end) that can be used in rotation (one filling, one 'cooking', one available for use on the garden). But this scenario is unlikely in the average London garden, where your best bet is either to make a single bay (old skip timber or pallets work well) or to buy a commercially produced wooden or plastic bin (many local authorities offer hefty discounts on such products to encourage home composting). An ordinary plastic dustbin actually works fine, too – just pierce the base and sides with holes at least ½ inch wide to let liquids drain out. Some sort of lid (even a scrap of old carpet or tarpaulin) is necessary to keep the rain off and the heat of decomposition in.

The next step is to fill it. Fruit and vegetable peelings, leftover cooked or rotten vegetables, garden waste (weeds, prunings, grass clippings, etc.) and faded cut flowers are among the most commonly composted materials, but don't forget old newspapers and tissues, eggshells, coffee grounds, leftover pasta and rice, stale bread, and the husks from peanuts and other nuts. I even came across one man who saved up his family's nail clippings and hair from their hairbrushes to add to the compost heap, but that might be taking things too far for most. Never be tempted to include fish or meat as the smell will attract rats and other vermin. You can just add all the ingredients to the heap willy-nilly and hope for the best, but your greatest chance for success is to take a tip from the Centre for Alternative Technology's decades of composting experience and aim for their 'compost lasagne' of alternative layers of 'soft' material (most kitchen waste, softer garden waste such as lawn clippings) with 'dry' carbon-rich materials such as waste paper (best scrunched up or shredded, to incorporate air, another vital ingredient) and woodier garden waste (best shredded, if you have access to a shredder). The layers can be up to six inches deep for larger piles down to two or so for plastic bins. This method should avoid the compost becoming too wet or too dry – and you can adjust the balance accordingly.

You'll find that the bin or bay will never fill in practice, as the volume of waste keeps rotting down. If you've only one heap, stop adding new material when it is about three-quarters full, and put the new waste into a heavy-duty bag that can be stored on top of the rest of the contents. When you turn out the bin a couple of months later, the bag can be emptied on top of some fresh garden waste in the base of the bin to begin the new heap. For the best results, you ought to turn the compost at least once – many people swear this is unnecessary, but it introduces more air into the mix, and mingles the well-decomposed waste with the half-composted stuff (twigs, eggshells, citrus peel and teabags always seem to lag behind). This is the stage at which you can add more shredded paper if the mix is too slimy, or more lawn clippings or leafy waste if it seems too dry. If you make regular trips to the seaside, seaweed is a great addition to the compost heap, rich in vital nutrients and micro-organisms. If not, you might sprinkle a handful of calcified seaweed pellets every three or four layers – or a concentrated chicken manure preparation such as '6 X'. Manure (including strawy stable sweepings) and dead autumn leaves (especially when shredded, as they break down faster) are also good ingredients and best added in layers. Some people swear by compost activators to speed up the process – there are preparations in the shops, but nettles and comfrey are a good natural alternative, as is urine (now you know why so few allotment plots have lavatories). It's a bit 'muck and magic' but a herbal preparation sold as 'QR' based on a recipe devised by Miss Maye E. Bruce in the 1930s – available from the Organic Gardening Catalogue (▶ 252) – is said to produce 'rich, sweet, friable compost' in just 4–6 weeks. I've tried it and it did seem to work – her advice to re-layer a slow-burning winter heap with grass clippings (and the precise application of the activator) in spring had near miraculous results in just over a month.

If you don't have room for a compost heap, a worm bin may be a good alternative (see page 254 for suppliers). I have one in my front garden to complement the large double bay at the allotment, and it voraciously eats up all our kitchen waste, turning out a bin full of fantastic chocolatey-brown compost twice a year along with many bottles of dark brown liquid manure that can be diluted down ten parts to one to make an excellent plant feed. Worm bins can be tricky to get started, even if you follow the instructions to the letter. The worms are quite sensitive to changes in temperature, and the bin may need an insulating jacket in winter and to be shifted into the shade in the summer if you are not to lose your worms. Replacement packs are available by post, but it is always dispiriting to think you have killed off all those diligent workers. They can become almost like pets to some people. But do not despair! I gave up on worms one year, thinking I'd managed to kill off a couple of batches, but carried on using the bin as a regular compost heap. A few months later I opened the lid to find it positively heaving with worms.

The only other problem with wormeries is that they are not the simplest things to empty. The conventional ones have to be tipped up and emptied, and all the worms picked out from the compost and returned to the bin. For the squeamish, there are new models available – marketed under the name 'Can-O-Worms' (▶ 255) – which are made up of a stack of trays that can be removed in sequence as the compost is ready and the worms move on. The best system might be to have two conventional wormeries, side by side, so that one could be 'cooking' while the other is being filled.

The other, very simple form of composting that can be done in your garden is the creation of leaf mould from fallen autumn leaves. Make a square or cylindrical column of chicken wire supported by canes stuck into the earth and pack it with dead deciduous leaves – from your garden, from the street, and (with permission) from the local park. Soak with water. And then just let it be. Leaf mould is slower than compost, but should have rotted down to a rich, dark crumbly soil conditioner in anything between nine months and two years. (Again, there are activators that can help.) Use it as a spring mulch, or to protect the crowns of tender plants from frost. For a nutrient-rich potting mix, add comfrey leaves to one-year-old leaf mould and leave for a couple of months before adding to two parts soil or proprietary compost.

Recycling

Composting your kitchen and garden waste may make you more mindful of other items that can be recycled. Here are some ways in which you can do your bit for the planet while also saving money and (if you use your creativity) making stylish and original additions to your garden. Every item recycled is not only an item saved from a landfill site, it's also one fewer new item manufactured, marketed and transported at cost to the environment. Try salvage yards for unusual alternatives to shop-bought garden furniture and planters. Where you have to buy new, try to buy from local, environmentally sound sources. Or commission a local craftsperson or artist to make a one-off piece for you – this can sometimes work out cheaper, and you'll have something totally unique (see page 49).

- Recycling rainwater by way of a water butt. Plastic water butts can be bought cheaply from mail order companies and can harvest rainwater from roofs via the guttering and downpipes. A tight-fitting lid will avoid algae, evaporation, mosquitoes and clogging from dead leaves. Raise the butt up on a block or pile of bricks so you can fill a watering can easily from beneath; if it's higher still, you may even get good pressure from a hose pipe.
- Grey water from baths, washing machines, dishwashers and washing vegetables, etc., can be recycled in the garden, provided it is uncontaminated with harmful soaps, oils and detergents. Most of the environmentally sound products available in the shops are fine for plants, but it is inadvisable to use grey water on edible produce, and it may be harmful to acid-loving acers and azaleas. Waste pipes can be fitted with a diverter to collect the water on its way to the drain. Rotate grey water applications around the garden to avoid any potential build-up of substances in the water.
- Before you rush out to the garden centre for hard materials for your garden, take a long hard look at what you already have on site; even the most unprepossessing of materials can form the basis of a great idea that will truly be rooted in the place. The garden designer Ivan Hicks does this to great effect in the gardens he designs. He weaves magic out of nothing, as fragments of rock set in a spiral pattern on a bed of moss become a striking sculptural maze; pieces of broken mirror are propped in dark corners or strung from the branches of trees; lengths of twisted rusted metal become arty plant supports, or frame a distant view. On a more pragmatic level, you may have lengths of old timber that can be used to make paths or planters; or a stack of old bricks or tiles that could be laid as a terrace. The decking in my garden was made from old scaffolding planks, which are much sturdier than the wood generally used. Could the mirror from an old wardrobe door bring light into a dark corner? Might some scrappy old chairs be given a new lease of outdoor life with a coat of the right colour paint? And remember, if you can't use it, somebody else may. One man's meat . . .
- Think twice before throwing anything away that might make an attractive container – old buckets, waste bins, enamel bread bins and other kitchen paraphernalia can look good in the right style of garden, and old metal dustbins make a good home for young trees. Just make

sure to drill some holes in the base. Don't chuck out chipped mugs and bowls if they're pretty – use them for planting small species bulbs or hyacinths (see pages 104–6). Make new troughs and containers from wood offcuts, recycled cupboard doors, or slate roofing tiles. You can paint them all the same colour (or various shades of one colour) if you want more uniformity.

• Recycle your plastic plant pots. If you propagate your own plants, you'll be glad of pots in all sizes for potting-on your seedlings as they grow larger, and the large sizes can be used for planting bulbs that can be plunged into the soil, pot and all, to fill a gap in the border, or hidden inside a pretty cachepot for display indoors. Even if you have no use for your old pots, ask your local garden centre if they have a pot recycling scheme.

• Mulches – a layer of matter on top of the soil that keeps moisture in and weeds down – can be made from all manner of recycled materials. I've seen old oyster, mussel and cockle shells used to good effect; spent wine corks, washed walnut shells, old pine cones, even old nuts, bolts and washers. The right material can reinforce the underlying theme, or style, of the garden. At an allotment, or under densely planted bushes where it will not be visible, newspaper or other paper makes a good mulch, watered well and weighted to keep it in position. The poet Linda Hasselstrom wrote lyrically about recycling her old love letters in this way. Alternatively, there are mulches made from recycled materials available on sale in the shops – crushed shells look pretty, recycled glass chippings of various colours, even coloured beads. A mulch needs to be at least an inch thick (at best, two) to be effective.

• Look round your local allotment for some of the most ingenious recycling ideas. You'll find everything from snipped-up old tights used as plant ties and sawn-off plastic bottle cloches to old sash windows made into cold frames, and unwanted CDs strung up as bird-scarers. Some of these may not be the most attractive options for use in your private garden, but the spirit is infectious. Since having an allotment I have turned into the sort of person who saves elastic bands and stray lengths of string.

- I've seen old wine bottles upended into the soil as a surprisingly attractive edging for paths. Rainwater collects in the dented bottoms to glint fetchingly in the light and give small birds such as sparrows the chance of a bath. They can also be stacked one on top of the other to make a wall (or section of wall – this idea is best used in small spaces): the different shades of green glint in the sunshine. Old bottles stuffed with fairy lights and strung along a wall also give a new twist to the song 'Ten Green Bottles'. . . Don't use just any old bottles for special features – it's worth collecting nice ones, such as the bright blue bottles used for a particular brand of mineral water.
- Recycle the garden itself: use your flowers as pot pourri or pressed on to cards – just a single pressed autumn leaf on a post card is a thousand times nicer to receive than most shop-bought greetings cards. For more ideas and resources, visit www.recycleforlondon.com.

Bio Pest Control

'Exterminate! Exterminate!' we want to cry as we lose a prize heuchera to vine weevil or lament our latest crop of lettuce seedlings, snaffled to the bare stalks by slugs and snails. It's all too easy to reach for the insecticide spray or can of pellets in our understandable urge to zap the enemy then and there. But before you do, spare a thought for all the other beneficial creatures (not to mention yourself, your children and your pets) who might also be harmed by them. And don't forget the microscopic organisms that live in the soil and toil away unseen to break down organic matter and maintain the balance of nutrients, body and texture. Some of the so-called 'eco-friendly' products on the market may claim not to hurt pets and birds if correctly used, but little has been done in the way of research into their effect on worms and smaller, soil-dwelling creatures. And besides, if you are growing food to eat, are you ready for all those residues to be served up on the plate, too? Once you start composting and becoming aware of the natural cycles of gardening and the wider issues beyond the instant solution, the chances are you will begin instinctively to turn away from pesticides. There are enough toxins in the London soil and air without us adding more. And there are alternatives to chemical warfare, even for the most persistent of pests. Good sources of bio-pest controls include Green Gardener (▶ 254) and the Organic Gardening Catalogue (▶ 252). The pests most commonly found in London gardens can be dealt with as follows:

Slugs and snails are some of the most troublesome garden pests, and London (along with Bristol and most of Wales) is one of the top slug and snail hot-spots in the country. Slug pellets (particularly the blue ones containing methaldehyde) might seem an effective way of controlling them, but may actually end up making the problem worse. A snail can lay up to 1,500 eggs in its short lifetime, which are programmed to hatch in batches by a growth retardant enzyme present in the adults' slime. This ensures there isn't a sudden mad competition for food. By killing all the adults we effectively override this natural control and can end up causing a snail population explosion. The other problem is that a substance in many pellets positively attracts slugs and snails to your garden – good news for the manufacturers of the products, but a nightmare for you. Don't be fooled by the manufacturers' claims that their products are harmless to birds and animals if correctly used. The government's annual study 'Pesticide Poisoning of Animals' shows that animals, including cats, dogs, wild birds, hedgehogs and predator beetles *are* poisoned every year by slug pellets, even when the instructions have been followed to the letter. And there has been no conclusive study so far on their effect on worms and soil micro-organisms.

Here are some safe and organic methods of controlling slugs and snails; you may need to use a few in conjunction for a failsafe 'belt and braces' approach:

• Encourage natural predators. Birds can be lured in with feeders and nesting boxes, frogs and toads (who will eat slugs and young snails) will quickly populate even the smallest wildlife pond (see page 68). Or acquire a pet hedgehog – send a self-addressed envelope marked 'Hedgehog Factsheet' and £1 in stamps to St Tiggywinkle's Wildlife Hospital, Aston Road, Haddenham, Bucks HP17 8AF (01844 292292).

• Use biological controls or nematodes. 'Nemaslug' and 'Slugsure' are the brand names for natural microscopic parasites that can be applied to the soil via a watering can. They stop the slugs feeding, so that they die underground, unseen. Nematodes are only effective on slugs and very small snails, and have to be renewed every 6–8 weeks, but I have found them extremely helpful in reducing slug levels. Green Gardener offers an annual programme of six 6-weekly packs that are sent out from spring onwards.

• Make a barrier around beds, borders or plants themselves using a substance that slugs and snails dislike. Very sharp grit can be effective (normal gravel is not sharp enough), and I have heard (but not tested) reports that coffee grounds, pine needles, troughs of salt water, sawdust and wood ash also work. Crushed eggshells (the by-product of many a Nigella-style cake-baking session, patiently dried in a low oven, crushed and stored in a large jar) were *not* a success for me. But a relatively new product called 'Slug Stoppa', available from garden centres, was. It works by absorbing the moisture in the creatures' slime to (literally) stop them in their tracks. It can be quite expensive, however, for all but your most treasured hostas or vulnerable seedlings, and has to be reapplied after heavy rain.

- Coarse sandpaper and copper-backed tape also repel slugs – lay it across the greenhouse entrance or around the rims of pots. Slug-repellent mats and collars (previously only available to the horticultural trade) are also sold by Green Gardener. They come in a variety of sizes and can be placed beneath pots and tubs both inside the greenhouse and in the garden.

- Divert the slugs with something else they like to eat. Sow sacrificial lettuce seeds around treasured plants such as hostas, or lay a wreath of freshly cut comfrey leaves. Bran is also extremely effective. Scatter it on the soil around vulnerable plants and the molluscs will gorge themselves so excessively overnight that they will be unable to move and can be cherry-picked the following morning. I've even heard of slugs exploding with this method, but don't think I'd fancy witnessing that over breakfast.

- Traps are another age-old remedy. 'Slug pubs' (diluted beer in old yoghurt pots sunk in the soil) do work, but disposing of the drowned slugs may be messy, and other beneficial creatures may also meet a boozy death. Raise the rim slightly above soil level to ensure that beetles (many of whom eat snail eggs) won't stumble in. I've also tried laying old squeezed grapefruit and orange cups around the garden in the hope that slugs will congregate beneath them – the theory is that you can scoop up the cups, with the slugs hiding beneath them, in the morning. After a particularly successful cocktail party our allotment looked like a Brit-Art installation, but it didn't really attract enough slugs to make the effort worthwhile.

- Buy *The Little Book of Slugs* (Centre for Alternative Technology, £4.99), a light-hearted and useful book born out of CAT's 'Bug-the-Slug' campaign ('Tough on slime; tough on the causes of slime'). Bringing together tips from CAT's twenty-five years of gardening in slug-ridden Wales with hundreds of innovative contributions to their www.ihateslugs.com website, it lists ideas in terms of 'the good' (gathering slugs at night and driving them to safety on nearby wasteland); 'the bad' (snipping them with scissors, spearing them with a screwdriver or throwing them in the path of passing cars); and 'the ugly' (swallowing them as a nutritious source of protein – urgh!). In among the more outlandish ideas are some pretty useful ideas, including using near-empty beer cans as traps (the slugs are attracted by the smell and can't get out over the sharp inward openings), old Marmite jars and large cabbage leaves as lures, and using milk instead of beer in slug traps in the hope that a hedgehog might come along and finish off the lot.

- Perhaps the best – and certainly the simplest – solution is the night-time patrol, armed with a torch and bucket. (I've often longed for one of those old miner's helmets with a light on the front so I could have both hands free.) In a small urban garden you'll become familiar with the places where slugs and snails like to lurk – behind the larger leaves of ivy, in snug corners of trellis and on the lower, shaded stalks of large plants such as acanthus, arum lilies, phormiums and macleaya. Then all you have to do is decide what to do with them. Don't be tempted to throw them over the neighbours' wall: apart from being anti-social, it won't work. A report on the *Today* programme on BBC Radio 4 found that snails which had had their shells marked with Tippex before release into the local environment migrated back to the same garden within days. The eco-inclined might take them to the countryside (though whether the countryside really wants our townie slugs is doubtful). I'll leave that last choice up to you.

Aphids (otherwise known as greenfly and blackfly) are a drag in the garden or vegetable patch, appearing as early as February in sheltered London gardens when there are fewer natural predators around to eat them. They cluster around the growing tips of roses and other plants, sucking sap from the leaves which can cause stunted growth and distorted leaves as well as the spread of viruses from plant to plant. They also excrete honeydew, which is sticky and unsightly and encourages mould, which further saps the plants' vigour. One of the best ways to combat aphids is to encourage birds and other predators into your garden (see pages 67–70) – I love watching blue tits balance precariously on whippy young rose stems as they peck off the pests one by one. Ladybirds and lacewings and their larvae are the other great predators, and you can encourage them to set up home in your garden by providing suitable sheltered places in which they can overwinter. (Wooden ladybird houses and lacewing chambers are sold by many mail order companies.) Get them off to a flying start by ordering a pack of the creatures themselves, along with sachets of attractant and food (Green Gardener do a 'Gardener's Friends Pack' including 25 ladybirds and 500 lacewing larvae). All you do is tap them gently out of their box and on to affected foliage once they arrive and watch them get chomping. You can even hatch your own ladybirds with a special box kit, which is great for children. Ladybirds and lacewings will also tackle other pests including red spider, woolly aphid, scale and thrip.

Aphids in the greenhouse and conservatory can be dealt with by introducing nematodes (*Aphidius* or *Aphidotoles* nematodes), as can whitefly. The only trouble with most of the biological controls mentioned is that they can only be used when ladybirds and lacewings and their larvae are naturally at large, which could be too late for the earliest aphid infestations. A good preventative cure that I have found effective is to plant garlic around the bases of your rose bushes – the essence of the garlic penetrates the rose sap and makes it impenetrable to many pests. But if all else fails, use a soft soap spray (available from garden centres) which breaks down the aphids' waxy coating and kills them, or simply squash them between your fingers. I have become shamefully unsqueamish about this last method – it's quick, it's immediate, and it's absolutely free!

Whitefly causes much the same damage as aphids, with stunted growth, malformed leaves, sticky honeydew and the spread of viruses the principal problems. The insects tend to be smaller than greenfly or blackfly and, unlike aphids, fly off the plant as soon as they are disturbed. Inspect plants from early on in the season to catch the start of an infestation, as it may be difficult to treat later on. In greenhouses and conservatories, where whitefly can be a huge problem, a natural parasite called *Encarsia formosa* can be introduced when the average temperature is above 10°C (50°F). Earlier in the season, or if huge numbers are present (in which case the *Encarsia* will have a job to catch up), use a soft soap spray or sticky glue traps. There is some evidence that the scent of French marigolds (*Tagetes patula*), when in flower, may help keep whitefly out of a greenhouse.

Vine weevil. Horror movie music plays in my head whenever I spot one of these horrible matt black beetles in my garden. Ugly though they are, however, it is not the beetles that do the worst damage to your plants. While they take notches out of the sides of leaves before laying up to 1,500 light brown pinhead-sized eggs each summer (curiously, all vine weevils are female), it is the creamy, crescent-shaped grubs (with a darker brown head) that are the real killers. All autumn and winter they feast unseen on the roots of your plants, with camellias, herbaceous perennials such as heucheras and vines (of course) their favourite delicacy. Plants in containers (including hanging baskets) are particularly prone, as the weevils seek out the warmest soil temperatures available at that time of year. The first sign of infestation may be the sight of the grubs when you are re-potting or planting bulbs in autumn – in which case, act fast! If you're unlucky, you may simply notice that a plant looks sick and then, on further investigation, find it has no roots left to speak of and will need to be replaced.

Obviously you should kill the adult beetles whenever you see them – they can be hard to spot, but once seen are slow-moving and easy enough to crush underfoot. Zap them when you can – vine weevil beetles can travel an incredible three miles, including up vertical walls, in search of suitable egg-laying habitats, and even if you get rid of them from your garden they will carry on marching over from next door. A barrier glue can be applied to the rim of tubs, baskets and pots to stop the beetles climbing in. There are proprietary pesticides on the market to kill the grubs, but these are highly toxic and likely to harm much more besides. The best line of attack, in my experience, is to use nematodes that can be watered on to the soil. 'Nemasys' is available from garden centres and mail order companies and can be applied from early April to late October when the grubs are present. (In greenhouses and conservatories and sheltered London gardens it may be effective even earlier and later in the growing season.) All the soil in the garden will need to be treated.

Caterpillars can be a real problem, stripping the flesh from leaves of hollyhocks and other susceptible plants in just a few days. The best defence – as with most pests – is to keep a vigilant check on your plants. Remember that caterpillars are the larvae stage of butterflies and moths, many of which are desirable in the garden. They can also be highly beautiful things in themselves. Where they are a problem, pick them off and relocate or crush them. There is a spray called 'Dipel' that stops the caterpillars feeding (available from Green Gardener ▶ 254) but this should only be used a) as a last resort and b) when you know what species of caterpillar you will be killing. Cabbage white caterpillars can be kept off cabbages with netting that will prevent the butterflies gaining access to lay their eggs.

GROW YOUR OWN FOOD

In this age of pesticides, preservatives and genetically modified crops it makes sense to try your hand at growing your own organic food – even in the heart of London. It's also great fun – not only can you grow unusual varieties you won't find in the shops, you can harvest and enjoy them at their freshest and best. If you're really serious about home-growing, an allotment is your best bet to secure the expanse of open, sunny ground that large-scale fruit and vegetable growing requires. But many crops can be raised quite successfully in a small back garden, and you can grow a fine crop of rocket on a windowsill.

Allotments

I don't think I could live in London without my allotment. Quite apart from the delicious organic food it produces, it is a wonderful place to get away from it all when the traffic, the telephone and the terrific pace of urban life become too much to bear. I love growing vegetables, from broad beans and peas to potatoes, wild rocket and sweet corn. But more than anything I just like being there, with only the birds in the trees for company, and maybe one or two fellow plot-holders at the top of the sloping site, toiling away in companionable silence as the rest of London rushes by around us.

London is full of allotments. You see them from train windows, or flickering in the rear-view mirror as you drive out of town. Their shanty-town landscape of old sheds and rickety beanpoles is as much a part of the London landscape as the Thames at night. The Victorians saw them as a way of keeping the 'labouring poor' off the streets and out of the gin palaces, and when the middle classes were urged to 'Dig for Victory' during World War II, the number of allotment holders trebled. Demand for allotments declined during the 1950s and 1960s, and for a while they seemed old-fashioned and obsolete. However, in the past decade the tide seems to have turned, and allotments are popular again with Londoners, with long waiting lists at the more central sites. Once the preserve of people who drove sensible cars (preferably with a caravan in tow) and wore cardigans with leather patches on the elbows, allotments are now home to a new generation of growers who are more likely to sow organic rocket and radicchio than compare giant onions with their neighbours. Allotments offer urban gardeners their best chance to grow their own food (most London gardens being too small and shady to yield bumper crops) and many younger people are discovering the satisfaction of eating fruit and vegetables they have nurtured from seedlings and tended without pesticides. In some sites there's an almost comical rivalry between the 'old-timers' with their battery of chemicals and time-worn methods, and the eco-friendly newcomers with their trendy vegetables and shiny new spades. It can make for an interesting exchange of ideas. The communal aspect of allotments – long, thin plots lined up hugger-mugger – means you are never far from advice, whether asked-for or unsolicited. Remember that among your fellow plot-holders there will probably be many who are not only more experienced than you, but also wise to the vagaries of the local soil and weather conditions. You may even get offers of leftover seed or seedlings. Don't expect the sort of conversations you might have outside the allotment gates, though; stick to the 'three Ws' – weather, weeds and weevils – and you're sure to be accepted.

One of the many appealing aspects of allotment culture is the makeshift, make-do mentality. Nobody uses a brand new plant tie when a snipped-up pair of old tights will do. It is a matter of pride (no matter what your ecological leanings) to recycle what you can – old carpet and plastic sheeting keep the weeds down, timber offcuts become beanpoles and an old tennis net makes a support for climbing beans. The shed is the nerve centre of any allotment plot and is usually home to an array of tools, a few old deckchairs, endless empty plastic pots and the background burble of Radio Four. It will probably have been tacked

together from old doors and windows found in skips and crowned with corrugated plastic, but to the happy Londoner sitting inside sipping a thermos of tea it will be a much-treasured refuge – not least from the rain.

None of this makes allotments particularly smart places to be seen in; they are at best slightly scruffy round the edges and at worst a real eyesore. But they do have an undeniable and very English charm. London has its share of extremely picturesque allotment sites. Hampstead, as you might expect, has a crop of rather rarefied allotments – relatively small sites such as that at Fitzroy Road where the atmosphere is gentle and the plot-holders share gossip and gardening tips around rickety tables and chairs. Fulham has one of the largest – the Fulham Palace Allotments in Bishop's Avenue. As befits an outpost of medialand, you may even spot a TV celebrity or magazine editor among the carrots and turnips. Here, as on most allotment sites, there's a jolly, communal atmosphere, with frequent barbecues and a shop where surplus seedlings and produce – as well as tools and seeds – are on offer. But for the best view in town you can't beat the Grange Lane allotments on a gently sloping hillside off what looks like the perfect country lane near Dulwich College (▶ 200). The light at the end of the day here is stupendous, and on a fine summer's evening lucky south Londoners can sit back, relax and savour the sunset over the city before taking their freshly picked vegetables home for supper.

If you think you'd like an allotment, apply to your local council, which may have the cheapest plots to rent (the average plot costs around £20 for five poles – 150 square yards to the layman). Railway sidings, local schools and land owned by public utilities companies are other possibilities. The National Society of Allotment and Leisure Gardeners (▶ 267) should be able to advise on allotments in your area. If there's a waiting list, don't be discouraged. Put your name down anyway and there's a chance that at the committee's next Annual Purge enough recalcitrant plot-holders will be thrown off to shunt you to the top. Think twice about getting an allotment more than ten minutes' drive from your home – one within walking distance is the ideal, and you'll spend more time there if you can wander over after work. For minimum upkeep, at least one visit during the week and a good few hours at the weekend are required – more if it's a dry summer. A fun way to spread the work and watering is to share a plot with friends or another family – at least you will be able to get away for weekends and holidays without feeling guilty. After all, allotments are supposed to be relaxing.

The Back Garden Larder

Though you'll get bigger yields from the open expanse of an allotment, you can still grow good fruit and vegetables in an average-sized back garden. Many Londoners section off a part of their plot as a kitchen garden, and if you have pets or football-playing children it will pay to invest in a protective fence. You should also buy in as many sacks of well-rotted manure or mushroom compost as you can afford and work them into the soil before planting – you'll be rewarded with far superior crops. If you're short on space, forget about rows and rows of onions and potatoes – they take up too much room and these days you can buy organic ones relatively cheaply, even at supermarkets. Concentrate instead on crops that are hard to come by in the shops or are expensive, especially as organic produce. As the veg patch is part of your garden, you might as well make it attractive: there is always something satisfying about straight lines of crops, with their different colours and textures – or how about a patchwork effect, with squares of deep green spinach contrasting with bright lime oakleaf lettuce or frilly pink 'Lollo Rosso'? A few cornflowers or nasturtiums can be planted in between – they look pretty and will encourage beneficial insects (see pages 67–70).

Another approach is to grow some of the more attractive fruit and vegetables among the shrubs and flowers in your borders. This can look surprisingly smart – think of the fine-cut silver leaves and tufty violet heads of globe artichokes and cardoons, or the glaucous grey-green leaves and indigo spears of purple sprouting broccoli. I've seen this done beautifully in the tiny Stoke Newington garden of Pedro da Costa Felgueiras (sometimes open through the NGS ▶ 263). Portuguese-born Pedro sets tomatoes, runner-bean tepees and towering 'walking-stick' cabbages among his roses, irises and tree ferns to great effect. Raspberries mingle well with roses – they're unobtrusive until the pretty crimson fruits appear, and make a delightful snack when you're weeding. In the garden of his Paris headquarters, the fashion designer John Galliano grows raspberry canes interspersed with fragrant old-fashioned roses and swishing bamboos. Lower growing lettuces and herbs such as crinkle-leaf parsley can be used to edge the beds.

Here are some crops that are worth trying in a London back garden – even if you're a complete beginner:

• Rocket is the ideal London garden crop: it is extremely easy to grow, self-seeds like mad, and is a real saving on the tiny plastic bags of the stuff that cost the earth in the supermarket. Try wild rocket (from Seeds of Italy ▶ 253) with its narrower, delicately cut leaves for a slightly different flavour – it's also less prone to flea-beetle holes than the cultivated sort.

- Globe artichokes are great for a sunny spot – once planted out they pretty much take care of themselves, and should come back for four or five years if you protect the crowns in winter with straw or cloches. Established plants produce the largest number of edible flower-heads. Sow under cover in early spring and you could be eating your first artichokes with melted butter or vinaigrette by late summer.

- Courgettes are easy to grow provided they are sown or planted on a mound of soil mixed with well-rotted manure and given enough water. Two good plants will feed a family all summer – try Simpson's Seeds and Seeds of Italy (▶ 253) for attractive striped, ridged or yellow varieties. If you have a slug and snail problem it's best to raise them in pots and plant out when the seedlings are big enough to withstand damage.

- Broad beans and peas are well worth the effort of watering and weeding around the seedlings – and nothing beats the fresh smell and flavour of the first crops. Use twiggy tepees or woven willow cones to make the supports into a feature in your garden. November-sown beans will get a head start and are more likely to beat the blackfly that often covers the growing tips by spring.

- Dwarf French beans are easy provided you protect from slugs and snails. If you have room for climbing beans, try some of the more ornamental varieties such as 'Trionfo Violetto' (purple), 'Meraviglia of Venice' (yellow) and the crimson-streaked borlotti bean (much loved by the *River Café Cookbook*) whose name 'Lingua di Fuoco' translates as 'tongue of fire'. A few fragrant sweet peas interspersed with the beans not only look lovely, they also aid pollination.

- Lettuce is the ideal crop for home growing. The average shop-bought 'Iceberg' has been sprayed up to sixteen times with various chemicals before it reaches your salad bowl. And the crisp, squeaky freshness of newly picked lettuce is in a league of its own. Look for attractive and flavoursome varieties such as red salad bowl, oakleaf and red-streaked 'Quattro Stagioni' (slugs don't seem to like red leaves) or try the 'cut-and-come-again' Mediterranean seed mixes that include endive and radicchio and are marketed under names like 'Mesclun' and 'Saladisi'.

- Tomatoes are easily grown in the garden, where you can harvest them whenever you want – there's nothing like popping a cherry tomato, still hot from the sun, in your mouth as you gather the vegetables for supper. Bush varieties do away with the need for complicated pinching out, and 'Tumbler' can cascade from containers or hanging baskets. Try some of the unusual striped, black or yellow varieties to perk up your garden and cooking alike. Simpson's Seeds (▶ 253) is a good source of seeds and young plants of unusual varieties. Mexican tomatillos are grown in the same way – seed from Future Foods (▶ 252) – and are great for making *salsa verde*.

• Rhubarb is the ultimate trouble-free crop, and will reward total neglect with gorgeous pink shoots in late January and February when there is little else to harvest. Invest in a terracotta rhubarb forcer for the pinkest, longest, earliest shoots and an attractive feature in the garden all year round. Soft fruit is a real treat, and less trouble than it sounds. A row of ten or twenty raspberry canes and a couple of red- and blackcurrant bushes will provide you with the makings of a good few summer puddings. Currant bushes and gooseberries can also be purchased as standards. Strawberries make an attractive edging for vegetable beds – but protect from the birds if you don't want to lose the cream of the crop!

• Finally, don't forget about the ultimate trouble-free home produce – fruit from your own trees. (See page 51 for more information.)

Some crops can be sown *in situ*, but to make sure the slugs and snails don't get them all, raise in smaller pots inside or on shelves well off the ground. Or buy ready-to-plant seedlings from garden centres or mail order companies. (See pages 28–30 for more advice on raising your own plants.)

Container Garden Harvest

Even if you live with your head in the clouds in a block of flats, or have only a tiny courtyard garden, you needn't deny yourself the delights of home-grown produce. Many types of fruit and vegetables can be grown in containers, and you can even grow a fine crop of rocket in a window box – just open the window and snip. The drawbacks are that yields from pots will never be as high as in open ground – apart from tomatoes, which don't seem to mind having their roots restrained – and that you'll need to feed and water rather more. On a south-facing terrace or balcony twice-daily watering may be necessary in a hot summer, so don't embark on a container kitchen garden unless you're prepared to put in the leg- (and arm-) work or invest in an automatic irrigation system. In an exposed spot, you'll need to put up mesh netting inside the railings or erect some sort of screening to filter the wind.

I grow a long line of tomatoes in pots in my tiny garden every summer, and often get better yields than at my allotment, where blight can lay the plants low overnight. I also grow salad crops in one of two large galvanized metal grape-treading vats that I bought from Brick Lane market – similar ones are described as bath tubs in Manners mail order catalogue (▶ 257), or you could try the metal baths sold by builders' merchants. 'Cut-and-come-again' mixtures that include a range of different varieties of lettuce, radicchio and endive look pretty – and because you only pull off a few leaves at a time and leave the plant to re-sprout, a single sowing can last for months. A late-August sowing of hardy varieties sees me through the winter with enough home-grown leaves to perk up shop-bought produce. Not all crops are suited to container growing, however. One year I tried growing runner beans in pots on my study windowsill. I tacked up some wires on either side, and had visions of the plants surrounding my window with a flowery and leafy frame – not to mention a delicious crop of beans – but the plants never got into their stride and my harvest was precisely three pods. (I've since learned that beans like richer soil and more root space than I had been able to provide.) More successful were the squashes sown in three large tubs on the little flat roof on top of our ground-floor bay window. They took a bit of watering, but produced six sizeable fruit among the madly spreading leaves and tendrils. Some self-seeded nasturtiums from the year before romped happily among them and down in front of the window, providing a pretty floral screen. It was fun to peer out and see people's surprise at spotting a pumpkin on a Brixton rooftop.

The real queen of container veg growing in London is Penelope Bennett, whose little book *Windowbox Allotment* is an inspiration to urban gardeners everywhere. A writer in her early sixties, she lives in a first-floor flat on a busy road in Chelsea with two cats and several hundred plants. Her west-facing terrace measures just 16 x 8 feet, and was an unpromising patch of asphalt before she decked it over, but it now keeps her in fresh fruit and vegetables almost all the year round. Crammed on this little rooftop are several fruit trees, including a Comice pear, a Victoria plum and a cherry, troughs of year-round perpetual spinach and perennial herbs, and in summer, all manner of containers spilling over with dwarf beans, tomatoes, oriental salad greens and lettuce. Penelope even grows root crops in containers – carrots, parsnips and beetroot are harvested while still small, like the expensive 'baby vegetables' sold in trays at Marks & Spencer – and she grows new potatoes in 8-inch pots (a couple of seed potatoes produce a healthy single portion). Aubergines and cucumbers clamber up a sunny wall, and alpine strawberries fringe an old plastic water tank.

Penelope raises her plants with the protective instincts of a mother rearing her young. Each spring, her bedroom is turned into a 'seedling kindergarten' with removable shelves fitted across the window frame to house trays of basil, lettuce, tomato and aubergine seedlings until the weather becomes warm enough to establish them outside. She likens the 'hardening off' process (in which plants raised under cover are gradually acclimatized to the great outdoors) to 'putting a baby outside in its pram for the first time' and once left a dinner party early because she had forgotten to take her young melon plants in for the night. More unusual fruit and vegetables are attempted every year: Penelope has tried her hand at oyster mushrooms, wheatgrass and saffron crocuses, as well as gourmet and heritage varieties of radish, garlic and shallots, all with great success. She even finds room for a compost bin and wormery – and swears by the brown liquid feed produced as a by-product of the wormery process as a tonic for all her plants.

If you're a total beginner, try a few easy things first, like rocket or bush tomatoes, choosing the largest pot you can and following the planting advice in the section on container gardening (see pages 40–42). If you have nowhere to raise seedlings, and don't fancy sharing your bedroom with them, you might find some vegetable seedlings on sale at garden centres. A few of the mail order seed companies, such as Simpson's Seeds (▶ 253) and Sarah Raven's Cutting Garden (▶ 252), can also send out seedlings in season, which can be costly, but cuts out a lot of the work. A container crop of potatoes is well worth trying – you'll only need about six seed potatoes for a large container – a dustbin is ideal, or even a stack of old car tyres. Place the potatoes in an eggbox on a cool windowsill for a few weeks with an 'eye' pointing upwards so they develop firm stubby shoots. Put 6 inches of compost in the bottom of the pot (or bottom two tyres) and space out the potatoes with the sprouts uppermost. Cover with 6 inches more compost and water well. As green shoots break through the surface of the soil, keep adding more compost (and tyres), and watering once a week until the pot is full. New potatoes take about three months to be ready. So if you plant them on the traditional date of St Patrick's Day (17 March) you could be celebrating Midsummer's Day with a dish of the most delicious freshly dug potatoes ever.

Places to go for inspiration:

Centre for Wildlife Gardening (▶ 205)
Chumleigh Multicultural Gardens (▶ 206)
Culpeper Community Garden (▶ 189)

The River Café (▶ 215)
Roots & Shoots (▶ 207)

Herbs

We tend to think of herbs as culinary plants, but the true definition is much wider, embracing trees, shrubs, biennials, annuals and herbaceous perennials that have aromatic, medicinal and cosmetic as well as culinary uses. In many, it is the foliage that is used; in others the flowers, seeds or even roots – and sometimes all four are useful. On top of all this, many herbs make beautiful garden plants and are grown for their appearance alone. Walking out into a garden where lots of herbs are grown is a wonderful experience. On a warm summer's day, when the warmth on the leaves has released the plant's essential oils into the air, you can almost get high on the aroma. In one large garden I visited, where the herb garden was contained within high hedges, the effect was amplified to such an extent that the gardeners used to fight over who should work there, and those suffering from colds and other ailments claimed to be miraculously cured after an afternoon's toil. Urban gardens may not have room for a separate herb garden, but if you are keen on herbs you might find room for a small herb potager, or a container herb garden outside the back door. I grow twelve different types of herbs, most of which compete for space in the second of my old grape-treading vats. They have been given a mulch of purple aquarium gravel, which not only complements the leaves of the sages and the flowers of marjoram, chives and thyme, it continues to look good over winter, when many of the plants have died down. Rosemary and bay are grown in large pots separately, owing to their size, as is mint, due to its habit of spreading and taking over. (I also have a 'mint plantation' at my allotment, where I grow six or seven different varieties, mainly for fresh mint tea and summer cocktails such as the delicious *mojito* from Cuba.) Basil is planted out separately in summer and eaten as fast as it grows. The main trick with herbs is to grow enough. If you eat a lot of curries, or like making pesto or adding chopped flat-leaf parsley to everything, your stocks in an average London garden are never going to keep up, and you may need to think about an allotment. It would be worth it – herbs can be expensive to buy, and the silly little supermarket sachets don't stretch far. Other herbs, such as chives, thyme, sage and fennel are attractive enough to mingle with ornamentals in the flowerbed, and the lower growing herbs can make a pretty edging. If you like Thai food, you could try growing lemongrass – buy some fresh from the shops, place in a jar of water for a week, and wait for roots to develop before potting up. Here are some tips for my top twelve garden herbs:

Basil is one you definitely shouldn't be without – the scent of the leaves on even the tiniest seedling seems to hold all the essence of summer. It can be grown successfully from seed in early spring, using the warmth of an airing cupboard or propagator to aid germination. Sow directly into pots or plug trays, as basil has long tap roots and doesn't like to be disturbed. It is also prone to damping off disease, so avoid over-watering and never water after midday. If, like me, you sometimes fail with basil, you can cheat by buying a pot from the supermarket: gently separate out the individual plants and re-pot in rich, well-drained soil in full sun. However you grow basil, pinch out the growing tips to promote bushy growth. Grown among tomato plants, it repels many pests and will benefit from the extra feeding and watering.

Bay is often grown as smart clipped standard trees in pots to flank a front door, and you could use the prunings in the kitchen. I treat my small pyramid bay in the back garden this way; its annual haircut keeps us in bay leaves for cooking all year, and the tree comes inside every Christmas as part of the decorations. Don't buy too small a plant; you'll be waiting for ever for a decent harvest, as bay is slow to grow. It can be tricky to raise from cuttings without a heated propagator and mister. The main pest to look out for is scale insect, which covers the plant in black spots and needs to be washed off with soap and water. Like basil, bay likes full sun and a sheltered position, particularly when young.

Chives can be grown from seed, but a small plant or two, bought from the garden centre, will soon increase if the clumps are lifted and divided every few years in spring. They grow best when planted at least 6 inches from other plants and given rich moist soil. (In poor soil the leaves turn yellow and then brown at the tips.) Keep well watered. The leaves can be cut to within an inch of the ground four times a year to maintain a good supply; cut only a section of the plant if you have only one. The flowers, too, can be added to salads. Garlic chives (or Chinese chives) can be grown in the same way; they have strappier leaves that taste of garlic.

Coriander in abundance is a boon for lovers of curries and Middle Eastern dishes. It can be grown easily enough from seed, but should be sown directly where it is to grow, as it dislikes disturbance. When put under any kind of stress, the seedlings bolt straight into flower, producing only the feathery top leaves and omitting to produce the larger lower growth which is used for cooking. To keep coriander happy, give it light, well-drained soil in a sunny position and water well when young. Seed can also be harvested for use in the kitchen. One of my fellow allotmenteers swears by rubbing the seed between his hands and soaking in a damp flannel overnight to promote better germination.

Dill in the garden is great for making your own gravadlax or other fish dishes. The trick is to stop it from bolting; like coriander, it will miss out on the leaf production stage if disturbed or upset. Raise from seed in pots or plug trays or where it is to grow; it prefers well-drained poor soil in full sun. Protect from the wind and thin plants to 8 inches apart so they can spread. Push twiggy stakes around the seedlings to support them and water well in hot dry spells. Dill makes a good companion with chervil, the seeds of which will germinate and overwinter just as dill is giving up the ghost. The two herbs should co-exist quite happily, re-seeding every year.

Mint is a must for every garden. The family includes many different varieties including spearmint, peppermint, ginger mint, eau-de-cologne mint and apple mint, all of which have subtly different leaf shapes, textures and flavours. Grow a few and experiment with their use in mint sauce with roast lamb, chopped into tabbouleh and Middle Eastern salads, or crushed into drinks such as *mojito* or Moroccan mint tea. Just a sprig of young leaves crushed in the bottom of a glass with hot water added makes a delicious refreshing drink; for the cocktail, substitute hot water for fizzy spring water, a spoonful of sugar and a measure of white rum. Mint prefers full sun but will tolerate a fair amount of shade. Restrict its growth by growing in pots or a deep tin or plastic container sunk into the soil. Mint tastes best before it comes into flower, so keep cutting back to encourage bushy growth. Before it dies down in winter, bring a pot inside where it will continue to supply you with leaves till spring.

Marjoram and oregano are closely related plants of the genus *Origanum*, whose spicy aromatic leaves are indispensable in Greek and Italian cooking. There are, in fact, many different varieties with subtly different uses, but if you pick up a plant at the garden centre the chances are it will have been mislabelled, so you may want to have a go at growing from seed or cuttings. Pot marjoram (*O. onites*) is the one to choose if you want to use the leaves fresh, while the leaves of Greek marjoram (*O. vulgare* subsp. *hirtum*) keep their flavour best when dried. The golden oregano (*O.v.* 'Aureum') makes an attractive yellow splash in a herb garden and combines well with vegetables in the kitchen. Well-drained sunny dry soil is a must, and the plants grow well in containers.

Parsley is one of those herbs you can never have enough of: it is worth setting aside at least a square yard for a mixture of flat-leaf and curly varieties. Some swear that the curly leaves are more flavoursome, in spite of the fact that the flat leaves, chopped, are a vital ingredient in French and Italian cookery. To cover this amount of ground it is cheaper to grow from seed, but you'll have to be patient – parsley seed takes 2–3 weeks with heat and 4–6 weeks without. Raise the seedlings in pots or plug trays in early spring to avoid root disturbance and plant out only when the soil and air temperatures have begun to rise, and the seedlings are large enough to withstand slug damage. Cut the leaves down frequently to ensure bushy regrowth; it may even overwinter in a sunny sheltered spot but the plants will run to seed rapidly in the second year, so make another sowing in August to be sure.

Rosemary, like bay, can be grown most attractively as a standard bush or tree; its mauve-blue flowers look pretty in early summer and the scent of the leaves makes me long for roast lamb. It can be raised well from cuttings, but impatient gardeners will probably prefer to buy a potted plant. Give it well-drained soil in a sunny position, as befits its Mediterranean origins; against a south or south-west facing wall is ideal. Prune – quite hard, if you like – immediately after flowering; do not prune in autumn as new growth is susceptible to frost damage. Sprigs can be picked for cooking, however, all the year round.

Sage is worth growing simply so you can nip out into the garden and pick enough leaves to make the simple butter and sage sauce ('*burro e salvio*') to melt over fresh-cooked pasta or ravioli. It is also attractive enough to be grown for its appearance alone, though the most showy varieties, including purple and variegated types, do not have the best flavour. Again, you are probably best off buying a plant or two and keeping it in a pot or border in sunny, well-drained soil. Prune well in spring to encourage young shoots with a strong flavour, and also after flowering in late summer to prevent the plants growing leggy.

Tarragon is a treat in the garden for adding to chicken and fish dishes. Stuff a mixture of soft butter and chopped leaves beneath the skin of a chicken before roasting, or add just a few leaves to sliced courgettes before steaming. French tarragon (*Artemisia dracunculus*) is the type you want, rather than the less tasty but more vigorous Russian tarragon (*A.d. dracunculoides*) which is often wrongly labelled and sold in its stead. French tarragon cannot be grown from seed, and cuttings can be tricky, so buy a plant from a reputable herb nursery and plant in a warm dry position. Remove the flowers, and pick leaves for cooking all year round. As the plant dies down in autumn, protect its crown from frost with mulch, straw or horticultural fleece and pot up some sections of root for extra insurance in case the mother plant doesn't make it.

Thyme is an evergreen and will add immeasurably to your garden with its green, grey or golden leaves, its pretty flowers in all shades of pink through to white and dark purple, and the bees that will buzz around it when in bloom. On top of that, its culinary uses are many – add it to stocks and marinades, stick a few sprigs in an onion as stuffing for chicken or sprinkle in a pumpkin risotto. Different varieties of creeping thyme can be grown as a 'patchwork carpet' in a sunny spot, or in cracks (or intentional chessboard gaps) between paving. It can also make a good ground cover for sun-loving trees and shrubs in pots. The crucial condition is well-drained soil and protection in harsh winters. Thyme can be raised easily from softwood cuttings, but if you buy even quite small plants they will soon spread. Prune after flowering to prevent the plant becoming too woody.

Places to go for inspiration:

Aveda Institute Roof Terrace (▸ 120)
Barber-Surgeons' Hall (▸ 160)
Chelsea Physic Garden (▸ 150)
Chumleigh Multicultural Gardens (▸ 206)
Eltham Palace (▸ 184)
Fulham Palace Park (▸ 214)
Geffrye Museum Gardens (▸ 173)
Hall Place (▸ 209)
Herb Garden, Battersea Park (▸ 199)

Indoor Edibles

Even if you have no outdoor growing space at all, you can still grow herbs and salad greens in pots on a sunny windowsill. Supermarket basil plants can be kept going for longer if you pinch out the growing tips first, and harvest leaves from different parts of the plant. (Buy the biggest plants, as the little ones will be used up in one go.) With coriander and parsley you might even get a second sprouting if you cut the first growth almost to the soil. The plants will look a lot nicer if you hide the plastic pots in something prettier – even an old painted mug will do. A kitchen always looks – and smells – better with fresh herbs growing in it.

And have you ever thought about raising home-grown organic mushrooms? Grow-your-own kits can be found in garden centres or ordered from Future Foods (▶ 252). Follow the instructions, which invariably involve emptying bags of spawned compost and a peat 'casing' into a box and keeping them at a series of strictly controlled temperatures for a set number of days. An airing cupboard is useful, especially in the early stages – and you'll enjoy that faint smell of damp woodland every time you open the door. Mushrooms don't need much care after the initial starting-off period; all you have to do is wait, water, watch – and keep the box dark and warm. They seem to come from nowhere – the spores are too small to see – and arrive without warning, silent and stealthy like those in the poem by Sylvia Plath. Once they have appeared – a few dots of whiteness at first against the dark compost at the edges of the box – they grow at an astonishing speed, and can double in size in one day. At this stage you can start to thin and eat the mushrooms; the flavour and cool, clean texture are out of this world and you'll find it hard to stop. A mushroom-growing kit would make a fun present for a teenager or curious child gardener, and the entire family will enjoy the produce.

If field or button mushrooms are too commonplace for you, there are even kits for growing oyster mushrooms on cardboard tubes. Again, the spore-impregnated rolls need a bit of juggling about between airing cupboard and fridge to shock them into their fruiting cycle, and it's crucial to keep them moist. I have yet to try this, but it must be such a thrill to see the frilly pale brown mushrooms forming inside the plastic bags – and even more of one to serve them up for supper. Mushrooms have the added advantage of growing well over winter.

Wheatgrass is one of those wonder foods that is packed with all manner of vitamins and minerals and is sold in expensive juices in smart health food shops like Fresh & Wild and Planet Organic. A few years ago the bright green juice was the favourite drink of actresses and supermodels *en route* to a yoga or pilates class. But wheatgrass is simplicity itself to grow at home on a tray like a little indoor lawn. The grass will be ready to use in a few weeks – just snip off a section of the green fringe as you need it. A juicer is necessary to get the full benefits from wheatgrass, unless you're a cat. Cats love to nibble at a wheatgrass lawn and pet shops in the United States are full of 'kitty lawn' kits.

Even the laziest London gardener can sprout some seeds and pulses. These, too, are incredibly nutritious. No self-respecting detox regime should be without them and they bring a crisp texture and fresh taste to salads and sandwiches. There are special kits and trays available, but the simplest way to sprout seeds is in a large jar with a piece of muslin stretched over the opening and held in place by an elastic band. Mung beans are an easy choice to start with, and they taste pretty good, too. Place a heaped tablespoon of beans inside the jar, fill it with water and shake to clean the beans before straining through a sieve. Refill the jar with water and soak the beans for twenty-four hours, during which time they will have swelled to double their original size. Secure the muslin over the mouth of the jar and drain it of water. Fill with water to clean the beans again, and drain once more. Then place the jar in a dark place – an airing cupboard is too warm but under the sink would be fine, or covered by a box or thick paper bag. Repeat the washing, draining and covering every day – morning and night if you can remember. By day three the beans will be sprouting. You can start eating them now, as Indian people do, or wait till the creamy white sprouts are an inch or more long – or even sprouting small pointed leaves. Alfalfa and wheat are easy to sprout in the same way – though some sprouted seeds are an acquired taste, or even toxic if eaten raw in large quantities. If the idea of sprouting appeals, you should buy a copy of *The Sprouter's Handbook* (from the Organic Gardening Catalogue ▶ 252) for further information and inspiration. It was written by a man who overcame ill-health by making sprouts a regular part of his diet.

While on the subject of sprouting seeds, don't forget mustard and cress. A small tray (such as those in which vegetables are sold in supermarkets) and some blotting paper or thick paper towel are all you need: just add water and wait. The sprouts will be up in a matter of days. For adults they are a fresh peppery addition to salads; for young children, whose names have been written in the seeds on a sunny windowsill, they are the closest thing to magic.

❦ INDOOR GARDENING

Houseplants

Some people are snobbish about houseplants – and there's no doubt that the dusty old rubber plant and brown-tinged yucca of student bedsits are best avoided. But a house full of growing things is for me a happy and vibrant house. Plants improve our air quality and combat pollutants in the environment, while looking beautiful at the same time. Choose the right ones for the right places, take good care of them, and your house will feel and look better for the effort. It's a personal preference, I know, but I try to steer clear of what I call 'office plants': cheese plants and other glossy-leaved specimens that seem to have been chosen for their ability to withstand low light levels and cups of coffee being emptied on their roots. I go instead for things with a bit more active life in them – succulents, with their fleshy glaucous leaves and surprising flowers, or scented-leaf geraniums, which can fill a room with their perfume. There are many good books on the different types of houseplant and how to keep them. What I'm interested in here is unusual ways of grouping or growing them that seem particularly suited to life in the city. Here are some I've experimented with myself or seen elsewhere:

- Most houseplants grow best when grouped together. I don't know why – is it something to do with the increased humidity or are they sociable souls like ourselves? To avoid mess and make watering more manageable, set your pots on large trays filled with porous clay granules (available from garden centres). This gives the plants access to moisture without leaving the roots sitting in water; and many houseplants will benefit from slightly moister air around their leaves.

- Plants can be grouped in windows as a living screen for privacy from passers-by – much smarter than muslin curtains and constantly changing through the year. A bank of plants on staggered shelves can fill the bottom half of a bay window in your average Victorian house, and though you'll lose a bit of light, you'll get some wonderful effects as the low morning or evening sun shines straight through the foliage and casts shadows on the walls. Be sure to choose plants that are suited to the conditions (light levels/direction/temperature, etc.). If your windows start quite close to the ground, take your lead from Chinese takeaway restaurants and let a few money plants (*Crassula ovata*) and scented-leaf pelargoniums sprawl all the way up to the top. If you need curtains, too, it's usually possible to arrange the pole so the fabric can pull clear of the foliage.

• Rather than hang a blind in our top-floor bathroom, which is overlooked by a neighbouring building from one side, I've just crammed the deep dormer windowsill with plants. A peppermint-scented *Pelargonium tomentosum* seems to thrive in this position and filters the sunlight – not to mention our neighbour's view – quite beautifully. Other plants that might enjoy the hot humid conditions of the average bathroom include the umbrella plant (*Cyperus involucratus*) – which should stand in water – and some bananas and bamboos. These all need at least some light. Mist the leaves with a sprayer every few weeks to keep them happy and healthy.

• Stretching shelves across a window is a great way to cram in more plants and increase your privacy. I first saw this done at the beautiful Kettle's Yard in Cambridge where a south-facing window has been transformed into a living tableau of plants, beach pebbles, glass fishermen's floats and inscriptions on glass that sparkle in the sunlight. The shelves at Kettle's Yard are of slatted wood, but chunky glass would also look good and maximize light, although you'd have to keep up with the dusting. I've also seen it done to great effect in a kitchen in a mansion block that looks out on to a light well with neighbours directly opposite; as he is on the top floor with reasonable light, my friend is able to grow culinary herbs there. Again, you need to choose the plants with the light levels and temperature in mind – a sunny window would be a great place to raise seedlings if you don't have a greenhouse. The effect is pleasing from inside and out. Strolling the streets of Greenwich Village in New York I came across a corner house that must once have been a shop, whose floor-to-ceiling windows were jam-packed with succulents and other small potted plants that didn't need too much watering. It looked stunning – the only problem was that everyone else thought so too, and crowded closer to get a better look, so the original aim of providing privacy was somewhat compromised.

- Sometimes, just one big plant in a room makes a huge dramatic impact. I often bring in a large potted brugmansia from the garden when its fragrant pendent flowers (earning it the common name angel's trumpets) are in full bloom, and it makes a great centrepiece on a low table. The interior designer John Stefanidis had one magenta-flowering bougainvillea picking up the hot pinks of the furnishings and paintings in his 'Indian sitting room' and a rare incense plant, *Calomeria amaranthoides*, towering in front of a window.

- If you work at a computer, spider plants are particularly effective against the harmful emissions that can emanate from the back of terminals. The dragon tree (*Dracaena*) is also good at this, which may explain why its spiky variegated leaves on a tall central stem are frequently seen in work places. Group some plants around the computer on your desk, stand taller specimens on the floor in front and they will protect you while you work. Happily, all this heroic effort on the part of the plants has no ill effects on them whatsoever – all they ask is to have their leaves occasionally sprayed with water and carefully wiped with a cloth to remove dust. What better excuse to create an urban jungle in your study?

- Aloes make great houseplants and the 'medicine plant' *Aloe vera* has extraordinary healing properties. The outer leaves of plants three or more years old can be snapped off and the gel inside used direct on the skin to heal burns or sun damage, or speed up the healing of cuts and grazes. Sliced up and left in cold water overnight, the flesh also makes a refreshing and healing tonic to drink. I keep a plant on the bathroom windowsill; it would be good to have one in the kitchen, too, to have at hand in case of burns. Make sure you are buying a real *Aloe vera* and not a substitute. Aloes need good light levels or their leaves, which should be perky and upright, will start to sag.

'Paper White' Narcissi

From late November through to February or March, my house is filled with glass bowls of fragrant 'Paper White' narcissi, grown on pebbles in water. They must be one of the simplest things to grow and are endlessly rewarding. For just the price of a few bulbs, and the minimal effort of arranging them on a container full of pebbles and adding water, you have many weeks of pleasure. The shoots start to sprout almost immediately, forming buds that should open within four or five weeks into heavily scented clusters of starry white blooms. 'Paper Whites' are perfect for impatient gardeners – and children will be thrilled by the day-to-day progress of the bulbs. Plant them at the end of November and you should have a bowlful blooming in time for Christmas. They are a lot prettier – and cheaper – than most of the cut flowers available at this time of year.

Order the bulbs in late summer to early autumn – and err on the side of generosity, as a bowl of them coming into bud makes a wonderful Christmas present. (Garden centres also stock them, but you'll end up paying more – the mail order supplier Peter Nyssen offers a good discount for fifty bulbs or more ▶ 252.) For a continuous supply of flowers throughout the winter you'll have to stagger the plantings, so unpack the bulbs and place all those you don't need in a cold dark dry place, with the sprouting ends all pointing upwards (in a box in a shed or unheated bedroom is ideal – make sure they have some air circulating or they may go mouldy). Those you want to start now can be planted straight away – the bulbs have been specially prepared so there is no need for 'forcing' in the dark as you do with indoor hyacinths.

'Paper Whites' will grow in soil, but I love the look of them on pebbles in glass bowls, where I can see the white roots snaking down to anchor the plants as they grow. I use shallow round and chunky square glass containers bought at wholesale prices at New Covent Garden Flower Market (▶ 230), but any clear receptacle at least 3 inches high will do. Ceramic containers or cachepots can also look good – and this is one occasion when you *don't* want drainage holes, as the water has to be retained. Carefully fill the bowl or pot with pebbles to an inch or so below the rim. I use Scottish beach pebbles which can be bought by the sackful from builders' merchants or DIY superstores such as B&Q (▶ 249) as I like the combination of pink, grey and cream pebbles. But gravel – or pea shingle, as the professionals call it – is cheaper and looks nearly as nice. You can even use coloured slate chippings or glass beads or marbles, or pop a few pieces of coloured glass in with the pebbles to catch the light. The crucial thing is to add a small piece of charcoal (a stick of the stuff used for drawing, broken into 1–2-inch lengths is fine) at this stage, as this is a most effective way to prevent the water smelling.

Arrange your bulbs on top of the pebbles, perhaps adding a few more pebbles around the bases to keep them sitting upright. Pack them quite closely for a good cloud of blooms – I have a couple of larger glass bowls that take ten to fifteen bulbs apiece, but three or four good-sized bulbs in a smaller pot will give a good display, as each bulb should put out at least two or three stems. Add water to *just below* the bases of the bulbs. Bulbs never like to sit in water, and the mere presence of moisture is enough to trigger the roots into action. Then just watch and wait. For the first few days the bulbs will sit there quietly, putting most of their energy into sending out roots to anchor them in position. Keep an eye on the water level, as the bulbs seem very thirsty at this stage. It won't be long before the green shoots start to stir, and once they do, there is no holding them. In a warm room, you can practically *see* them growing at an inch or more a day. Just keep topping up the water. After about four weeks (depending on the state of your central heating) the buds will start to burst and that gorgeous heady perfume will begin to pervade your house. At this stage, the stems tend to get a bit wayward, so it's a good idea to bind them loosely with some raffia or ribbon (string will do fine). Some people stake them, but I find gathering them together and twisting gently to splay the stems out in spiral fashion will keep them upright. You occasionally have to rescue a particularly renegade bunch of bulbs that keel over or try to jump out of their container overnight, but it doesn't take a minute to rearrange them.

The flowers should last for a good two weeks, the clusters getting larger and larger as more buds open. Then they start to fade and turn brown at the edges – which is when you can begin the entire process all over again. (I sometimes have quite a few bowls at different stages on the go, so I don't have to wait so long for new flowers.) Remove the bulbs, along with as many roots as you can, and rinse the pebbles in a colander. I have been known to put the pebbles, colander and empty glass bowl in the dishwasher, so they all come out clean and sparkling and ready for re-use, but I doubt very much if the manufacturers would recommend it. Then simply start off with a fresh supply of bulbs. The old spent bulbs have to be composted – there seems to be no way round it. For quite a few years running, I have experimented with drying them out in a shed till the foliage dies down and replanting, as you do with tulips, but have never got so much as a single bloom. I've even put them out to graze at my allotment, hoping for a further flush of flowers at some stage. Nothing. I can only think that with prepared bulbs such as these, so much of the energy of the plant goes into the first year's flowers that it can muster no more. When you get to the end of this year's supply of bulbs, wash the containers and store them, with washed pebbles inside, in a safe place. That way, when the dull drear days of November come round once again, they'll be ready for a new batch of bulbs to be started into life.

Small Bulbs in Small Pots

Planted in pots, some of the smaller spring-flowering bulbs can be brought inside when they are coming into flower. Their delicate patterns and flowers can be appreciated best at close quarters, and will cheer you up no end on a grey wintry day when it's too cold to go outside. It's best to plant them up outside and leave them there till the buds are showing – too much heat too early encourages excessive foliage.

I plant the bulbs in autumn, five to ten to a pot, and cover them with a layer of compost the same depth as the bulbs themselves and a little cap made from chicken wire to fend off foraging squirrels. (Before I began doing this, I would frequently arrive home after a weekend away to find my pots ransacked and the garden littered with bulbs with just one bite taken out of each. Infuriating.) It's fun to co-ordinate the colours of the bulbs with the type of pot – remember that old cracked mugs and galvanized buckets make good alternatives to plastic and terracotta. The pots in which the bulbs are planted should have drainage holes (with the exception, sometimes, of hyacinths, see below), but another possibility is to plant in plastic pots and slip them inside a pretty cachepot or other hole-less container as you bring them inside. Once the pots are planted up, group them in a not-too-prominent corner of the garden (they are boring to look at at this stage) and forget about them for a month or more – just check occasionally to make sure they are neither dry nor waterlogged.

Mid-January is the time to start watching out for buds, particularly among the earlier flowering dwarf irises and miniature daffodils. Bring the pots into the warm, acclimatizing them gradually if your house is extremely warm, and place where they can be seen to best advantage – on the kitchen table or where you eat, on a writing desk or bedside table.

When the flowers have faded, snip them off, leaving the foliage, and place the pots back outside. A dose of liquid feed will give the bulbs a boost at this stage, and the leaves will continue to feed the bulbs as they die down. Most bulbs treated in this way should flower again in subsequent years. I've had success with the following:

• Snowdrops – It is such a lovely surprise to see a clump of snowdrops growing inside in the depths of winter. They never seem to give too good a return when planted as bare bulbs. Buy a few little pots in bloom – or beg some from a friend who has lots – and they should continue to come up, and multiply, year by year.

- Dwarf irises are some of the easiest and loveliest bulbs to have inside, where you can see all the subtleties of their patterns and colour combinations. The little *Iris reticulata* varieties are particularly beautiful, and come up reliably again and again. Try *I.r.* 'Springtime', which has soft blue inner petals and deep violet 'falls' streaked with white and maroon; *I.r.* 'Natascha', which is almost white; and *I. histrioides* 'George', whose dramatic flowers are almost black at the tips when opening, with a yellow blotch on the 'falls'. *I. tuberosa* is curiously sombre, but none the less beautiful, in velvety black and lime green, while 'Katharine Hodgkin' is an absolute delight in shades of pale blue, soft yellow and cream.

- Crocuses look sweet in little pots or bowls inside, where you can appreciate the colouring of their petals as they close and open according to the light. One kind or colour per pot looks better than a mixture, and the plants are more likely to flower at the same time – plant the tiny corms seven or more to a pot. The winter-flowering varieties such as 'Bluebird' (mauve outer petals, white inside), 'Cream Beauty' (pale butter yellow) and 'Gipsy Girl' (pale gold with outside petals feathered with chocolate brown) will flower from late January onwards. I have also enjoyed autumn-flowering colchicums, whose large crocus-like flowers grow from big bulbs on ghostly pale stems – the foliage appears in spring. For indoors these can be grown, like hyacinths, in water or on pebbles rather than in soil.

- Miniature daffodils and narcissi can get lost in the garden, but are a cheerful and fragrant presence in the house. As well as the classic miniature 'Tête-à-tête', try 'Hawera', which bears up to seven delicate pale yellow blooms on a single stem; *Narcissus cyclamineus* with their pretty, backward-reflexed petals ('Jenny', in white and palest primrose is particularly pretty); and the jonquil types such as the lime-tinged 'Pipit' and pinkish 'Bell Song'.

- Grape hyacinths are unpopular with some gardeners due to their colonizing tendencies in the border, but this can be contained if you grow them in pots. I cram them fifteen or twenty bulbs to a small pot to make a dense cloud of blue when they open; the designer Anthony Noel used to plant them into a cone of compost held in shape with chicken wire, which was a real eye-catcher. The bulb catalogues offer many variations on the usual cobalt blue: from *Muscari* 'Cantab' (sky blue) and 'Valerie Finnis' (pale baby blue) to 'White Beauty'. The lower bells of *M. neglectum* are deep purply-black with neat silver rims, gradually turning paler blue towards the top.

- Delicate species tulips are as far from their big blowzy over-bred cousins as are dog roses from hybrid teas. Just a few inches high, their blooms have fragile pointed petals and can be found in some extremely beautiful combinations. *Tulipa humilis* 'Alba' is pure white with a slate-blue base to the petals, while *T.h.* 'Persian Pearl' is cyclamen-purple with a yellow base and 'Little Beauty' a vivid lilac-mauve with deep blue centre shading to moss green. *T. clusiana* has slim crimson petals with white, cream or yellow insides, while *T. turkestanica* has five to nine flowers to each single stem – creamy white with a green and bronze flush on the exterior.
- Snakeshead fritillaries are best seen *en masse* in a water meadow with the low spring sun shining through their fragile purple bells. But urban dwellers can appreciate their dusky charms close-to by planting them in pots. Be generous when planting, as a fair proportion may not flower the first year (luckily they are relatively cheap), and don't let the soil dry out. There is a white variety (*Fritillaria meleagris* 'Alba'), but the purple is really what you want for that subtle chequerboard pattern, unlike that seen in any other flower.

It's possible to buy many of these already potted up from a nursery or garden centre, though you won't get the more unusual varieties and you'll end up spending a lot more. Slip the plastic pot into a pretty container or cachepot and you'll have the instant effect without any of the bother – or a lot of the fun.

Hyacinths and Amaryllis

Indoor hyacinths and amaryllis need just a little more attention to produce the best flowers. They are the classic Christmas flowers, and I like them best in white, when the blooms are like moments of quiet among the visual cacophony of all the cards and decorations. Coaxing a hyacinth bulb into flower for Christmas Day is, however, more difficult than you might think. While they are easiness itself outside, hyacinths need special treatment to flower indoors – which is where you really want them, in my opinion. The flowers – especially the pale pinks – are hard to place in the border, and can look a little awkward and stunted. And who's going to be out there in the cold on their hands and knees to appreciate their wonderful heady scent?

Indoor hyacinths can be grown in conventional pots of compost, or in jars of water. Unlike most other plants, they can also be grown successfully in containers without drainage holes, enabling you to press anything from old painted mugs to small enamel buckets and pretty soup tureens into use for the purpose. The two absolutely crucial things to remember are: a) to give the planted bulbs enough time in the dark, and b) never to let the compost dry out. Bringing the bulbs into the light too early results in weak and over-leafy growth; while dry compost at any stage of the growing process can seriously damage and distort the flowers – an all-too-common problem with home-grown hyacinths. If planting on soil, place the bulbs on a bed of damp compost and cover with more compost until only the very tops are exposed. I usually do three to a 6 or 7 inch pot and just one in each of a number of old Italian painted mugs which are too chipped to drink from but too beautiful to ditch. In mugs and other containers without drainage holes, it's not a bad idea to place a layer of gravel in the base of the pot to avoid waterlogging. If there's room for the pots outside, so much the better, as there will be less chance of them drying out. Wrap the pots right over the top with a thick layer of newspaper to exclude all light and protect from frost. Inside, they can be stored in a cool, dark, well-ventilated place where the temperature stays below 10°C (50°F) – a cellar or unheated spare bedroom is ideal. Cover with newspaper or empty cardboard boxes to be sure of total darkness and check every week or so, watering as necessary.

For the earliest blooms, buy 'prepared' bulbs that have been specially treated by the growers to activate the flower buds for flowering a few weeks earlier than untreated bulbs. Planting in September or early October provides the best chance of those elusive Christmas flowers. Hyacinth bulbs need ten to fourteen weeks plunged in the dark to develop a complete root system and for the buds to appear. Only when the bud is clearly visible between the emerging leaves should the containers be moved into the light. Acclimatize the plants in a dim corner for a few days – they'll look a little yellowy and anaemic at first but will soon colour up and spurt into growth. An even temperature of about 18°C (65°F) suits them best. Slowly, the fat bulbs will swell and begin to open from the bottom first – they should be in full fragrant bloom in another few weeks.

Hyacinths also look pretty grown in water in forcing jars, where the spiralling patterns of their long white roots add to the effect. Clear hyacinth jars can be found in good garden centres for just a few pounds, but if you hunt around in junk shops you might find some of the stylish coloured glass ones that were made in the 1950s. I have some in dark green and purple in unusual graphic shapes – the purple ones look lovely with the magenta hyacinth 'Woodstock', which, like the more common blue hyacinth, has a pinkish bulb. Fill the jars with clean cool water to just below the base of the bulb – they will go mouldy if the bulb sits in water. Then put them in a cool dark place, as above, until the top growth is about 4 inches tall. This should take about eight weeks, after which the jars can be placed in a light, but not overly bright place, where the temperature does not exceed 21°C (70°F). As with most flowers, they will last longer in a cooler environment. When the flowers are over, the bulbs can be planted out in the garden, where they will flower somewhat less spectacularly the following year (prepared bulbs may 'rest' for a year before flowering again).

Amaryllis (or *Hippeastrum* as they are correctly, but less commonly, known) can only be grown in pots indoors in this country, though I've seen them in sun-baked borders in Morocco and the Mediterranean. There are many colours of amaryllis beside the classic white and screaming scarlet: 'Apple Blossom' is white tinged with pink, while 'Picotee' has a fine red edging around its pure white petals. There are also smaller-flowered amaryllis with names like 'Movie Star' and 'Naughty Lady', some of which produce up to three stems per bulb, and double-flowered varieties, which I find rather hideous. They are all easy to grow the first year, requiring no time in the dark, but repeat flowers in subsequent years require a little extra effort. The enormous bulbs – often 4 or 5 inches across – are packaged up in boxes as a classic Christmas present, but you'll need to plant in late October for a yuletide bloom.

Amaryllis can be grown in soil, or just in water, supported by pebbles or coloured chippings, but the soil level must never be higher than half way up the bulb, and the water touching the roots only. The pot should, ideally, be only an inch or so larger in circumference than the bulb. Place in a warm sunny spot – the more light the better. Amaryllis can be slow to get going, but once that fat shoot is on the move, it can put on half an inch in a day in a warm room, and should flower within six to ten weeks of planting. The plants are almost obscene at this stage, but compelling to watch as the growing point swells to reveal four or more buds, each of which opens into a bloom of breathtaking beauty that can be 8 or more inches across. Feed weekly while in active growth and continue fortnightly after flowering until the leaves die down – you can extend the life of the flower by pulling off the stamens. Then place in a cool dark place and allow the pot to dry out. In autumn, lift the bulbs out of their pots, taking care not to damage the roots; shake off the old soil and soak for an hour in warm water. Re-pot, place in a warm bright spot and resume watering, and you ought to be rewarded by a further flush of blooms.

Inside Out Gardening

Certain plants really lend themselves to what I call 'inside out' gardening, which was touched on in 'Containers' (see page 42). As well as moving potted plants around your garden, to ring the changes as different plants come into their own, why not move some in and out of the house at different times of year? This is a fun and little-explored area of gardening that can create some stunning effects both inside and out. Most outdoor plants will not mind a quick sojourn indoors, provided the change in temperature is not too extreme – if you have your central heating up high, you may need to acclimatize the plants gradually in a reverse process of 'hardening off' ('softening up'?), and they'll require extra watering.

Sometimes, the smaller potted plants in the garden can be overlooked in their moment of glory, particularly in the winter months, when you don't often venture out. A few snowdrops or crocuses in a pretty pot can look lovely on the kitchen table or make a welcome surprise by a guest's bedside. And when auriculas are in flower in May, it's a treat to be able to study their exquisite painted faces on a sunny coffee table or writing desk. Throughout the year, other, larger plants can be used to good occasional effect inside. How about a line of potted lavender plants along a mantel- piece, a tree fern in a shady corner, or a pot of the beautiful pineapple lily, *Eucomis bicolor*, as a centrepiece in your sitting room? Using 'outdoor' plants in this way can be handy for decorating a room for a party – and will certainly save you money in flowers. For a few weeks each December, I commandeer a potted bay pyramid and an ivy trained as a spiral as impromptu Christmas decorations – with a few tiny white fairy lights woven among the foliage, they look extremely festive. None of the above is a houseplant by nature, but they will all be happy enough inside for a few weeks, provided they are watered well and their light requirements are respected.

The principle works the other way around, too. Many houseplants will actually enjoy a holiday outside in summer – and if there should be a warm downpour, as there so often is in June and July, it's worth hauling all of your houseplants into the garden or on to a flat roof and allowing the rain to wash off all that dust. Many of the frost-tender plants, such as pelargoniums, cymbidium orchids and most succulents, prefer to be outside all summer, where they will often put on a surprising spurt of growth, but they must be brought back in again before the first frosts of winter. This twice-annual exodus can be quite an upheaval if, like me, you have a lot of this type of plant, but it galvanizes me to get the house and garden into order, and is a good way of marking the changing seasons. In spring, when all danger of frost is over, many of my scented-leaf pelargoniums, echevarias, aeoniums and other succulents are marched outside and arranged on garden tables or grouped around the French windows. (They'll be taking the place of the potted spring bulbs most of which, bar the late-flowering tulips, will be over and can be moved out of the way.) There they will stay all summer, where they often flower profusely – and the scent of the pelargonium leaves is a real pleasure. If one of the plants is looking particularly ravishing – and I'm a sucker for the frilly grey leaves and dark magenta blooms of *Pelargonium sidoides* – it might be brought in again for a short spell, as I like to have something beautiful to look at while I work. But well before the first frosts in autumn, it will be time to bring them all back inside, thus making room to plant up your spring bulbs.

In my house, the smaller pelargoniums have some staggered shelves below a skylight at the top of the house, where they sit on trays of porous clay granules along with the houseplants that stay inside all year, while a larger, rose-scented one fills my study window. Sometimes my plants have put on so much growth outside that it's hard to get them through the doors. If your pelargoniums have grown too unruly at this stage, it's possible to strike cuttings of many varieties by snapping off a growing shoot a few inches long, gently pulling off the lower leaves and sticking the lower couple of inches of stem straight into moist compost. The succulents become 'coffee table plants', their pots grouped on round aluminium trays that are placed in the best light possible. I love to see the fat fleshy leaves and subtle colours of crassulas and echeverias at close quarters, as well as through the window. By spring they will all be itching to get outside in the sunshine again.

Christopher Lloyd is a master of 'inside out' gardening at Great Dixter in East Sussex. All summer long there is a flamboyant display of huge succulents, bright annuals and scented lilies in a cluster of pots around the main entrance to the house. And inside, in the Great Hall and ground floor study, he often has 6-foot spires of the chimney bellflower (*Campanula pyramidalis*) flanking the fireplaces. It's wonderful to see herbaceous garden plants such as this in unexpected situations. The designer Tricia Guild likes to use foxgloves in a minimalist interior, where their wayward spires, twisting this way and that, bring a welcome whiff of wildness while looking surprisingly graphic and modern. Inside out gardening requires a bit of a change in the way in which you think about plants, but once you get started, the possibilities are endless.

Part Two

LONDON GARDENS

THE WEST END

From Mayfair to St James's

In spite of recent tree-planting initiatives, Oxford Street and Regent Street themselves have little in the way of natural beauty; in fact, they are probably at their greenest in the lead-up to Christmas, when every shop front is festooned with evergreens and fairy lights. Step off the main thoroughfares, however, and you will find much to delight and inspire. The roughly square-shaped area bordered by Oxford Street to the north, Regent Street to the east, Piccadilly to the south and Park Lane to the west contains a fascinating range of gardens, from the leafy grandeur of Berkeley and Grosvenor Squares to ritzy Mayfair window boxes and perky pelargoniums on the balconies of the Peabody Trust mansion flats off Oxford Street.

PEABODY GARDENS
W1. Bond Street or Marble Arch Tube. Accessible daily.
Turn off Oxford Street into Balderton Street (just opposite the famous Selfridges clock) and you stumble into a delightful enclave of red-brick Peabody buildings on the streets that run parallel to Brown Hart Gardens and Weighhouse Street. The residents are obviously keen gardeners who don't let lack of space put them off. Balconies bristle with bright red pelargoniums, jasmine and golden hops clambering over the smart black ironwork, and even the darkest basement wells are crammed with shade-loving *Fatsia japonica*, spotted laurel and spider plants and hanging baskets in summer. The communal garden between Binney Street and Gilbert Street is a wonderful shady haven in high summer: the huge plane trees that tower overhead have a leafy cuff of ivy around their bases, while box-edged beds contain bluebells and variegated foliage plants. Travelling south down Gilbert Street, you pass another well planted garden on the right and, if you turn right at the end down Brook Street, you will find yourself in Grosvenor Square.

GROSVENOR SQUARE
W1 (020 7298 2000). Marble Arch or Bond Street tube. Usually open daily 7.30am–dusk. Royal Parks Agency.
After September 11, 2001, the park at Grosvenor Square became pretty much out of bounds, due to security surrounding the American Embassy at the western end. A wide path links sculptures commemorating President Roosevelt and the Eagle Squadron, while crisp hedging, low

stone walls and large expanses of close-clipped grass make for an elegant, sophisticated atmosphere. Formal unfussy planting is concentrated around the Roosevelt Memorial, with banks of acanthus, lavender, euphorbias and *Crambe cordifolia* flanking rows of wooden benches and backed by neatly pleached limes. A memorial garden in honour of those killed in the World Trade Centre attack has been opened on the eastern side, with a rose-covered pergola and central stone floor panel inscribed in a spiral with the names of those who died. A girder from the ruins of the towers has been buried beneath it.

MOUNT STREET GARDEN
Mount Street W1. Green Park tube. Open Mon–Sat 8am–dusk,
Sun and Bank Holidays 9am–dusk. City of Westminster.
This little L-shaped garden between St George's Church and the white-painted Grosvenor Chapel on South Audley Street is much loved by the

few Londoners who know about it. Judging by the inscriptions on the rows of wooden benches, these include many of the Americans who have come to live and work in the area. (One is dedicated to 'An American who could not find a park like this in New York City'.) Its sheltered aspect, hugged on all sides by tall buildings, allows an *Acacia dealbata* and a Canary Island palm (*Phoenix canariensis*) to flourish, along with other attractive ornamental trees. The wedding cake tiers of *Cornus controversa* 'Variegata' preside over a central bed containing rhododendrons, hostas and acers, while bamboos and more shrubs to the west conceal more benches in secluded enclaves. Birds in the trees and rustling leaves create a wonderful feeling of peace.

The smart window boxes of the antiques shops and restaurants on **South Audley Street** are worth checking out as you walk south. Turn left into Hill Street and some of Mayfair's most stylish streetside planting can be glimpsed on the façades of the houses on **Hay's Mews** (west) and **Chesterfield Hill** just a little further east. Continue down Hill Street to arrive at Berkeley Square.

BERKELEY SQUARE GARDENS
W1. Green Park tube. Open daily 8am–dusk. City of Westminster.
My heart always leaps when I walk or cycle through Berkeley Square. Its majestic plane trees are some of the oldest in London – the trunks and lower branches are misshapen like mad sculptural beasts, while the uppermost twigs interlace against the sky. Though too circumnavigated by noisy traffic to be truly peaceful, the all-enveloping canopies of the planes in high summer do seem to exude an air of calm, and the line of benches down the middle is well frequented. A stone statue of a nymph (originally a fountain) stands at the south end, and there are handsome tubs planted with topiary and seasonal bedding. The moneyed restraint of the planting is in keeping with the façades of the surrounding houses, offices and flashy car showrooms. In the centre of the garden is a covered shelter that looks as if it ought to house an old-fashioned band playing the famous song, although I've yet to hear a nightingale sing in Berkeley Square. Have a peek down **Bruton Place**, on the north-east corner of the square, where there are some interesting pots and window boxes adorning the brightly painted mews houses and Guinea Grill pub.

Walking north up Davies Street from the north side of Berkeley Square, take a look at the smart little courtyard garden of **Bourdon House** on the left – as the headquarters of Mallett antiques it sports some elegant lead planters and antique stone fragments. There are also some smart hotels to check out – not least **Claridge's** (on the corner of Davies Street and Brook Street), where immaculate seasonal planting flanks the entrances and spills out between the smart black-painted railings. (The **Raffles Brown Hotel** in Albemarle Street is the epitome of discreet elegance with trailing ivy and clipped box and pale silver-grey railings.) Brook Street links **Grosvenor Square** in the west with **Hanover Square** in the east.

HANOVER SQUARE
W1. Oxford Circus tube. Open daily. City of Westminster.
Surrounded by busy thoroughfares, Hanover Square is hardly a tranquil retreat, but dense planting around the periphery provides some respite from the traffic and a degree of privacy for the office workers who sunbathe there at lunch times. Shade-loving shrubs such as *Fatsia japonica*, phormiums and ornamental grasses abound, with some pretty acers and lilacs bordering the four pathways that cross in the middle. The central roundel is more formal: potted camellias give way to curved beds with palms. Though most of the visitors loll on the grass, there are a few benches from which to spy the models on their way in and out of Vogue House on the square's southern side.

PARK LANE
W1. Marble Arch or Hyde Park Corner tube. Accessible daily.
If you ever find yourself walking or cycling from Marble Arch to Hyde Park Corner, it's far more peaceful to take the Broad Walk – the plane-lined avenue just inside Hyde Park's eastern boundary. But you would be missing a few little horticultural gems on the far side of the road. The tiny strips of garden outside **Grosvenor House** are an exercise in chic urban topiary, with different types of ivy trained into balls and around openwork spheres. Neat box-edged gravel beds contain ferns, phormiums and the odd seasonal splash of bedding, while painted Versailles tubs are home to slender multi-stemmed birches. A few hundred yards south, there is more relief from car showrooms at the **Dorchester**, where a tiny formal garden in front of the hotel is kept in immaculate condition beneath a large illuminated plane tree. Pocket-handkerchief lawns of bowling green quality are interspersed with stone paths, simple fountains and geometric beds filled with fresh green and white planting. The cool expanse of **Hyde Park** (▶ 143) can be glimpsed through Park Lane's central reservations, whose elaborate shows of spring and summer bedding, beneath more

enormous plane trees, are an attraction in themselves. For the best views over the park, however, reward yourself with a cocktail in the Windows on the World terrace bar in the London Hilton (22 Park Lane).

GREEN PARK

Piccadilly W1. Green Park tube. Open daily 5am–midnight.
Royal Parks Agency.

In spite of being bordered by busy Piccadilly to the north and Hyde Park Corner to the south-west, Green Park has a perennially serene atmosphere. The further you venture into its 53 acres of trees and grass, the more distant the noise and the hustle of the city become. No fancy flower beds here, just soothing expanses of green, interrupted only in springtime by carpets of crocuses and daffodils, and in autumn by the changing colours of the trees. Rent a green and white striped deckchair and feel as if you're part of a *pointilliste* painting, or stroll down Queen's Walk (on the eastern boundary, beside the Ritz) and check out the rear façades and gardens of the grand buildings that look out over the park – some can only be glimpsed between gaps in the fences and railings. The garden of Spencer House is particularly elegant, with white roses, acanthus and cardoons in box-edged beds around a circular lawn.

The far end of the path offers a view of Buckingham Palace and the gilded Queen Victoria Memorial (often surrounded by patriotic red, white and blue planting) to the right. The 39 acres of **Buckingham Palace Gardens** are hidden behind a high brick wall. Parts of them can be viewed on a guided tour of the Palace (August and September only, ring 020 7766 7300 for details), but your best bet is to try to get invited to one of Her Majesty's summer garden parties. I always smile when I think of the two German tourists who scaled the wall ten years or so ago and pitched their tent unwittingly on her lawn.

ST JAMES'S PARK

The Mall SW1. St James's Park tube. Open daily. Royal Parks Agency.
Café, lavatories, children's playground.

St James's Park has a magical atmosphere that sometimes seems more the stuff of fairytales than central London. Perhaps it is the view from the bridge: the south-eastern skyline is punctuated by the improbable turrets and spires around Horse Guards Parade. Or perhaps it is the pelicans that patrol the lakeside – I once saw one (very politely) steal an ice-cream from an unsuspecting child. The walk around the lake is dreamily romantic, weaving in and out of planting, beneath huge weeping willows and ancient London planes. Check out the charming **Duck Island Cottage** over near the fountain. Built in 1837 for the Ornithological Society of London, it is still surrounded by wildfowl and now houses the offices of the London Parks and Gardens Trust (▶ 261). The planting in this park is particularly inspired – an unusual range of perennials, graded according to height, fills a variety of irregular-shaped island beds and borders. Shade-loving plants are to be found in the north-facing beds bordering Birdcage Walk, whose name dates back to James I, who established an aviary here (as well as a menagerie featuring crocodiles and an elephant).

ST JAMES'S CHURCHYARD
*Piccadilly W1. Piccadilly Circus or Green Park tube. Open daily
8.30am–6.30pm. St James's Church. A little café is attached to the church or,
for a touch of luxury, Fortnum and Mason's is a few steps down the road.*
Fight through the craft stalls that often crowd the front yard of this beautiful Christopher Wren church, skirt the café to the right and climb a few steps to a pleasant raised garden furnished almost entirely with plants that are mentioned in the Bible. Attractive painted labels inform you of plant, chapter and verse. Wooden seats around a central lawn are popular with local workers at lunchtime, but the place always has a peaceful air befitting its location. Peace poles and other commemorative sculpture are half-hidden in shady borders, and there are sometimes special displays. William Blake was christened in the church, which has an unusually fine display of potted plants along the window ledges. Later in life he apparently used to cavort, naked, with his wife in his own garden, and tell friends they were playing 'Adam and Eve'.

ST JAMES'S SQUARE
*SW1. Piccadilly Circus tube. Open Mon–Fri 10am–4.30pm, closed weekends.
St James's Square Trust.*
Sandwiched between Pall Mall and Piccadilly and enclosed by railings and dense greenery, St James's Square looks pretty impenetrable, like one of the private, key-holders-only squares. Find one of the entrances, however, and you'll enter a well loved and well used space, beautifully maintained for the use of all Londoners by the St James's Square Trust. The Trust was appointed by Act of Parliament in 1726 to 'clean, adorn and beautify that Great Square, place or piece of green called by the name of St James's Square', and is still doing a good job. The 1854 Nash layout survives, with four paths leading to a central roundel and benches backed by yew hedges or bamboo or

surrounded by pretty planting that includes hostas, lavenders, euphorbias, hellebores and hydrangeas. Particularly graceful London planes throw a dappled light across the lawns, and there are some other good trees: a *Cornus mas* with its puffs of chartreuse blossom in spring, a weeping mulberry and a catalpa whose lime green foliage is like a splash of sunshine.

To the north, Duke of York Street leads up to Jermyn Street and St James's Piccadilly (▶ 118). Pause on your way to admire the window boxes of **Chatham House** on the left (once the home of former Prime Ministers Pitt and Gladstone) and No. 4 in the north-east corner of the square, the former home of Nancy Astor, the first woman MP. And if your visit coincides with pub opening hours, the Red Lion just up the street has one of the best original mirrored interiors of any pub in London.

Covent Garden and the Environs of Tottenham Court Road

In spite of its name and history, Covent Garden is rather lacking in green spaces – though those it has are well looked after, thanks largely to the excellent Covent Garden Open Spaces Association (020 7379 3187). It is well worth heading off the busy, beaten tracks of Charing Cross Road, Shaftesbury Avenue and Tottenham Court Road to find some of the gems that are described below. The spaces are small – no major parks here – yet incredibly varied, and offer heaps of inspiration, from the sleek minimalism of the Sanderson Hotel Courtyard and Aveda Institute Roof Terrace to the vibrant spirit of the Phoenix Community Garden.

PHOENIX COMMUNITY GARDEN
21 Stacey Street WC2 (020 7379 3187).
Tottenham Court Road or Leicester Square tube. Open daily 8.30am–dusk.
Covent Garden Open Spaces Association.
From the moment you set foot in this garden, tucked away behind tall buildings in the crook between Charing Cross Road and Shaftesbury Avenue, it is clear this is no municipally run set-up. Most of the benches are

made from logs and rough-hewn timber, the paths are uneven and the planting wild and eccentric in places. People loll on grassy mounds in the sunshine, keep an eye on their kids in the play area or meditate in quiet corners. There's some esoteric sculpture, a wildlife pond, a daily weather notice and poems pinned to the trees. All in all, Phoenix Community Garden is a charming place and totally deserving of its own claim to be 'the greenest space in the heart of the West End'. The garden was founded in the mid-1980s, when a group of local residents approached Camden Council with a plan to turn a third of an acre plot formerly used as a car park into a community and wildlife garden; the result is clearly a popular space with local people, birds and butterflies alike. An assortment of chairs on a deck by the community building seems to invite you to get involved – there are eco-activities for children in the school holidays and an 'Adopt a Plot' scheme to help bring the wilder reaches of the garden into cultivation.

NEAL'S YARD
Off Shorts Gardens WC2. Covent Garden tube. Open daily.
The buildings that surround this little courtyard are festooned with trailing plants and window boxes as colourful as the paintwork. Fuchsias, salvias, morning glory and bright pelargoniums cover the façade of Neal's Yard Remedies and its neighbours. There are even trees on the roof and I seem to remember a wall of sunflowers along the top-floor balcony when I used to take yoga classes there. The place has a slightly hippy, but none the less groovy, urban atmosphere. The Neal's Yard Salad Bar is a good spot for a healthy lunch – there are tables under parasols or, for takeaways, clever wooden seats surrounding the painted oil drums in which young trees, shrubs and phormiums have been planted. For gardening-sustained ailments, try the walk-in back rub clinic and Neal's Yard Remedies, packed with wholesome goodies.

AVEDA INSTITUTE ROOF TERRACE
The Aveda Institute, 174 High Holborn WC1 (020 7759 7350).
Open Mon–Fri 9.30am–7pm, Sat 9am–6.30pm. Access to the garden is for clients only, but try asking at the desk upstairs – or use it as an excuse to book an appointment.
An exercise in eco-minimalism, designed to provide a peaceful summer hangout for staff and clients of the green cosmetics company Aveda. Constructed on two levels, it makes good use of a few pared-down materials: pale stone paving for the main area, timber decking for paths and simple bench seating around the edges; beach pebbles as infills

between paths and paving and wicker hurdles as fencing and to screen the enormous (and highly un-green) air conditioning units. The planting is in bold blocks and consists largely of aromatic herbs such as sage, lavender, thyme and rosemary and a variety of ornamental grasses. This style continues on an upper level, with paving paths among waist-high plantings of phormiums, astelias and larger grasses such as *Stipa gigantea* and miscanthus – on closer inspection these are hiding more unsightly technology. The electric purple heads of *Verbena bonariensis* look great here interspersed with silvery cardoons and artemisias, mauve asters and blue-grey tufts of *Festuca glauca*. Large terracotta pots of bamboo flank your re-entry to the Institute, where the scent of the lovely Aveda products hits you with such an impact I defy you not to treat yourself on the way out. There is also an excellent organic café on the ground floor.

CRABTREE FIELDS
Colville Place/Whitfield Street W1. Goodge Street tube. Open daily dawn–dusk. London Borough of Camden.
This is a well loved little garden just a stone's throw from tacky, trafficky Tottenham Court Road and directly opposite the local police station, which should deter ne'er-do-wells. If you visit at lunchtime you will be lucky to find a spot on the grass, let alone space on one of the benches, as workers from surrounding shops and offices compete for a picnic spot. A pergola loaded with wisteria and kiwi vines divides the grassy outer area from a quieter paved courtyard with fastigiate fruit trees – pears, definitely, and one would have thought crab apples – planted in a strict grid formation. At the far end is a small children's playground. Paths around the periphery are planted with shade-loving *Fatsia japonica*, mahonias, bamboos and ivy, and there is a neat beech hedge around the gate. Trees include a large robinia and a group of silver birches. **Colville Place** – a forgotten pedestrianized Georgian terrace – has a few nice collections of pots around some of the doorways that open straight on to the pavement.

THE SANDERSON HOTEL COURTYARD
50 Berners St W1 (020 7300 9500).
Oxford Circus or Tottenham Court Road tube. Open daily.
Very modern, very urban, very sophisticated. The oh-so-cool, dimly lit interior (designed by Philippe Starck) leads seamlessly out into a stunning courtyard water garden with rills and mini-waterfalls, pebble paths and sculptural blocks of evergreens and trees in zinc planters. It's a glamorous spot for lunch by day; at night the atmosphere changes to become

mysterious and romantic, with subtle lighting and secret hidden places to sit among the plants and water. In winter the courtyard is tented over and is popular for parties. This minimalist de luxe style is continued outside the hotel, where oversized pots of lavender and severely clipped conifers stand sentry. Judging from the healthy fringe of bamboo on the skyline, the Sanderson must have a great roof terrace, too – but you have to be staying there to see it.

SOHO SQUARE
W1. Tottenham Court Road tube. Open daily. City of Westminster.
A pretty, well loved shady square, whose most remarkable feature is the quaint mock-Tudor shelter in the centre. Mature trees (mainly planes) give welcome shade to picnicking office workers in summer, while shrubs around the periphery make a bid for privacy. Plantings of exotic-looking shrubs and ornamental grasses have been successful on the whole, and there are well planted tubs with seasonal bedding in the summer months.

WESTMINSTER AND PIMLICO

The monthly Royal Horticultural Society Flower Shows (▶ 258) are a good excuse to explore some of the gardens – both the grand and the everyday – in this often-overlooked area of London.

VINCENT SQUARE AND ENVIRONS
SW1. Pimlico or Victoria tube. RHS open Mon–Fri 9am–5pm (020 7834 4333).
Vincent Square is one of the largest residential squares in London. The Horticultural Halls where the RHS Shows are held are just round the corner on Greycoat Street. If there's no show on, console yourself with the gardening books, both ancient and modern, in the newly restored RHS Library (▶ 259) in the main building on the north side of the square. Or take a stroll around the surrounding

streets where many of the residents, no doubt benefiting from the monthly proximity of the country's best nurserymen, do seem to have made an effort with their front gardens and window boxes. The high Victorian terraced houses on the north and east sides of Vincent Square and the cottages on adjoining **Maunsel Street** and **Elverton Street** have some pretty examples in a variety of different styles. If you're walking to Victoria station, check out **Ashley Gardens**, with its well planted communal gardens belonging to the red-brick tenement blocks on Thirleby Road and Emery Hill Street. **Vauxhall Bridge Road** is surprisingly good value for gardeners considering it's such a busy thoroughfare. There's the small but well stocked **Tachbrook Tropicals** water gardening centre up towards Victoria at No. 244 (▶ 242) and, as you walk south towards Pimlico tube, a spectacular potted garden above the garage on the corner of Hatherly Street. On the other side of the road, towards the west, admire the ambitious planting that adorns Charlwood House and Henry Wise House on the right hand side of the road. Huge strapping phormiums, euphorbias and kniphofias fill the beds in front of and around the flats, while large shrubs and trees sprout forth from tiny balconies and roof terraces – a fine example of how good planting can redeem even the most unpromising architecture.

BESSBOROUGH GARDENS
Vauxhall Bridge Road SW1. Pimlico tube. Open daily dawn–dusk.
A pleasant little garden in front of white stucco houses which, though they look old, were built in the last couple of decades. Ornamental grasses are used to good effect around the periphery, with shade-loving fatsias, ferns, ivy and bergenias beneath the large plane trees. Colour is concentrated around a dolphin fountain at the far end, with beds overspilling with roses, peonies and catmint in high summer, and sculptural tiered towers for summer bedding.

Head south over Vauxhall Bridge for **Bonnington Square** (▶ 157) to the east and the **Museum of Garden History** (▶ 155) to the west – and look out for a piece of planting in front of the strikingly modern **St George's Wharf** development on the banks of the Thames.

TATE BRITAIN GARDENS
Millbank SW1 (020 7887 8734). Pimlico tube. Open daily 10am–5.50pm.
Café and lavatories inside gallery.
Next time you're visiting an exhibition at the Tate, take a look at the gardens to either side of the main steps. Plenty of inspiration for

minimalist gardeners with expanses of pale stone paving, lawns edged with zinc, geometric hedging and pared-down benches. The area in front of the Clore Gallery to the right has a simple shallow pool and grapevine pergola, with well designed wooden seats interspersed with the planting along the gallery wall. Notice how dappled shadows of leaves transform large expanses of paving in an effect akin to an art installation. It was a shame that on my last visit the inspired original planting of bronze fennel, *Verbena bonariensis* and 'Velvet Queen' sunflowers had been replaced by blocks of bright bedding plants. (NB: a new boat service every 40 minutes will take you from the pier on the other side of the road to Tate Modern (▶ 153) in just 18 minutes.)

ST JOHN'S GARDENS
Horseferry Road SW1. Pimlico or Westminster tube. Open daily 7am–9pm BST; 8am–4pm winter. City of Westminster.
This former churchyard was opened as a park in the 1880s and the original layout, with a circular pool and fountain with York stone paths radiating out like the points of a compass, remains. The grassy areas between the paths are shaded by enormous plane trees and feature large beds of seasonal plants, some with oleander bushes in their centres. Other trees include the ancient gingko, the cut-leaved Norway maple and the Camperdown elm, and there are box balls around the fountain and new-ish plantings of shade-loving plants and grasses around the edges. The elegant classical building on one side is actually the headquarters of the maintenance staff. Sadly the peace of this leafy garden is often disturbed by the noise of heavy traffic and building work.

WESTMINSTER ABBEY
SW1 (020 7222 5152). Westminster tube. Open Mon–Wed 10am–4pm, BST 10am–6pm. Dean and Chapter of Westminster.
It's worth braving the queues of tourists for a look at the two hidden gardens within Westminster Abbey. Enter, if you can, through Dean's Yard, where the ancient walls are clad in creeper, with some pretty window boxes near the gateway to the Chapter House. The first cloister, known as The Garth, is just a bare patch of grass, but if you follow the signs to the **Little Cloister Garden** you'll be rewarded by a gem of a garden that can be glimpsed only through railings from the surrounding stone cloister and looks all the more cool, green and lovely for its inaccessibility. Created in the eighteenth century, it has a pretty stone fountain playing in the centre of a handkerchief lawn, with immaculately tended borders of green and

white plants – euphorbias, hellebores, lamiums, box balls and white foxgloves on the shady sides and a pair of olive trees, iris, poppies, santolina and lambs' ears in the sun. Just down a short dark corridor is the **College Garden**, a much larger space and one of the oldest gardens in continuous cultivation in the country. On the site of the Abbey's first Infirmary Garden in the eleventh century, it still has borders full of herbs and medicinal plants, and a small well maintained knot garden to the right of the entrance. Don't be put off by marquees and garden furniture on the lawn – wander right around the borders, and explore the shady paths behind the fountain at the far end, where ancient stone fragments and sculpture are hidden among the hostas and hydrangeas.

Back outside, the planting schemes in **Westminster Square** are nothing to write home about, though there's a nice stone bench around the base of a London plane near Dean's Yard, with roses and clematis scrambling high into the branches, and some smart pleached limes in front of the Houses of Parliament. The catalpa trees, with their clusters of orchid-like blooms, are beautiful in July. From here, it's just a hop across the river to the **Museum of Garden History** (▶ 155) and the bohemian enclave of **Bonnington Square** (▶ 157).

EBURY SQUARE GARDEN
Buckingham Palace Road SW1. Sloane Square tube. Open daily 8am–dusk. City of Westminster.
A small square, whose unexciting layout is more than made up for by interesting planting. A central fountain is surrounded by standard elaeagnus bushes and a harmonious blue, white and yellow colour scheme prevails.

ECCLESTON SQUARE
Belgrave Road, Pimlico SW1 (020 7834 7354). Victoria tube/train. Open only through the NGS (▶ 263) and London Squares Day (▶ 262). Residents of Eccleston Square. Plants and trees for sale on open days.
It's well worth waiting for one of the few public open days to view this gorgeous 3-acre garden. Dense planting around the outside prevents all but the odd glimpse of the interior, and all one can do is envy the lucky residents – both for their keys to the garden and their luck in having resident garden writer Roger Phillips at the helm of the Garden Committee. (His correspondence with an American gardener comparing their two gardens has been published as the hugely entertaining *The 3000 Mile Garden*.) Benefiting from the fruits of Mr Phillips' plant-collecting

travels, the garden is packed with rare and interesting plants, including the National Collection of ceanothus, more than a hundred camellias, four hundred or more roses – including some rare Chinese species – and some unusual trees and shrubs, including a handkerchief or ghost tree (*Davidia involucrata*) and the foxglove tree (*Paulownia tomentosa*).

BLOOMSBURY SQUARES

Perhaps I'm biased because I used to live in this area, but to me Bloomsbury is still one of the most fascinating parts of London – where east meets west; academia rubs shoulders with grotty Tottenham Court Road, and a multitude of quiet leafy squares provide respite from the shopping thoroughfares and villagey enclaves. Russell Square tube station is as good a starting point as any for a walk around the area.

RUSSELL SQUARE
WC1. Russell Square tube. Open daily 7.30am–10pm.
London Borough of Camden. Café.
The centrepiece of the Bloomsbury estate laid out in the late eighteenth century, Russell Square has had a chequered history. Humphry Repton had a hand in its original design, and a recent redevelopment, fuelled partly by the council's frustration at the square's increasing use as a nocturnal gay hangout, has replaced the undeniably scruffy 1960s scheme (hexagonal concrete pavers and concrete planters) just when it was getting fashionable again. The new scheme, which looks back to the square's Regency heyday with the aid of archive paintings, has serpentine paths leading from the entrances on each corner, and weaving among the lawns and flowerbeds. A horseshoe path, which is being planted with a tunnel of pleached limes, leads around the central fountain plaza, where the height of the jets is controlled by computer. Much of the planting has a suitably frothy Regency air with roses, mignonette, pinks and violets; the larger beds on the eastern and western corners are planted in a more Mediterranean style, with sun-loving phlomis, fennel, iris, stachys, lychnis and nepeta. The dense bushes around the periphery have been replaced with a new hornbeam hedge and lower, more open planting. There are also spanking new railings and an ornamental gate.

BLOOMSBURY SQUARE

WC1. Russell Square tube. Open daily 7.30am–dusk.
London Borough of Camden.

This square, which is surrounded by some of the finest Georgian architecture in London, was still under much-needed renovation at the time of going to press, but all the signs are excellent. Much of the former scruffy shrubby planting has been removed to make way for a highly elegant scheme based on earlier designs, which is much more worthy of its setting. A young hornbeam hedge has been planted around the periphery, and large circles beneath the spreading plane and ash trees have been planted with swathes of shade-loving ferns, tellimas, hostas, epimediums, foxgloves, periwinkles and *Euphorbia amygdaloides*, which should be especially pretty in spring. Four paths meet at a central paved circle, which has attractive borders of pink shrub roses, irises, lavender, nepeta, cistus and hardy geraniums behind a young box hedge. However the circle seems to lack focus beyond a plaque set in the paving engraved with an entry from John Evelyn's diary in 1665, recording a dinner with the Earl of Southampton while he was in the process of building this 'square or Piazza, a little Towne'. The detailing in this new scheme is impressive: zinc edges to the flowerbeds and sleek black metal benches with waste bins to match. There is a small modern children's playground in one corner.

BEDFORD SQUARE

WC1. Tottenham Court Road tube. Only open on London Squares Day (▶ 262).
The Bedford Estate.

London's only complete surviving Georgian Square (note the decorative use of Coade stone in the round-headed doorways) has a suitably grand garden in the centre. Unfortunately, this perfect green oval can only be entered by key-holders, but you can peer over the railings at the south side to take in the quietly elegant composition of trees, lawns and shrubs – particularly attractive in the dappled light of a sunny afternoon. The artist John Piper called this square (on quiet Sunday afternoons) an 'almost hallucinatory piece of preservation of eighteenth-century London'. The Architectural Association at No. 34–36 offers a good course in historic garden conservation (▶ 277).

TAVISTOCK SQUARE

WC1. Russell Square or Euston tube. Open daily 7.30am–dusk.
London Borough of Camden.

This pleasant place might as well be called 'Peace Square', dominated as it is by a bronze statue of Gandhi, cross-legged and head bent and surrounded by offerings of flowers, cards, candles, scrawled messages, necklaces and other talismans. A number of trees, including a handsome copper beech, have been planted by politicians and other public figures with dedications to peace – note the cherry commemorating the victims of Hiroshima. At the northern end of the square a large carved and inscribed boulder honours the conscientious objectors of the Second World War. Indeed, considering the presence of busy Woburn Place just to the east, the atmosphere in the garden is surprisingly peaceful. The four quartered beds around the statue are model exercises in municipal bedding, a patchwork throughout the year of spring bulbs, summer bedding and lots of dwarf dahlias in high summer. Joggers jog around the periphery, students revise in the shade and red-leafed prunus and laburnum form a backdrop for Gandhi in the centre.

GORDON SQUARE

Bloomsbury WC1. Russell Square or Euston tube. Open Mon–Fri
dawn–dusk. Closed weekends and public holidays, except London Squares
Day (▶ 262). Gordon Square Garden Committee.

Just to the west of Tavistock Square is this smaller, much quieter garden. Managed by the Gordon Square Garden Committee rather than the council, the square has a rather wilder, more natural feel, though whether this is intentional or not is unknown. Having said that, the limes on the eastern side have been pollarded to within an inch of their lives, allowing you to see the façades of the houses where various members of the famous Bloomsbury Group (including Virginia Woolf and her sister Vanessa Bell, John Maynard Keynes and Lytton Strachey) lived at different times. Inside the scrappy wire-link fence the place feels like a private rather than a municipal garden; you can't help but try to imagine the square's former illustrious residents walking its shady paths or sitting, deep in discussion, on the benches beneath the trees. There are some charming touches: Victorian tiles edge the beds while climbing roses and jasmine scramble up into the cherry and weeping pear trees.

Just to the south, **Woburn Square** is in a parlous state: parched lawns and bare flowerbeds behind ugly wire fences and an uninspired children's playground at one end. Surely some of the local residents and academic institutions (the Slade School of Art and the Warburg Institute overlook it) could do something to revive it?

Heading west towards Tottenham Court Road, the hotels at the lower end of **Gower Street** put on a festive display of window boxes and pots flanking the steps in summer, while the little garden belonging to **University College** on Malet Street is worth a quick glance if you are passing. Set back and sunken down from the road level, it is little more than a rectangular lawn beneath the usual plane trees, but provides a pleasant shady haven away from the traffic for UCL students and employees.

FITZROY SQUARE
W1. Warren Street or Great Portland Street tube.
Only open on London Squares Day (▶ 262). Residents of Fitzroy Square.
Thought by many to be one of the finest squares in London, this is strictly speaking in the area fashionably known as Fitzrovia rather than Bloomsbury, but the fact that Virginia Woolf once lived at No. 29 and Roger Fry set up the Omega workshops at No. 33 begs its inclusion in this section. The elegant Georgian terraces on the eastern and southern sides of the square were built by the Adams brothers in the 1790s, while the remaining two sides were completed some twenty years later. In 1815 the local residents, fed up with having the green space in the centre used as what they referred to as a 'cow yard' and 'a playground of children of the lowest classes', enclosed it as a private garden for themselves. And so it has remained – an enviably quiet space ringed with railings and pedestrian-only paving that can be entered only in the company of a key-holder or on London Squares Day (▶ 262). Luckily the garden, designed by Sir Geoffrey Jellicoe, can be glimpsed most satisfactorily through the railings. It is simplicity itself – just grass, shrubs and ivy-clad plane trees – but the surprise lies in the seductive undulations of the turf. The one real focal point is a modern abstract sculpture by Naomi Blake.

QUEEN SQUARE
WC1. Russell Square tube. Open daily 7.30am–dusk.
London Borough of Camden.
Old-fashioned, unremarkable formal garden arranged in a long rectangle and surrounded by tall apartment blocks and hospitals. Worth mentioning simply because you pass through it when walking from Bloomsbury Square to Brunswick Square, Coram's Fields and St George's

Gardens. Square and round rose beds abound – sparsely planted when in bloom and totally uninteresting for the rest of the year. Borders flanking the tarmac paths are thick with spring and summer bedding beneath slightly incongruous spiky chusan palms. And yet this space is clearly popular with workers, patients and visitors from the surrounding hospitals.

BRUNSWICK SQUARE
WC1. Russell Square tube. Open daily 7.30am–dusk.
London Borough of Camden.
A mass of paling and wire fencing when I visited, this space is undergoing renovation as part of the same scheme as Bloomsbury Square (and has an identical notice promising to 'improve lines of visibility' by removing shrubs and realigning paths and implementing a new scheme 'based on earlier designs'). The layout looks less severe than Bloomsbury Square, retaining the wavy paths and a central area of planting. Cherry trees around the periphery of the square look wonderful in spring – and you might catch a glimpse of the sheep that live in Coram's Fields next door. While you're passing, look up at the concrete balconies that ring the much-maligned Brunswick Centre – a few of them are quite inspiring.

CORAM'S FIELDS
Guilford Street WC1 (020 7837 6138). Russell Square tube.
Open to adults with children Mon–Fri 8.30am–dusk, Sat–Sun 9am–dusk.
Coram's Fields Charitable Trust. Café, lavatories, under fives club.
'No adults unaccompanied by children' reads the sign on the gate, making this children's park a godsend for Londoners with children; if you don't have kids yourself it's worth borrowing those of a friend in order to enjoy it. Originally part of a foundling hospital (its museum is round the back), its peaceful lawns and play areas are flanked by rows of squat Palladian-style buildings that now house some of the resident sheep. Majestic plane trees provide shade in summer and the atmosphere is surprisingly tranquil considering the number of children usually playing on the well designed swings and monkey gym, and the floodlit football pitch at the far end. The flowering cherry trees around the entrance make it a local landmark in spring, as does the incongruous sight of sheep grazing behind the railings on Downe Terrace.

MECKLENBURGH SQUARE GARDEN

WC1. Russell Square tube. Only open on London Squares Day (▶ 262).
Enquiries to London House/Goodenough College, Mecklenburgh Square
(020 7837 7800).

Though you can't get into the garden without a key, this leafy, square, tucked directly behind Coram's Fields, is worth visiting for its stunning Georgian architecture alone. The houses (mostly converted into flats) are vast, with wide doors and ornate fanlights. I used to fantasize about living in one of the white stucco-fronted ones with an ironwork balcony looking out over the gardens, but the nearest I got was having a birthday picnic there thanks to a friend who was a key-holder. A dense privet hedge all the way around certainly affords privacy; but you can peer through the narrow gates at the majestic planes and cherries, well tended borders and tennis courts. There is also an area dedicated to plants from New Zealand. It looks particularly beautiful at the end of a summer afternoon with leafy shadows dappling the lawns.

INNS OF COURT

You can weave your way through the Inns of Court, from Gray's Inn down to the Thames, trying not to get lost in a world of enclosed gardens, courtyards and buildings that, in many places, has changed little since medieval times.

GRAY'S INN GARDEN

Theobald's Road WC1. Chancery Lane tube. Open Mon–Fri 12–2.30pm.
The Honourable Society of Gray's Inn.

This ancient garden was once a busy thoroughfare from formerly rural north London to the City markets further south. The central Great Walk flanked by young oaks now marches along this route, and the gardens are a haven of peace and quiet, not least because of the restricted opening hours. The planes here must be some of the oldest in London, towering against the sky and casting welcome dappled shade, while the catalpas, with their attractive, orchid-like blooms in July and bean-like fruits in autumn, may be even older. The grassy ground is terraced, with a sloping bank much favoured for sunbathing in summer, and some well planted borders around the periphery and flanking some of the many wooden benches. Gray's Inn garden is perhaps at its prettiest in spring, when the grass is carpeted with different types of daffodil and huge old magnolias are covered in white blossoms right down to the ground. The colours of the trees on a sunny autumn day are wonderful, too.

LINCOLN'S INN FIELDS

Holborn WC1 (020 7974 1693). Holborn tube. Main square open daily dawn–dusk, Lincoln's Inn private gardens open Mon–Fri 12–2.30. Lincoln's Inn/London Borough of Camden. Café, lavatories.

The seven acres of green space just to the east of Holborn tube survive from common grazing land and were for centuries used for fairs and popular sideshows and frequented by thieves and beggars. The area is now the height of respectability thanks, largely, to the presence of the Law Courts, and the main public square is the largest in the capital. On a summer's lunchtime it can seem crowded, with a mixture of students and be-suited lawyers sprawling on the grass and queueing at the tented café.

But the place is full of surprises for the keen gardener. Beyond the tennis courts and bandstand is an impressive collection of subtropical plants – swishing bamboos and pampas grasses, tree ferns (*Dicksonia antarctica*), spiky yuccas and agaves, bushy fan palms and the curious-looking toothed lancewood (*Pseudopanax ferox*). At the far south-east corner there is also a dry garden, where sedges, grasses and spring bulbs, selected to survive without irrigation, have been planted among carefully placed rocks and stone fragments. This is the point at which you can cross the road and pass through the porter's gates into **Lincoln's Inn** itself. The atmosphere here is akin to that of an Oxbridge college – the green squares are enclosed by fine buildings including a chapel and a library, enhanced by ornamental brickwork. To the right, behind the splendidly sculptural Brewster Gates, is **New Square** – the lawn was being excavated when I visited, but there is a pretty garden on its far side, with borders of day lilies, geraniums and *Verbena bonariensis* spilling out between the railings. To the left, you pass some fine borders in front of the library (which, rather interestingly, can also be viewed from the terrace above) and well planted lead planters, to arrive at the secluded private gardens which, a notice announces, are open to the public only on weekday lunchtimes 'for the enjoyment of rest and quiet'. The lawns here are green even in high summer, and the borders and pots around the surrounding buildings well tended. The long border at the top of a steep bank is impressive all summer long, with roses, delphiniums, lavender, poppies and clouds of *Crambe cordifolia* giving way to day lilies, crocosmias, echinacea, the plume poppy (*Macleaya cordata*) and sprays of purple buddleia. On the way out, check out the minuscule crenellated brick cottage with its neat sign saying 'Head Gardener'.

Before you leave the area, the **Sir John Soane Museum** at 12 Lincoln's Inn Fields is well worth a visit (open Tues–Sat 10am–5pm, admission £3) – the couple of clipped bays outside are uninspiring, but there is plenty of inspiration for urban gardeners inside, with inner courtyards crammed with statuary and architectural fragments covering walls.

MIDDLE AND INNER TEMPLES
Temple Lane EC4. Temple tube. Middle Temple open May, Jun, Jul, Sept Mon–Fri 12–3pm (020 7427 4800), Inner Temple open Mon–Fri 12–3pm (except during legal holidays) (020 7797 8250). Middle and Inner Temples.
Off Temple Lane are to be found some of London's very oldest gardens: it is reputedly from the Middle Temple Gardens that the white and red roses were picked at the start of the Wars of the Roses, and parts of what is now the

Inner Temple Garden were under way long before the Third Crusade in the twelfth century. The Middle and Inner Temples only became separate institutions in 1732, when the larger **Inner Temple Garden** was divided into Nuttery Court, the Nut Garden and the Great Garden; the latter has a simple, spacious layout with well kept lawns and fine ornamental trees. From 1888 to 1913 the annual RHS flower show was held here, until it was moved to its present site at the Royal Hospital, Chelsea. Recent research has discovered a Tudor Garden laid out in 1591, which original manuscripts describe as 'ornified with beautiful banks, curious knots and beds of fragrant flowers and herbs of sundry sorts and scents'. In the **Middle Temple Gardens**, ancient tradition has been kept alive by the recent replanting of sixteen bushes each of the red *Rosa gallica* var. *officinalis* (for the House of Lancaster) and white *R.* x *alba* 'Maxima' (for York); as a symbol of peace, an equal number of the stunning red and white striped Rosa Mundi (*R. gallica* 'Versicolor') have been added alongside. Fountain Court is dominated by a single jet fountain and ancient plane trees that throw filigree shadows on the pale paving. (Charles Dickens has strong links with the Middle Temple, and it is here that he set the meeting between John Westlock and Ruth Pinch in *Martin Chuzzlewit*.) An impressively old wisteria is entwined among the railings that mark the boundary between the courtyard and the main gardens. The **Lower Temple Gardens** leading down to the river are closed to the public but can be seen clearly through the railings – immaculate lawns, beautiful blossom in spring and colourful rose beds in summer.

MARYLEBONE AND REGENT'S PARK

CAVENDISH SQUARE
Wigmore Street W1. Oxford Circus tube. Open daily 8am–dusk.
City of Westminster.
Just behind John Lewis, this little square has more to commend it than you'd guess from the busy traffic whizzing round it and the underground car park beneath. True, it's a lot noisier than when sheep used to graze here in the eighteenth century, and the layout by Charles Bridgeman (a celebrated contemporary of 'Capability' Brown) was replaced in 1971 when the car park was constructed. But the square is a pleasant shady haven away from the hubbub, with a central circular holly hedge surrounding wooden benches and magnolias in stone urns beneath the

towering plane trees, and some pleasing planting in box-edged beds around the periphery: huge strapping phormiums, *Cotinus coggygria*, different types of lavender and white roses. The stunning architecture glimpsed through the branches enhances the effect.

On the north-west corner of the square, **Harley Street** makes a pleasant 10-minute stroll up to **Regent's Park** (▶ 136) – Georgian London at its finest, with some of the smartest window boxes and doorstep planting in town. Thankfully, the expensive doctors on Harley Street see fit to spend some of their proceeds on greenery!

PORTMAN SQUARE AND MANCHESTER SQUARE
W1. Marble Arch or Bond Street tube. Private.
A little further west, you come across two private squares that are worth a glimpse through the railings, even if they are not open to the public. **Portman Square** is surrounded by splendid Georgian buildings to the north and the Churchill Continental Hotel with its impressive display of palms on the east. (Check out also the smart topiary gardens outside the Radisson Portman Hotel on the north-west corner). The square is pretty secluded, with only a few gaps in the clipped privet hedge to offer glimpses of the rose gardens, benches in the shade of plane trees, children's play area and tennis courts that can be enjoyed only by the lucky local residents, who must relish its peace and quiet in the heart of the West End. Just a little further east, **Manchester Square**, in front of the fabulous Wallace Collection, has a pretty private key-holders' garden that can be glimpsed through the railings. A circular lawn is ringed by gravel paths, with stone urns at intervals, which are usually well planted. The square itself is colourful in summer, with attractive window boxes adorning the Georgian façades and hanging baskets on the lamp posts. Just south across Wigmore Street, **St Christopher's Place** is pretty in summer, with window boxes above the ranks of chichi shops and cafés and a Kasbah-style potted garden on the pavement outside the Ayoush café on the corner of Wigmore and James Streets, with mosaic paths and planters, leopardskin chairs and low brass tray tables among the hookah pipes.

RIBA ROOF TERRACE
Portland Place W1 (020 7631 0467). Great Portland Street tube.
Open Mon–Fri 8am–6pm; Sat 8am–5pm. Bookshop, restaurant, lavatories.
This smart first-floor roof terrace was opened in 1998 and features suitably architectural planting (clipped yew cubes, spiky phormiums and ferns) in

square zinc planters and a modern kinetic water sculpture by William Pye. It's attached to the RIBA café and restaurant, and the shiny chrome-frame tables and chairs are in keeping with the contemporary design. When I visited, the garden was looking a little scruffy, but it's still worth coming in here to experience the stylish Art Deco architecture and browse in the bookshop (which has a good landscape architecture section). If you take the stairs up to the top you can look down on the roof garden (and another a few floors up) from the stairwell windows.

PADDINGTON STREET GARDENS
W1. Baker Street or Regent's Park tube. Open daily 8am–dusk.
City of Westminster. Lavatories, children's play area.
These pleasant shady gardens have the air of a neighbourhood park just a stone's throw from the centre of town. It is a former graveyard and still consecrated ground, but there is little sign of the 80,000 graves, except for a small mausoleum which is now decorated with hanging baskets. Converted into a recreation ground in 1885, the gardens now contain a large well designed children's playground, a small bandstand and some immaculate lawns and flowerbeds. The trees have their canopies clipped to make room for interesting horizontal views beneath, and the geometric beds of salvias, lobelia, African marigolds, cleomes and rudbeckia create a bright (some might say garish) patchwork in high summer. There is another smaller, less interesting garden over the other side of Paddington Street.

ST MARYLEBONE PARISH CHURCH GROUNDS
Marylebone High Street W1. Baker Street or Regent's Park tube.
Open daily. City of Westminster.
Just opposite the Conran Shop, this small shady space offers a quiet respite from retail therapy. A huge London plane provides the centrepiece, with others around the periphery and benches beneath. Peace and quiet prevails – no bright bedding, just the patterns of light and shade on the cobbles and against the white church façade.

REGENT'S PARK
NW1. Regent's Park tube. Open daily dawn/7am–dusk. Royal Parks Agency.
Café. Open-air theatre.
One of the many treats of living in the capital is to drive (or, preferably, cycle) around the Outer Circle when the trees are frothing with blossom in April and May. Enclosed by palatial Nash terraces to the east, Quinlan

Terry's latterday villas to the west and London Zoo to the north, Regent's Park is one of London's best-loved parks. It offers gardens within gardens, secret enclaves, an open-air theatre, lakes and wooded areas, but has enough open expanses of sweeping lawns to prevent it from feeling over-crowded, even on a hot summer Sunday. The most elaborate planting is concentrated within the Inner Circle in the area collectively known as Queen Mary's Gardens. **Queen Mary's Rose Garden** is rightly famous, with more than 60,000 roses of 400-plus varieties – the Technicolor hybrid teas in radiating beds in the centre and old-fashioned scented climbers and ramblers forming floral swags, Fragonard-style, on ropes slung between wooden posts round the outside. Also within the Inner Circle are a romantic lake with a waterfall and rocky alpine garden and some stunning Mediterranean-style planting and topiary-edged beds up towards the open-air theatre. Leading south off the Chester Road, a 5-minute walk from the Rose Garden, is the formal **Italianate Avenue** designed by William Nesfield in the 1860s and a riot of colourful spring and summer bedding. This main axis continues north beneath a foxglove tree, large chestnuts and London planes to **London Zoo**, where you can peer over into the camel house and see the mountain goats on their fake mountains, silhouetted against the sky. Further west, just north of the London Mosque, you can steal a discreet glimpse into the garden of **Winfield House**, home of the American Ambassador to the UK and, at 12½ acres, one of the largest domestic gardens in the capital. The western reaches of the park are quieter and more domestic in scale, with a boating lake and a pretty bridge over its northern stretch with pebble beaches and some pleasant waterside planting, and lots of nesting boxes – also a good café. Back around the lake to Regent's College, whose **Botany Garden** is open through the National Gardens Scheme (▶ 263). But the real jewel in Regent's Park's crown is the little-known **St John's Lodge Gardens** – a series of secret gardens reached via a wisteria-clad tunnel off the west side of the Inner Circle. Conceived in 1888 as 'a garden fit for meditation', it is still a delightfully peaceful spot, with a central circular rose garden underplanted with lavender and irises, a double border between scalloped yew hedges leading down to the Lodge, and secluded enclosures with attractive wooden benches beneath rose arbours. Because of its unpromising entrance, it is often empty save for a few young mothers and children or elderly people with books, all smug and happy about their discovery of this hidden gem. A high quota of staff keeps the lawns and borders in tip-top condition.

ST JOHN'S WOOD CHURCH GROUNDS
Wellington Road NW8. St John's Wood tube. Open 8am–dusk.
City of Westminster.
This fascinating garden is only a few minutes from Regent's Park's Hanover Gate (by the London Central Mosque). But if you are travelling by tube, the walk south down **Wellington Road** takes in some good examples of London municipal and pavement-side planting. St John's Wood station itself is leafier than most, with some impressive foliage planting outside the entrance, and the route southwards passes some well planted gardens around blocks of flats on the left and the Technicolor balconies of Wellington Hospital on the right, a veritable cascade of trailing ivy, petunias, geraniums, etc., in the brightest of reds and purples in high summer. (One wonders if the patients with a view of the plants get better faster, as research has sometimes claimed.) St John's Wood Church Grounds is a delightful amalgam of formal municipal planting, children's playground and wildlife garden, all in 6 acres of still-consecrated ground. Just across from the well designed children's

area, ancient graves are half hidden among the cow parsley and ragged robin; round the corner you can borrow a deckchair to sit among pots of bright annuals on the lawn. The main wildlife area to the east has a thistle meadow (to encourage goldfinches), a glade that is ablaze with bluebells in spring, a wildlife hedge providing breeding and feeding places for birds and a nectar bed for butterflies. Heading south, a well planted woodland walk emerges in a dazzling formal garden, where there is always a fine display in the circular beds, often featuring more unusual plants such as plumbago, daturas and morning glories trained up tripods. Head out of the gates towards Regent's Park and the roundabout just outside is usually planted up with similar style and panache.

PRIMROSE HILL

Prince Albert Road NW1. Chalk Farm tube. Open daily dawn–dusk.
Royal Parks Agency. No café but lots on Regent's Park Road.
North of Regent's Park, the grassy mound that is Primrose Hill offers little in the way of horticultural delights, but does give Londoners one of their few chances to look down on their city. Clamber to the top for vistas

stretching from the television mast of Crystal Palace to the London Eye and hear the otherworldly sound of wolves howling from the zoo. The primroses that gave the hill its name are no more in evidence but there are wilder patches with long meadow grass and wildflowers over to the north and west. More of a park for picnicking and dog walking than plant-spotting – buy your picnic from one of the great cafés and delis on Regent's Park Road (where there is also a good florist selling potted plants), admiring the pretty front gardens of the pastel-painted stucco houses on the way. The network of residential streets to the east of the Hill are good places for a bit of discreet front garden snooping – **Chalcot Square** is particularly pretty.

LITTLE VENICE AND MAIDA VALE

LITTLE VENICE GARDENS
Blomfield Road W9. Warwick Avenue tube. Accessible daily.
Little Venice, where the Grand Union Canal converges with the Regent's Canal, is a great area for garden-lovers, with the wonderful **Clifton Nurseries** close to hand (▶ 232) and lots of fine gardens to admire in front of the Georgian villas that line the canals. **Blomfield Road** is the heart of it all, with beautiful front gardens on one side of the road (every style from well clipped formal to lush *rus in urbe* roses and hydrangeas) and the jaunty deckhead gardens of the canal boats on the other – as bright and cheerful as the liveries of the boats themselves. The towpaths alongside inhabited boats are mostly private, but you can get a good view from the railings on the pavement.

Look out for the **Lady Venice**, home of Dennis Moore who has gardened here for twenty-five years and has regularly won the London in Bloom competition for his efforts (although, as he is at pains to point out, he has never actually entered himself). Brightly painted blue and yellow, the boat has a gondola-shaped planter on its roof, surrounded by other unusual containers, including five in the form of swans, with pelargoniums spilling from between their wings. The sides of the boat are almost hidden behind beautifully planted hanging baskets full of angel pelargoniums and trailing lobelia. The garden then jumps the towpath, via a wisteria-clad pergola made from old scaffolding, to take root along the roadside. Beds jam-packed with colour and incident continue a good 500 yards along the towpath in front of at least ten other boats (Mr Moore used to look after the lot but now, in older age, is encouraging his fellow boat-dwellers to tend the plots outside their boats). Every year he tries something new – turf topiary in the shape of a lion and a unicorn, for instance, or a salvaged boat planted with runner beans to make the sails.

When you've had your fill of garden-spotting, make your way over the Westbourne Terrace Road Bridge to the Waterside Café, itself a converted barge, which offers fine light lunches and teas and boasts a pretty potted garden with tables just under the bridge.

REMBRANDT GARDENS
Warwick Avenue W9. Warwick Avenue tube. Open daily 8am–dusk.
City of Westminster.
These 1½-acre sunken gardens are a model of old-fashioned municipal planting, with geometric beds spilling over with bright hybrid tea and shrub roses in high summer. Grapevines and ivy march around its perimeter, providing a backdrop for borders with a fine, if slightly regimented, display of gaudy favourites such as African marigolds, red and blue salvias and the odd brugmansia. For the less able-bodied, a viewing terrace above has benches from which to enjoy the bright patchwork laid out below, with large wooden troughs and sculptural towers filled with seasonal planting. Walk back down **Warwick Avenue** to the tube, admiring some of the fine front gardens as you go.

QUEENS PARK
Kingswood Avenue NW6 (020 8969 5661). Queens Park tube. Open daily 7.30am–dusk. Corporation of London. Café, children's playground, sports facilities, pets corner, paddling pool.
Thirty acres in the dappled shade of grand London planes, with expanses of grass, sports facilities and well maintained seasonal planting make Queens Park a popular place with families, dog walkers and plant-lovers alike. The garden in the south-east corner is a delight – meticulously kept with smooth lawns and neat circular and crescent beds. Clipped yew cones, a tree-of-heaven and old hawthorn provide structure, with shrub borders around the edges containing a fragrant mix of roses, philadelphus and cherry trees. The beds are the star of the show, though, planted up with the Corporation of London's customary flair – a riot of pelargoniums, fuchsias, canna lilies, castor oil plants, begonias and nicotianas in late summer. A traditional 'shield bed' raised up at an angle is carefully planted in an intricate design each year. Benches are provided to enable you to savour the show.

VIOLET HILL GARDENS
Violet Hill NW8. Maida Vale or St John's Wood tube. Open Mon–Sat 8am–dusk, Sun and Bank Holidays 9am–dusk. City of Westminster. Lavatories, children's play area.

A tiny jewel-box of a garden, well tended and obviously well loved by local residents – both the mothers and children who frequent the well designed play area in one corner and others who prefer to sit in the shade of the cherry and tulip trees and admire the neat geometry of the bedding displays, edged with spider plants or silvery senecio. Every inch of space is utilized – there are even troughs of begonias along the hedge dividing the immaculate lawn (Keep Off!) from the playground, and morning glories festoon the railings around the entrance and old-fashioned park attendant's shed, with its pitched roof and net curtains.

From here, it is a 10–15-minute walk down **Hamilton Terrace** (where some of the impressive villas have interesting front gardens behind portcullis-type gates) to Edgware Road. Pass **Paddington Green** – a welcome triangle of grass and plane trees on the borders of the Westway – and resist the temptations of **Alfie's Antique Market** down Church Street (sometimes good for garden furniture and quirky ornaments) to arrive at ▶

THE WATER GARDENS
Edgware Road W2. Edgware Road tube. Open daily. Hyde Park Estate.

These stunning modern water gardens are a must to visit, and I can't think why they are not more widely known. The only clue that there is something going on behind the unprepossessing exterior of the Hyde Park Estate (largely hidden behind Safeway) is the gorgeous little sculpture garden outside the doctors' surgery on the corner of Sussex Gardens and Edgware Road – like an abstract painting using slate, paddlestones, blue glass chips, shiny curves of metal and porous clay granules among off-centre cubes of box and yew, small pine trees and tufts of *Festuca glauca* grasses. Wander through an entrance gate just a little further up Sussex Gardens and you enter the Water Gardens proper – a fabulous series of pools and fountains enclosed by the dark brick 1960s tower blocks. Some have geometric islands with abstract sculptures; others are almost lost in a jungle of water plants or overhung by huge weeping willows. There are Japanese-style gardens with low ground-cover shrubs and conifers, Mediterranean-style planting in sunnier spots with huge phormiums and cordylines and cacti sunk in pots into the soil, and bridges from which to watch the fish and walkways to admire the views from above. Higher levels offer more amazing treats, with more of the gardens officially open, together with temporary art installations, for viewing on London Squares Day (▶ 262). Artist Tony Heywood, who took the job of gardener on the estate in 1984, is largely responsible for the transformation. Carry on down Edgware Road and you will reach **Hyde Park** (▶ 143).

ST GEORGE'S FIELDS
Albion Street W2 (www.st-georges-fields.co.uk). Marble Arch tube. Only open on London Squares Day (▶ 262), partially visible from Bayswater Road. St George's Fields Estate.
Known locally as 'the hanging gardens of Bayswater' because of the trailing plants that clothe five levels of the ziggurat-style 1970s architecture. The well designed flats allow for garden spaces in and around the linked buildings, with surprisingly large lawns mown in fluid curved lines, one of London's oldest plane trees and impressive mature planting in the borders, including spiky cordylines, tree ferns and New Zealand tea tree plants. Many a garden-lover might fantasize about owning a London *pied-à-terre* here one day.

HYDE PARK, KENSINGTON GARDENS AND KNIGHTSBRIDGE

HYDE PARK
W1 (020 7298 2000). Marble Arch or Hyde Park Corner tube. Open daily 5am–midnight. Royal Parks Agency. Lavatories, cafés, cycle paths, horse riding and boats for hire. Map available from Hyde Park Corner information centre, details of events from Park Manager (020 7298 2100).
At 350 acres of largely open space, Hyde Park is one of London's principal 'green lungs' – and you'll need a good pair of lungs yourself if you are to explore all its hidden corners. The points of horticultural interest are fairly

far-flung, but good signposting means that you shouldn't get lost. Starting at Marble Arch you can take in Speaker's Corner and enjoy a stroll down the **Broad Walk** beneath some of the finest plane trees in London; if you begin at Hyde Park Corner you'll cut this section out and kick off with the Victorian-style **Carpet Bedding** and enclosed **Flower Gardens** in one of the few really intensively cultivated areas in the park. Here, climbing roses on chain swags surround an inner circle of more roses grown up metal obelisks with benches in between and a central fountain. Paths lead through a series of smaller rose gardens, interplanted with lavender, lamb's ears and contrasting dark elder and cotinus, to a line of pleached limes and a romantic double pergola planted with rambling roses. From here, make for the Serpentine, via a small birch grove with large carved boulders that makes an atmospheric **Holocaust Memorial**. The enclosed **Dell** garden beside the waterside café is a much-loved garden within the park, a sheltered hollow with its own little stream, waterfall, grassy banks and foliage planting. In spring the grass is studded with snowdrops and other small bulbs and the magnolia is stunning. The café has great views and is a good spot for refreshment before continuing along the south bank of the **Serpentine**, where you may see Horse Guards and others exercising their horses along Rotten Row; the area to the south was the site of the Great Exhibition of 1851. Go past the **Lido**, where there is another café, and cross the Serpentine Bridge – the view towards the towers of Westminster and the London Eye is always breathtaking, whatever the weather. Nearby is the site for the **Diana, Princess of Wales Memorial Fountain**, designed as a modern circular rill by Kathryn Gustafson and scheduled to open in summer 2004. Despite all the controversy, it should provide a welcome modern element in what is largely a traditional park. Down West Carriage Drive, hidden behind trees, is the **Nursery** – a powerhouse of twelve huge greenhouses in which more than half a million bedding plants are raised every year for use throughout the Royal Parks. Pass the **Rima Monument** next door and head eastwards for the **Ranger's Lodge** and **Old Police House**, two old-fashioned buildings that look surreally out of place in the wilder reaches of the park. The red brick Police House has some suitably formal planting in front and a lone lamppost. North of here, paths lead through ancient woodland and in the **Meadow** the grass grows long in summer, buzzing with bees and butterflies. Many visitors do not venture this far and so it makes for an unusually remote and romantic place to linger on a sunny afternoon. From here it is easy to head north or east towards Bayswater Road or Marble Arch.

KENSINGTON GARDENS

Kensington Gore SW1 (020 7298 2000). Lancaster Gate, Queensway or (for south side) High Street Kensington tube. Open daily 6am–dusk. Diana, Princess of Wales Memorial Playground open to adults with children daily 10am–dusk (closed Christmas Day) and for horticultural viewing 9.30–10am. Royal Parks Agency. Children's play areas, tea room and restaurant in Orangery.

Crossing the great divide of West Carriage Drive, which separates Hyde Park from Kensington Gardens, the change of mood is almost palpable: from a large 'people's park' we move into a more elegant and intimate and somehow more feminine atmosphere. Indeed royal women have strong links with this park: it was Queen Caroline, wife of George II, who in the mid-eighteenth century carved off 200 acres of Hyde Park to create the gardens, and ordered the planting of stately avenues, the creation of the Serpentine and the linking of a series of fishing ponds to form the Long Water. Two hundred and fifty years later, Diana, Princess of Wales, who lived at Kensington Palace, became associated with the adjoining park, particularly after her death, when floral tributes carpeted a large area for many weeks. The **Memorial Playground** in her memory – up in the north-

west corner of the park and featuring a pirate ship, wigwams, a treehouse and crocodile – is deservedly popular. The famous **Peter Pan Statue** near by is also a draw for children and adults alike, as is the **Elfin Oak**, carved with brightly coloured elves and fairies emerging from the dead trunk. One of Kensington Gardens' most memorable features is the **Loggia** and **Italian Water Gardens** up at the north-east corner, decorated with stone urns overflowing with red pelargoniums in summer. The water from the four pools and fountains spurts down into the wilder **Long Water** below, where more naturalistic planting along the banks creates habitats for wildlife. From here it's a short walk (perhaps via the **Serpentine Gallery** (open 10am–6pm), to take in the stone circle by Ian Hamilton Finlay and the innovative temporary pavilions that are constructed in the grounds each summer) to the glittering Albert Memorial on the southern side, which marks the start of the **Flower Walk**. This is at its best in spring and summer, when the herbaceous beds are at their peak, but there are also some interesting old weeping trees, palms and succulents, and the scheme is set off by a backdrop of glossy evergreens. Half way along the walk, a path leads off to a spring garden planted with camellias, azaleas and rhododendrons. Moving northwards up the **Broad Walk**, you soon become aware of the elegant façade of **Kensington Palace**; on its northern side, the spectacular **Sunken Garden**, with its tiers of colour-graded plantings stepping down to a rectangular water lily pool, can be glimpsed through its pleached lime surround. The elegant 1704 **Orangery** next door is a good place to stop for refreshment and to admire the Grinling Gibbons carvings.

KNIGHTSBRIDGE SQUARES AND GARDENS

Many of Knightsbridge's squares and gardens are private, residents-only affairs, but the finest – among them Chester Square, Cadogan Place gardens and the six smaller gardens that make up Eaton Square – can be seen quite clearly from the road and are open through London Squares Day (▶ 262). When admiring **Chester Square**, check out the chic urban gardening in the basement gardens and balcony displays of the surrounding terraced houses – lots of clipped bay trees, topiary spirals and tree ferns. (Also worth a visit is **Woodhams' Flower and Garden Store** just around the corner on Elizabeth Street ▶ 246.) **Eaton Square** lives up to its reputation as one of London's grandest addresses with a series of enclosed gardens with good perennial planting around the edges of well kept lawns and fine specimen trees. Many of the flats on the Knightsbridge side have their own balconies above the smart colonnaded façade – some bristle with bamboos, silvery astelias and ornamental grasses, while others have sentry-like standard trees and topiary in pots. Over towards Sloane Street, **Cadogan Place Gardens** were originally laid out by Humphry Repton, but only glimpses of the lawns, shady sunken walks and modern sculptures can be gleaned through the gates that punctuate the high privet hedges. For those who love hidden corners of village London, **Kinnerton Street**, behind Harvey Nichols, is a cobbled enclave with pretty little courtyard gardens leading off it: one of these, **Kinnerton Place South**, has a raised walkway spilling with potted plants above **Judith Blacklock**'s florist and flower school. Large pots of bamboos flank the entrance to Egg – one of the most beautiful shops in London, housed in a former dairy and selling unusual Indian-made clothes and stunning ceramics – while the Nag's Head opposite is a wonderfully unspoilt old pub. On the other side of Knightsbridge and Brompton Road, just before you enter museum country, wander up to **Ennismore Gardens**, an award-winning Victorian garden first planted in 1870 and lovingly restored over the past twenty years (an ornamental urn commemorates the actress Ava Gardner, a long-time resident). It's open through London Squares Day (▶ 262) when all sorts of attractions including a rare plants sale and champagne and Pimm's bar are laid on for visitors. Nearby **Ennismore Gardens Mews** is a study in urban gardening, the pretty mews cottages decorated with climbing roses, jaunty window boxes and roadside planters spilling over with bright flowers all summer long. Cross the road to enter the tranquil grassy surrounds of **Brompton Oratory**.

KENSINGTON AND CHELSEA

KENSINGTON ROOF GARDENS
99 High Street Kensington (entrance on Derry Street) W8 (020 7937 7994). High Street Kensington tube. Open 9am–6pm most days if not in use for events (ring ahead to check). The Virgin Group.
Get out of the lift at the sixth floor and turn left out of the doors for one of London's most surprising horticultural treats. This 1½-acre roof garden, designed in 1936–8, is divided into three distinct areas that surround the central restaurant and conference room. The first and most spectacular is a **Moorish Water Garden**, with fully grown palm trees, a central pavilion, interconnecting pools, fountains and rills flanked with iris beds, and immaculate lawns with beds planted in an incongruous, if beautiful,

traditional English herbaceous style. Spiky phormiums and other more exotic-looking plants fill the borders in front of the barley-sugar cloisters that surround the garden on two sides. This looks great all year round, especially in autumn when the vines and creepers change colour, and is transformed in the evening by atmospheric lighting. Continue through to the **Tudor Rose Garden** – a series of secluded brick-paved courtyards where roses thrive free from aphids (which cannot survive more than 50 feet above ground) – and emerge in an equally surprising **Woodland Water Garden** with Japanese-style rocks, bamboos and bridges. Larger pools populated by mandarin ducks and pink Chilean flamingos are connected by a naturalistic stream that winds past peaceful lawns and seating areas and back to the lift entrance. The Roof Gardens are gardening at its most glorious, artificial best. In spite of the fact that the soil is only around 3 feet deep, nearly 500 varieties of trees and shrubs thrive here, and with the rustling of leaves overhead, you really need the odd glimpse out through peep-holes in the walls to remind you that you are far above the surrounding rooftops.

ST MARY ABBOTS GARDENS
Kensington Church Walk W8. High Street Kensington tube.
Open daily dawn–dusk. Royal Borough of Kensington & Chelsea.
Opposite Marks & Spencer on the High Street, a little alleyway signposted 'Gardens and Shops' leads to these pretty, secluded gardens – a peaceful haven just a few paces away from the High Street. The larger gardens to the left of the path have plane and birch trees, a brick pergola (sadly, most of it bare) and beds of roses and seasonal bedding among the tombs, but the real gem is the small circular rose garden on the other side of the path. Surrounded by neat yew hedging and with smart curving metal benches in the corners, it has a central sundial, lavender-hedged rose beds and a variety of ferns in the shade of a large mimosa tree.

Passing further north past the little shops that line Kensington Church Walk, you'll emerge on **Holland Street**, which has some pretty window boxes and roadside pots in front of the pubs, shops and houses. **Gordon Place**, just a few streets further west, has a short section at its southern end where the road runs out and the chic little front gardens, flanking a central path, almost meet beneath a tunnel of overhanging trees. Continue north for Holland Park (▶ 212) and Notting Hill (▶ 209).

NATURAL HISTORY MUSEUM WILDLIFE GARDEN

Cromwell Road SW7 (020 7942 5000). South Kensington tube. Open Apr–Sept 1–4pm, weather permitting. For group visits or education workshops ring 020 7942 5555. Lavatories and café inside the museum.

This beautiful oasis, just a stone's throw from the busy Cromwell Road, is one of London's best-kept secrets. A gate to the left of the close-clipped lawns of the entrance court leads into a secluded haven, where long grasses swish in the breeze and the air is filled with buzzing insects and birdsong. Branching paths lead over a bridge between two ponds, past a small meadow brimming with wildflowers (and sometimes sheep) and into a shady woodland area. Different sections of the site are devoted to different wildlife habitats, including heathland (featuring subsoil and turf from rural Dorset), hedgerows, fenland, reed beds, woodland, meadow and chalk downlands. Developed ten years ago in collaboration with the London Wildlife Trust with an aim to illustrate the potential for wildlife conservation through the creation of a variety of habitats in the inner city, the garden is the museum's first 'living exhibition'. Courses and workshops are held here for schools and other interested parties, and advice is available for those planning to create wildlife gardens in public or private spaces. Regular surveys of flora and fauna are conducted – the latest took the count to fifty types of bird and more than four hundred species of moth, with bats and foxes frequent visitors. The soil and air quality are tested regularly. Come here for ideas and inspiration, but also for the sheer peace and beauty of the place, and for the gloriously incongruous view across the reed-fringed pond to the museum's famous Victorian façade.

PIRELLI GARDEN

Victoria & Albert Museum, Cromwell Road, Kensington SW7 (020 7942 2000). South Kensington tube. Access only through museum, open daily 10am–5.45pm (except 24–25 Dec). Café and lavatories in museum.

By the time this book comes out the Pirelli Garden, last overhauled in 1987, will be well on the way to replacement with a contemporary redesign. Six designers with a modern edge were invited to submit plans – Martha Schwartz, Christopher Bradley-Hole and the Olin Partnership were eventually passed over and the final winner has yet to be decided between Kim Wilkie (central lawn with temporary water gardens), Adrian Geuze of West 8 (fastigiate cypresses on stilts) and Kathryn Gustafson (central lozenge-shaped pool that can be filled or drained at will). The results should be exciting – provided the original designs are not endlessly modified by committees.

CHELSEA PHYSIC GARDEN

66 Royal Hospital Road, Chelsea SW3 4HS (020 7352 5646).
Sloane Square tube. Entrance in Swan Walk. Open Apr–Oct Wed 12–5pm
and Sun 2–6pm. Also open every day 12–5pm for the duration of the Chelsea
Flower Show in late May and Chelsea Festival week in mid-June.
Admission £5/£3. Trustees of the Chelsea Physic Garden. Tea room,
lavatories. Often plants for sale.

If a visitor to the capital could look in on only three London gardens, this should be one of them – and it's amazing how many Londoners have never visited, perhaps put off by the restricted opening hours. Organize a weekday visit if possible, as Sundays tend to be more crowded, and attend one of the half-hour tours conducted by volunteers throughout the afternoon. The entrance on Swan Walk is just a gate in an old red brick wall – walking through it for the first time really is like entering a secret garden in the heart of this built-up area. At 3.5 acres it is a great place to wander, but not so large that you ever lose sight of the overlooking town houses and flats glimpsed through the treetops. (What an amazing view to have from your window.)

The garden dates back to 1673 when the London Society of Apothecaries bought the land to grow and study the plants of their trade. But its real hero is Sir Hans Sloane, physician and philanthropist, who bought and restored it in 1722 and leased it back to the apothecaries in perpetuity at an annual rent of £5 (which remains the same today, though an independent charity is in charge). Sir Hans' statue remains at the centre of the garden, alongside a pool surrounded by the UK's oldest (and Grade II listed) rockery, fashioned from stone from the Tower of London and Icelandic lava brought back as ballast by Captain Cook.

Some of the largest trees are originals from the eighteenth century, including the UK's biggest olive tree, a contorted black mulberry, a Mediterranean pomegranate and a Judas tree, while the warm walled microclimate encourages the National Collection of cistus to flourish (flowering at its best in May). The neat 'order' beds occupying much of the garden are laid out to accommodate plants of the same botanical family; other beds are devoted to plants introduced by famous plant collectors, to plants used in different systems of medicine throughout the world (Chinese, Ayurvedic, etc.) and by different schools of medicine (psychiatry, dermatology, oncology and so on). Everything is discreetly and informatively labelled. The interconnecting glasshouses and fernery are also not to be missed. These gardens are incredibly well tended, thanks to a large band of volunteers and students studying at the excellent English Gardening School that is based on the premises (▶ 277).

ROYAL HOSPITAL GARDENS (RANELAGH GARDENS)
Royal Hospital Road SW3 (020 7730 0161). Sloane Square tube. Open daily 10am–12pm and 2–4pm. Closed Christmas and New Year and for six days in May when entrance is only via the Chelsea Flower Show.
Royal Hospital, Chelsea.
This delightful 'garden within a garden' is in the grounds of the Royal Hospital, an elegant Christopher Wren building which looks at its best when glimpsed down Royal Avenue between gold-tinged lime trees on an early autumn afternoon. An impressive avenue of London planes now separates the open area in front of the main building from the leafy secluded gardens. For those who know these gardens only when they are crowded with the stands and exhibits of the annual Chelsea Flower Show in May, it is a treat to stroll among the serpentine paths and undulating grass knolls of this pleasantly tranquil place. Dense plantings beneath the huge old trees give way to naturalistic swathes of bluebells and cow parsley in spring. The gardens and benches around the Royal Hospital are always enlivened by the presence of the resident Chelsea Pensioners in their scarlet tunics and regalia.

CHELSEA EMBANKMENT GARDENS
Chelsea Embankment SW3. 10 mins from Sloane Square tube or take 22 bus. Open daily 7.30am–dusk. Royal Borough of Kensington & Chelsea.
A serpentine path winds through delightful gardens bordering the busy Chelsea Embankment. A shrub bed banks up one side, with the occasional commemorative bust or sculpture, and there are lots of spring bulbs and summer bedding. The houses of Cheyne Walk, home to rock stars and other celebrities, have small but pretty gardens. Thomas Carlyle's house at nearby **24 Cheyne Row** (020 7352 7087) is open Mar–Oct Wed–Sun and Bank Holidays 11am–5pm (last admission 4.30pm). Managed by the National Trust, it has a good back garden whose design remains largely unchanged since the great Victorian lived there.

While you're in the area, don't forget to drop into **R. K. Alliston** (▶ 242) and **The Chelsea Gardener** (▶ 232).

CHRISTCHURCH GARDEN
Christchurch Street SW3. Open intermittently (and daily during Chelsea Festival in mid–late June), but can be seen from the street.
The charming gardens on either side of this Victorian church have won numerous awards and prizes. The roses are glorious in high summer, but many other interesting plants and shrubs mean there is something to admire all year round.

Further up the King's Road towards Sloane Square, check out pretty private **Markham Square** with its well stocked flower borders and centrepiece planting of pink cosmos and *Verbena bonariensis* offset by silvery foliage plants, and the curious gravel expanse of **Royal Avenue** opposite, with its avenue of limes framing a great view of Wren's Royal Hospital at the far end.

A STROLL ALONG THE SOUTH BANK

You can do this walk from east to west, following the sun, or, if you fancy ending with some shopping at Borough Market on a Friday or Saturday, the other way around. Or just take in snatches of it when you are in the area.

GARDEN BARGE SQUARE
Reed's Wharf, Mill Street SE1. London Bridge tube/rail. Not open to the public except on London Squares Day (▶ 262), but can be glimpsed from Bermondsey Wall.
Mr and Mrs N. Lacey.
Just east of Tower Bridge, past all the Conran restaurants and the Design Museum, you'll see what looks like a floating village, fringed with green. Among the smartly liveried Dutch barges and Humber keels with their typical tubs of flowers are a growing number of 'eco-barges' whose entire deckheads have been planted up as gardens. Old Thames lighters which used to carry goods up and down the Thames, they were originally roofless, like large floating skips, but have since been converted by architect and owner Nicholas Lacey into covetable living spaces, popular with artists and musicians. One of the gardens is formal, in intention if not in practice, with box-edged beds spilling over with rosemary, lavender, purple sage and Michaelmas daisies; another bristles with spiky phormiums and cordylines and cactus dahlias; another has an orchard of fruit trees and a picnic table

and chairs. Bees and butterflies abound; while Greylag and Canada geese and a pair of coots nest on pontoons alongside the barges. An irrigation system using Thames Water powered by a windmill is in the pipeline.

From here it is a 15-minute stroll along the river, back past the Conran restaurants, the pleasant grassy **Potters' Fields** to the west of Tower Bridge, HMS *Belfast* and Hays Galleria to London Bridge.

SOUTHWARK CATHEDRAL GARDEN,
Southwark High Street SE1 (020 7367 6700). London Bridge tube/rail. Open daily 7am–6pm (Christmas Day closes 1pm).
This ancient cathedral, where William Shakespeare is buried, is worth a visit if you are in the area, and its grounds are a delight. Just outside the eastern façade, on the remains of an old stone wall, a small herb garden has been planted in box-edged beds, while ferns and other shade-lovers congregate beneath a huge London plane. The planting is rich in biblical associations: a grapevine and passion flower scramble the fence and railings, while roses and lady's mantle hug the church walls, where there are wooden benches. The best view of this little garden is from the road and steps that lead down to the churchyard proper – a larger grassy area more popular with the lunchtime crowd. Again, the planting is attractive and well considered, with a large fig and catalpa, and sun-loving irises, lavender and rosemary between the south-facing buttresses.

Borough Market is well worth exploring on a Friday afternoon and Saturday when the popular farmers' market is in full flow. Even on other days, the area is lively, with pubs, cafés, shops and local residents putting on a good display of window boxes, roadside and rooftop planting. Thread your way past the **Golden Hind** to the river, though you'll have to turn inland for a short haul before emerging again at the Anchor Bankside pub, with its Technicolor hanging baskets and window boxes. A nice bit of architectural juxtaposition follows, with Shakespeare's Globe Theatre followed by Tate Modern and the Millennium Bridge (leading to St Paul's Cathedral ▶ 166).

TATE MODERN
Bankside SE1. Southwark tube. Open Sun–Thurs 10am–6pm, Fri–Sat 10am–10pm. Gardens open daily.
Tate Modern is one of London's recent great success stories, and its riverside gardens, designed by Dieter Kienast, are as stylish and assured as the rest of the place. Urban groves of multi-stemmed silver birch trees

soften the industrial architecture while still remaining modern. Planted in simple geometric blocks, they create a rustling natural screen and divide the large lawn into more private areas. The garden – and the river view – looks particularly good from the terraces inside the gallery. At night, the birches are as dramatically lit as the gallery itself – a welcome new addition to the south London skyline. Continue down past Blackfriars Bridge to the Oxo Tower, Gabriel's Wharf and ▶

COIN STREET GARDENS AND BERNIE SPAIN GARDENS
Stamford Street SE1 (020 7401 2255). Waterloo tube/rail. Open daily.
Coin Street Community Builders.
Between the Oxo Tower and Gabriel's Wharf, a grassed area with plane trees and cobbled paths leads to a circle of lawn surrounded by a low brick wall, benches and lots of pretty planting – roses, silvery senecios, various bamboos, acanthus and day lilies – which is usually being appreciated by a group of men and their dogs over a few cans of cider. On the other side of Upper Ground, gleaming steel walls incorporating seating and wooden decks lead into the undulating lawns and well planted beds of **Bernie Spain Gardens**. There's a circular rose garden at the far end, with benches to sit on and sunny borders full of ornamental grasses, oriental poppies, crocosmias, buddleia and lavender. These gardens, and the brightly painted flats that look out on to them, were the result of years of campaigning by Coin Street Community Builders against one million square feet of office blocks that were scheduled for the area back in 1984. They are well cared for, and popular with local residents and office workers alike. (For more information about Coin Street Community Builders visit www.coinstreet.org or buy the 48-page booklet available from the Oxo Tower foyer (open 11am–6pm daily).

SOUTH BANK
SE1. Waterloo tube/rail. Accessible daily. London
Borough of Lambeth.
From here on, the South Bank makes a pleasant stroll or bike ride on a sunny day, with shade provided by the avenue of young plane trees and plenty of benches affording views out over the river. There is a fair bit of 'supermarket planting' with formulaic shrubs, particularly around the IBM building, but keep your eyes peeled for the odd nugget of interest – a pretty

little circular garden just tucked away on IBM's east side, with box-edged beds, a robinia tree and a half-moon-shaped patch of turf in the centre, the potted topiary around a Frank Dobson sculpture outside the National Theatre and the intriguing sculptural steps – a work of art by Richard Harris entitled 'Passage Paving' – outside the Royal Festival Hall. It's worth making a slight detour south of Waterloo Bridge to admire the ▶

IMAX TOWER
Waterloo Bridge roundabout SE1. Waterloo tube/rail. Accessible daily.
I can't be the only person to enjoy the ambitious use of climbers on the site of what used to be a scruffy old skateboarding haunt. The building itself is like a huge glass cylinder, and wires have been stretched all around it from the first or second storey to the ground at road level to provide support for climbers. Jasmine, creeping ivy, honeysuckle and Virginia creeper have begun to establish themselves, twirling along the supports to form a shady canopy for the floors below. It seems to work well, and it's good to see a modern building with its own time-weathered fringe of green.

MILLENNIUM GARDENS
Waterloo Road/Baylis Road SE1. Waterloo tube/rail. Open daily dawn–dusk. London Borough of Lambeth.
Contemporary gardens with large expanses of grass and a modern water feature with large naturalistic boulders and atmospheric planting.

JUBILEE GARDENS
SE1. Waterloo tube/rail. Acessible daily. London Borough of Lambeth.
Now a patch of well worn grass dominated by the fabulous London Eye, this garden has little to offer except an opportunity for those who either have been or are about to go on the Eye to lounge on the grass. And this is what they do. Beyond a hornbeam hedge on the far east side is a pleasant Parisian style avenue of cherry trees with simple granite benches and blocks to sit on. On the other side of Belvedere Road there is more municipal topiary, lavender beds and a dysfunctional water sculpture. From here it is not far to continue walking along the riverside to ▶

MUSEUM OF GARDEN HISTORY
St Mary-at-Lambeth, Lambeth Palace Road SE1 (020 7401 8865). Waterloo tube/ rail 10 mins. Open daily 10.30am–5pm. The Tradescant Trust. Café, gift shop.
The lovely old church of St Mary-at-Lambeth was saved from demolition

in 1979 and turned into a museum housing the largest collection of garden implements in the UK and run by the Tradescant Trust. The famous seventeenth-century plant hunters the John Tradescants, father and son, are buried in this attractive little churchyard and, behind the museum, a charming **Knot Garden** has been created in their honour. Designed by the Marchioness of Salisbury (in whose garden, at Hatfield House, the Tradescants worked for many years), it has been planted with shrubs and flowers either introduced by the Tradescants from Europe or America, or generally associated with the seventeenth century. A spiral of

variegated holly forms the centrepiece, and the surrounding box-edged beds contain daffodils, primroses, fritillaries and species tulips in spring, followed by a fragrant abundance of old roses, iris, geraniums, campanulas, foxgloves and herbs, all neatly labelled with the date of their introduction to Britain. Around the edges of the garden, stone seats have clever clipped evergreen backs and armrests, and there are plants for sale at the entrance. The museum interior is quiet and welcoming, with exhibits displayed in sculptural glass boxes. Low-key classical music fills the air and the café offers light lunches and delicious cakes. A programme of horticulture-inspired art or photography exhibitions is held here, along with gardening courses and a popular winter series of talks on aspects of garden history.

LAMBETH PALACE

Lambeth Palace Road SE1. Waterloo tube/rail, Westminster or Vauxhall tube 10 mins. The Archbishop of Canterbury's London residence open only through the NGS (▶ 263).

As the oldest and second largest private garden in London this deserves inclusion even if it is rarely open. The garden was extensively restored by Lady Runcie in the 1990s and contains a refreshing mixture of old and new, with sculptures by young contemporary artists displayed against the backdrop of ancient trees and thirteenth-century towers and chapels. Features include a rose terrace dating back to the 1900s, well stocked with pink and white varieties and bordered by a lavender hedge and impressive herbaceous border; an attractive pleached lime screen underplanted with dark blue agapanthus; a pond planted with irises and lilies; a wildflower meadow; a woodland walk (which is lovely in spring); and a monastic-style herb garden.

BONNINGTON SQUARE

SW8. Vauxhall tube. Community garden open daily – intended for use of residents. No facilities. Wheelchair access. Bonnington Square café and deli on nearby corners.

This lively Bohemian enclave is well worth a visit if you are in the area or visiting Tate Britain or the RHS just over the other side of Vauxhall Bridge. The tall Victorian tenements that surround the square have little to speak of in the way of conventional gardens, but every scrap of outdoor space, including window ledges, rooftops and street verges, is fringed with greenery. Every available container is pressed into use, from old bathtubs to dustbins, buckets and oilcans, and some of the planting is exquisite.

The garden designer Dan Pearson, an erstwhile resident, teamed up with New Zealander James Fraser to create the pocket-sized community garden – a real joy with its rusty old waterwheel, living willow bower, borders defined by chandler's ropes, scented climbers and Mediterranean-style planting. The garden is well cared for by local volunteers, many of whom are artists and architects.

 # THE CITY OF LONDON

The City of London's image as a bustling hive of money-making belies the reality of its many secret gardens. In certain parts of the Square Mile it is impossible to walk more than a few paces without encountering an intriguing green space – whether this be a historic churchyard, a piece of modern planting outside a state-of-the-art skyscraper or a jolly window box planted by one of the lucky residents of this fascinating area. For centuries, gardens of all types – ecclesiastical, secular, fruit and vegetable – have been cultivated in the City. Livery companies such as the Girdlers, Drapers and Stationers had gardens here as far back as the Middle Ages and John Gerard, the herbalist, created a garden at the Barber-Surgeons' Hall in the sixteenth century (▶ 160). Enthusiasm for gardening has continued to this day, and there can be few areas of any city in the world so packed with hidden gardens – some only a few feet square – in disused burial grounds and churchyards and in forgotten pockets of land along the remains of the ancient City wall, all overflowing with an inspiring selection of trees, shrubs, herbaceous plants and bedding schemes. The Parks and Gardens Department of the Corporation of London is well known for the pride it takes in its annual bedding schemes, the plants for which are all raised at West Ham Park (▶ 181). A wide range of species is selected not only for their dramatic good looks, but for their tolerance of what must often be a decidedly hostile environment. These little gardens have often been the recipients of London in Bloom awards (▶ 260) and the Corporation has its own annual Flowers in the City campaign and awards. The numerous brown signs make it easy to find the sites and gardens of the City. As you make your way from one to another, look out for the many trees with plaques donated by businesses and individuals and the many planter bins, decorated with the Corporation of London crest, that spill over with bright bedding plants throughout the year.

In and Around the Barbican
THE BARBICAN CENTRE
Silk Street EC2 (020 7638 6114). Barbican and Moorgate tubes.
Accessible daily. Corporation of London.
Built on a bomb site after the Second World War to provide a pleasing place for Londoners to live, work and enjoy the arts, the Barbican Centre was opened in the early 1980s. In spite of its confusing layout (which the current extensive foyer and entrances remodelling scheme should do much to improve), it is a remarkable place and its gardens – from the monumental water canal to the cascading window boxes – remain an inspiration.

From Barbican tube station you cross over the walkway to enter **Beech Gardens**, a raised garden above busy Beech Street and part of the Highwalk system. Here, manicured strips of lawn are interspersed with swishing bamboos and ornamental grasses, and banks of Corporation of London spring and summer bedding at its Technicolor best. Bulbs are a popular feature, with snowdrops, species tulips and narcissi in spring, followed by alliums, Madonna lilies and nerines. There are single wooden seats for solitary picnickers, longer benches for the more sociable and a variety of water features, including a minimalist fountain and a kitsch blue pool with a dolphin sculpture. I wonder if the designers realized that the way the paviours sweep up around the planting beds would create bags of fun for skateboarders.

From here, follow the Highwalk to the **Barbican Centre Sculpture Court** and **Conservatory**. The Conservatory (only open at weekends and Bank Holidays, 10am–5.30pm) offers glimpses of tree ferns, a massive date palm and weeping figs hanging like curtains from the balconies. An arid house with a great collection of cacti is on the second level, while a huge banyan tree dominates the eastern section. You'll also find koi carp, coconut palms, bananas, rubber trees, passion flowers and hibiscus. This lush urban paradise is available for hire for parties (020 7638 4141).

Come down in the lift to the Waterside Café to enjoy the Barbican's most spectacular piece of landscaping – its water gardens. On the **Waterside Terrace**, a string of fountains is enclosed in brick semi-circles, with steps down to the water and plenty of seating. An unexpectedly large expanse of still water dominates the view: a covered pergola to the right masks quiet private gardens of grassy slopes and chestnut trees while, towards the other end, a series of charming sunken circular gardens covered with bowers is surrounded on all sides by water. At the eastern end, water trickles from a large concrete pipe to provide a mask for traffic and other noise. This lake system practically surrounds St Giles' Church and is home to hundreds of fish, mallards, nesting moorhens and herons. Sadly for visitors, the sunken water gardens are among the spaces that can only be entered by residents, but the series of high walkways (St Andrewe's Highwalk) means it is possible to get a good view from above. Indeed, the gardens at the Barbican seem to have been designed with two main aims in view: to create pleasant spaces for visitors and residents, and also to be looked down on from the walkway system and the windows of the flats themselves. Judging from the curtains of colour descending from some of the blocks, many of the residents are very keen gardeners, and it is worth keeping your eyes open for attractive little front gardens or roof terraces as you stroll around the complex. If you feel you are getting lost, just keep following the signs! St Andrewe's Highwalk will take you to ▶

BARBER-SURGEONS' HALL
Wood Street EC2. Moorgate tube. Open daily. Corporation of London.
The public garden with its brightly planted geometric beds can be seen from the Highwalk, but to enter the little herb garden you have to descend the stairs and walk round to the other side of the hall and let yourself in through a small metal gate. Created in 1987 on the site of a former herb garden said to have been planted by John Gerard, author of the *Herball* (1597), surgeon and herbalist to King James I and master of the Company of Barber-Surgeons, this is an intriguing place, embraced by a curve of ancient wall that retains the scent of the herbs on hot summer days. Victorian tiles edge beds overflowing with all manner of plants associated with homeopathic and conventional medicine, including southernwood, santolina, foxgloves and salix. It is all the more charming for the contrast with the rather hideous modern formal garden in front of the hall – all white stone balustrading, stone balls and obelisks and clipped cones of yew. Up on to the Highwalk again, you will encounter the following gardens:

MUSEUM OF LONDON
London Wall EC2 (020 7600 3699). St Paul's or Barbican tube. Access only through museum, open Easter–Oct Mon–Sat 10am–6pm, Sun 12–6pm.
A compact exhibition in an inner courtyard brings to life the history of London's many plant nurseries from the Middle Ages to the twenty-first century, with plants introduced and sold by the various businesses displayed alongside fascinating potted histories. The small garden outside the restaurant is also worth a visit.

ST ALPHAGE GARDENS

Between St Alphage Gardens and Fore Street EC2. Moorgate tube.
Open daily dawn–dusk. Corporation of London.

Seen from the Highwalk, this looks like an unremarkable strip, with a row
of benches behind a neat beech hedge against a backdrop of ancient wall.
Venture down to explore, and you'll find a set of wooden stairs that lead
down to a tiny hidden sunken garden with just three quiet benches from
which to admire the tiers of terraced shrubs and seasonal bedding
dropping down from the street above. In late summer the latter included
pink pelargoniums, purple frilly basil, canna lilies, snapdragons and
nicotianas in all shades from cream through pale green and pink to
crimson. A gate in the wall offers a tantalizing view of the private Salters'
Garden next door.

SALTERS' GARDEN

Between St Alphage Gardens and Fore Street EC2. Moorgate tube. Usually
open on London Squares Day (▶ 262). Worshipful Company of Salters.

Privately owned by the Salters' Company, these delightful formal gardens,
designed by the late David Hicks, are best viewed from the steps leading
up to the Highwalk from the end of upper St Alphage Gardens. They show
Hicks' elegant fusion of formality with romance: yew and hornbeam
hedges enclose box-edged beds of lavender and roses,
punctuated by rose obelisks for height and potted hostas at
the corners, with strips of perfect lawn and wooden benches
in between. The air of seclusion and romance is
enhanced by three water features – a lion fountain in
the middle and bubble fountains in pools at each end.
The standard of upkeep is impressive.

ST ALPHAGE HIGHWALK GARDENS

London Wall EC2. Moorgate tube. Accessible daily.
Corporation of London.

If you're not already on the Highwalk, ascend the
stairs next to St Alphage House to find a roof garden
enclosed within trellis to protect from the wind but
offering stunning views of the 'Gherkin' and the
NatWest tower. The centrepiece is a semi-circular
garden with raised brick beds around Michael
Ayrton's 'Minotaur' sculpture: phormiums and tall
miscanthus swish in the breeze, while wind-tolerant

evergreen shrubs such as cistus, rosemary, choisya, abelia and
elaeagnus provide shelter for herbaceous irises, salvias, anthemis, poppies
and hellebores.

GOLDEN LANE ESTATE
*Aldersgate Street EC1. Private housing estate – only the common parts are
open to the public.*
Designed in the 1950s by Chamberlin, Powell and Bon, the Golden Lane
Estate was intended to be filled with plants and flowers. There are still
plenty of window boxes, and pots spilling down from front doorsteps, but
the common open parts are now bare expanses of concrete, with just a
small roof garden above the leisure centre. The roof garden on top of the
main tower must be due for a revival. (How about it, *Ground Force*?) Floral
glories remain, but guarded by a strict entryphone system – if you know
any friends of friends who live in Crescent House, beg an intro and go and
admire the potted gardens along the corridors of the coveted top-floor flats
with their crescent-moon vaulted ceilings. Even the occupants of less
sunny flats further down keep up the spirit with rows of pelargoniums in
their windows, and an annual flower contest rewards the best displays.

Around the London Wall

From Bastion Highwalk near the Museum of London you will also get a
great view of the modernist parterre around the Pompidou-style office
building on London Wall. Geometric stone-edged beds each planted with
a single type of plant (hebes, periwinkles, ivy and box) surround the
outside of the building, while the same scheme is continued within the
glass curtain walls with tropical-looking cadmiums and bromeliads. It
provides a wonderful contrast to the charming green gardens on the
former site of **St Olave's Silver Street** next door. Here, a robinia, oak and
other trees break up the monotonous straight lines of the modern
buildings, and there is a stone fish pond and raised beds incorporating
some ancient stone fragments (spot the skull and crossbones). Continue
down Noble Street to **St Anne and St Agnes**, where the foliage of the
golden robinia contrasts well with the warm red brickwork of the
Lutheran church. From a grassy patch in front of the church, a snaking
brick wall leads to a further section of paved garden with benches, raised
beds of shrubs and bedding, which in turn leads to another section of
Roman wall. A detour down Staining Lane leads to a tiny garden on the
site of the 1189 church of **St Mary Staining** – an immaculate lawn
dominated by a large plane tree, whose wayward branches relieve all the

straight lines of the surrounding office blocks. Corner beds are planted with lavender and spring and summer bedding, while climbers ascend the old wall behind.

CHURCHYARD OF ST JOHN ZACHARY
Gresham Street EC2. St Paul's or Bank tube. Open daily.
Worshipful Company of Goldsmiths.
This two-level garden – just opposite St Anne and St Agnes (see above) – was created on the site of a church destroyed by the Great Fire of 1666 and belongs to the Worshipful Company of Goldsmiths. Entrance is via impressive iron gates with gilded cats' heads and a stone path leads between two large plane trees on the right and some pretty woodland planting on the left. Steps lead down to a sunken garden with a square of immaculate lawn and a fountain in the centre. The retaining walls are covered in climbers, including roses, jasmine, grapevines, clematis and Virginia creeper, and benches in niches make the most of the quiet below traffic level. Colour in the peripheral flower beds is extended into late summer with day lilies, Japanese anemones and little cyclamen beneath the trees.

Further east along Gresham Street you will reach a pretty little pond and surrounding borders outside the church of **St Lawrence Jewry-next-Guildhall**. This is the spot where visiting dignitaries make their entrance via car to the **Guildhall** for official state banquets and is no doubt intended to impress. For state functions at Guildhall the Corporation of London imports hundreds and thousands of pot plants and cut flowers from its extensive nurseries at West Ham Park (▶ 181) and installing them is carried out with the planning and precision of a military operation. Tucked away behind Guildhall is ▶

ST MARY ALDERMANBURY
Love Lane EC2. St Paul's or Moorgate tube. Open daily.
Corporation of London. Lavatories.
Hedges of clipped box and yew mark out this garden in the ruins of a church designed by Sir Christopher Wren – you can still see the bases of the pillars lined up along the grass. A Victorian-style knot garden (the only example of a knot garden in the City) has its box-edged compartments planted with spring bulbs and other plants around a central cordyline. A *Magnolia grandiflora* stands to one side, while on the other, high hedges enclose a secret garden with a statue of Shakespeare and a planter in the form of a giant basket woven from living willow.

NO. 1 POULTRY ROOF GARDEN
1 Poultry EC2. Bank tube. Bar and terrace open Mon–Fri 7.30am–11pm,
Sat 6.30pm–11pm, Sun 12–4pm. Gardens open to the public during
opening hours. Owned by Coq D'Argent restaurant – for reservations ring
020 7395 5000. Available for private hire.

A high-speed lift from the shopping centre foyer rockets you up to one of
the most remarkable roof gardens in London. Owned by the Coq D'Argent
restaurant and designed by Arabella Lennox-Boyd in conjunction with the
architects who took over the development of this corner site when Sir
James Stirling died, it is half an acre in size with a soil depth of 30 inches.
Sixteen mature trees including acers, spring-flowering cherries, crab
apples, magnolias and a hawthorn flourish in the main dining area, while
tough sun-loving plants such as lavender, rosemary, acanthus, perovskia
and cistus thrive in the rooftop conditions. Other less tough plants such as
magnolias, roses and ceanothus are planted closer to the surrounding
walls, and an attractive oak pergola is festooned with white wisteria, *Vitis
coignetiae* and 'Fragola' grapes that can be picked and eaten. Through a
gate at the far end is the real star of the show – a simple formal garden that
has viewing platforms out on three sides, like the prow of a ship. The
design accentuates the flatiron shape of this corner site with an arrow-
shaped lawn, low box hedges in zigzag patterns and large pale stone
spheres lit from below. It is simple and elegant enough not to detract from
the stunning views out across the rooftops of the City.

From Mansion House to Smithfield

CLEARY GARDENS
Queen Victoria Street EC4. Mansion House tube. Open daily 8am–7pm/dusk.
Corporation of London.

An unremarkable brick and timber loggia at road level marks the entrance
to a fascinating series of enclosed gardens constructed around the
surviving walls of a building that was bombed in the Second World War.
The old pillars are now the supports for a pergola clad in climbers, while
benches are slotted into the gaps between the brick buttresses. On the
lowest level, the ruins of a much older Roman wall can be discerned. More
interesting for their history than their planting, the gardens were begun by
a shoemaker who decided to create some order and beauty from the rubble
by collecting mud from the Thames and soil from his own garden in
Walthamstow. A plaque dedicates the site to Fred Cleary (1905–84), a
former Corporation of London chairman who did much to encourage the
planting of trees and creation of new gardens in the City.

Heading towards St Paul's Cathedral, you'll see some impressive formal gardens on either side of the busy thoroughfare known as **St Paul's Churchyard**. A sunken rectangular lawn flanked by conical yews and seasonal bedding has a fountain at the far end and, above it, a semi-circle of dramatic planting (*Verbena bonariensis* and banana palms on my last visit) as a backdrop to Georg Ehrlich's lovely sculpture *The Young Lovers*. Just over the road, on the corner of New Change and Cannon Street, the lovely new garden in front of the **Fidelity Investment Building** (25 Cannon Street) is well worth a visit. An oval of perfect lawn is surrounded by bold yet tasteful planting in shades of green, silver, pink and white, with white roses, greenish mop-head hydrangeas, cranesbill geraniums, thalictrums and sedums in one wide border and lavender, lamb's ears, pinks and campanulas in a sunnier corner. Well designed wooden benches are hidden in the shade of silver birches and surrounded by ferns and euphorbias.

ST PAUL'S CATHEDRAL GARDENS
EC4. St Paul's tube. Open daily 7am–dusk.
St Paul's Cathedral/Corporation of London.
Forming a narrow horticultural frill around the huge cathedral, these gardens are pretty, well tended and surprisingly quiet, enclosed by impressive wrought iron railings made in 1714 – some of the earliest of their kind. The rose garden on the south side is the main attraction, with geometric beds of small rose bushes in shades of yellow, pink and orange (many still in flower in October) and rambling varieties (neatly labelled) climbing up wooden towers and over the railings. Sun-loving plants including a large *Fremontodendron* enjoy the shelter of the south-facing cathedral wall, while to the north there are well tended lawns and shrub beds and the only giant fir tree (*Abies grandis*) in the City. You can walk through the spanking new Paternoster Square to ▶

CHRISTCHURCH GREYFRIARS
Newgate Street EC1. St Paul's tube. Open daily.
Corporation of London.
Often glimpsed from the car when tackling the one-way system around St Paul's, this garden is

worth stopping for, especially in June and July when the roses are in full bloom. The ruined tower that stands alone at the western end is all that is left of Sir Christopher Wren's Christchurch Greyfriars, rebuilt after the Great Fire of 1666 using stone from a former Greyfriars monastery, founded in 1225. When Wren's church in turn was destroyed by bombing in 1940, the tower was rescued and now forms the backdrop to a stunning rose garden planted in the former nave. Box hedges infilled with rose bushes define the original pew areas, while ten sturdy wooden towers representing the pillars that once held up the roof have climbing roses and clematis scrambling up them and along ropes slung between them. The garden was opened in 1989 and is a beautiful if rather noisy place to sit and enjoy the sight and scent of roses (right through into early autumn) and a great view of St Paul's Cathedral.

POSTMAN'S PARK
King Edward Street EC1. St Paul's tube. Open daily 8am–7pm/dusk.
Corporation of London.
Taking its name from the postal sorting office near by, this little park contains a unique memorial to many everyday heroes and heroines who lost their lives saving others from fire, drowning and other accidents. The painter and sculptor G. F. Watts had the idea for a wall dedicated to such unsung acts of bravery – a patchwork of ceramic plaques denoting the names and details was begun in 1900 and is covered with a lean-to roof to protect it from the weather. The park was opened in 1880 and was pieced together from several former burial grounds – some gravestones remain, stacked around the periphery, and only seem to add to the peaceful atmosphere that prevails. This popular little park has other interesting features, including a small pond and fountain planted with water-loving plants near the church, a rose bed and ornamental flowerbed, and borders brimming with ferns, hostas, tree ferns, chusan palms and even the odd banana. Towards the other entrance on Aldersgate Street, the ground rises to form grassy mounds that are popular with picnickers and sunbathers in summer.

ST BARTHOLEMEW THE GREAT
Cloth Fair EC1. Barbican or Farringdon tube. Open daily 8am–dusk.
Walking down Little Britain past the hospital buildings towards West Smithfield you'll see a black and white Tudor arch leading to London's oldest parish church. The small garden to the right of the path lies on the site of the cloisters of a large priory that was founded in 1123; grass and

yews on a higher level to the left can be glimpsed from Cloth Fair, while sunken gardens around the back of the black and white patchwork church building can be seen from Bartholemew's Passage, where a row of pretty planters is filled with seasonal bedding. The church is said to be haunted by the ghost of a monk who appears at 7am on 1 July every year.

WEST SMITHFIELD
EC1. Barbican or Farringdon tube. Open daily dawn–9pm.
Corporation of London.
On the south-west side of the meat market, the one-time site of jousting tournaments, executions and the famous St Bartholemew's Fair, there is now a small circular garden in the middle of a roundabout, dominated by a huge statue. Trees including cherries, oaks and planes form a canopy around the edges, and a ring of wooden benches surround the stone steps leading up to the central statue. Somewhere to sit and read the paper rather than admire the planting.

From Broadgate to the Tower

FINSBURY CIRCUS GARDEN
EC2. Liverpool Street or Moorgate tube. Open daily May–Sept 8am–dusk,
Oct–Apr weekdays only. Café/restaurant open 11am–11pm (020 7628
8224). Corporation of London.
This is the largest open space in the City and also the capital's first public park, opened in 1606. The bowling green that dominates the site was installed in 1812 and is home to the City of London Bowling Club, and the pavilion is now a busy restaurant. The remaining land is given over to well kept lawns, municipal-style planting (including a raised 'shield' of bedding plants) and many fine trees – mainly planes but also the City's only pagoda tree (*Sophora japonica*) at one corner of the bowling green. The most adventurous planting is reserved for a snaking bed to the north of the green beside a weeping hazel; the peripheral shrub borders are also well stocked with camellias, *Fatsia japonica* and bamboos. Some quaint traditional buildings including the bandstand and a drinking fountain with a conical tiled roof enhance this popular garden. Coming out on to London Wall and turning left you soon arrive at ▶

ALL HALLOWS-ON-THE-WALL
London Wall EC2. Liverpool Street tube. Open daily. Corporation of London.
A small narrow garden hugs busy London Wall with the attractive church façade glimpsed through trees at the far end. One long bed is packed with

seasonal bedding, and there are miniature roses at the roadside. Take the next left and then right for ▸

ST BOTOLPH WITHOUT BISHOPSGATE
Bishopsgate EC2. Liverpool Street tube. Open daily.
Pass a curious little Moghul-style pavilion (incongruously now a pizza parlour) to enter these charming gardens around the church where the poet John Keats was christened. On your way in, admire the little church hall to the left, with its fine Coade stone figures and chest tomb. The garden's sheltered nature allows many slightly tender plants to thrive, such as silvery *Convolvulus cneorum,* abutilon and bay. A sunny herb garden has been planted beside the church, where benches on the raised lawn enjoy a good view of the new building known as the 'Gherkin'. The main stone path has a fine wrought iron arch bearing a central lamp, and an overhanging robinia tree. Towards the far end, a secluded little garden to the right is surrounded by small trees and shrubs with a modern fountain in the centre. Turn left into Bishopsgate and cross down Devonshire Row to arrive at ▸

DEVONSHIRE SQUARE
E1. Liverpool Street or Aldgate tube. Open daily. Corporation of London.
This had been dug up for renovations when I visited, but it looks as if the central circular bed for trees, flowers and shrubs will remain. Cross the square and enter the covered way for ▸

CUTLER STREET GARDENS
E1 (020 7626 8373). Liverpool Street or Aldgate tube.
Open daily 7am–dusk. Peabody/Dawnday Group.
This elegant series of interlinked gardens and courtyards was designed by Russell Page to enhance the surrounding Cutler Street offices. Most of the gardens have a pleasing restrained modernity: one of the finest has stone-edged pools and rills, simple fountains and neat box hedging beneath tall magnolia trees; others have been spoiled temporarily by over-fussy or gaudy planting. One small courtyard is dominated by a stunning sculptural fountain shaped like the spherical head of an allium flower; another has a modern sculpture of tenth-century King Edgar on horseback, hedged in with yew; another features a Moorish fountain with green tiles with a frog design. The high brick buildings all around are complemented by floor designs in sturdy stone cobbles.

Further down Houndsditch and into Aldgate High Street, exotic plantings surround the roundabout and entrances to **Aldgate tube, St Botolph's Aldgate** and **Beaufort House**. Cross via the subway to Minories and left into Portsoken Street for ▶

PORTSOKEN STREET GARDEN
E1. Aldgate or Tower Hill tube. Open daily 8am–dusk. Corporation of London.
A small sunny garden on a former children's playground that was under-used because of busy roads. A sunken garden but with good disabled access, the simple design features a central brick fountain and raised seating area with many fine trees and shrubs including the southern beech (*Nothofagus*) and an impressive collection of unusual bulbs in spring. Cross over Minories and down Crosswall to Crutched Friars and Seething Lane for ▶

ST OLAVE'S CHURCHYARD
Corner of Crutched Friars and Seething Lane E1. Tower Hill tube. Open daily.
A tiny green space in the grounds of this ancient unassuming church. Despite Charles Dickens naming it 'the church of the ghastly grin', the gardens are tranquil and private, with a few places to sit unseen among the trees and tombs – Samuel Pepys, who lived near by, is buried here. Just across the road is ▶

SEETHING LANE GARDEN
EC1. Tower Hill tube. Open daily 8am–dusk. Corporation of London.
A central bust of Pepys commemorates his association with the area. The long narrow garden spreads out to either side, with a ribbon of grass surrounded by shrub borders, benches and neat stone paths. Red roses growing in beds beneath the gingko trees that flank the entrance are used in an annual ceremony by the Company of Watermen and Lightermen of the River Thames, while the garden itself was given to the Corporation of London in 1972, preserving it in perpetuity in return for an annual rent of a posy of flowers. Some fine spring bulbs and autumn cyclamen flourish beneath the many small specimen trees along the roadside border. From here it is a short walk along Great Tower Street to ▶

ST DUNSTAN'S IN THE EAST
Dunstan's Hill EC3. Tower Hill or Monument tube. Open daily
8am–7pm/dusk. Corporation of London.
This lovely little garden is one of the jewels in the City's crown and you would never know it was here unless you glimpsed it from a side road. The

ruins of a Christopher Wren church with later Gothic Revival additions, bombed in 1941, have been transformed into a series of romantic secret gardens. Wren's tower remains, draped in creepers, and forms a dramatic backdrop for a central courtyard garden walled in by glassless Gothic windows that are festooned with wisteria, Virginia creeper and *Vitis coignetiae*. The latter two look stunning when they turn crimson in autumn. In the centre, two fastigiate oaks preside over a ring of benches around a tranquil bubble fountain, and an atmosphere of calm prevails. Around the walls, surprisingly exotic plantings of hoherias, chusan palms, Moroccan broom (*Cytisus battandieri*), strappy phormiums and banana enjoy the sheltered conditions. A mimosa and a spreading magnolia flourish in the narrow boundary gardens on either side, where stone slab graves are interspersed with granite setts in patterns, slate mosaics and mossy pebbled areas.

Heading back along Byward Street to the Tower, pass through **Tower Place** to admire its minimalist scheme of sleek slate benches (each with infills of box, a water rill and lighting from beneath) with Turkey oaks and young multi-stemmed trees among stepped box hedging to either side. The tiny churchyard of **All Hallows** is also worth a visit for its extremely pretty planting of standard junipers, silvery *Convolvulus cneorum*, roses, perovskia, hebes, spiky palms and wisteria against a backdrop of the Tower and Tower Bridge. Bright seasonal planting and sloping lawns surround the **Tower Hill War Memorial** across the road, while on **Tower Hill**, overlooking the Tower, attractive gardens with good shrubby borders (recently replanted with euphorbias, hellebores, geraniums with neat yew hedges and a row of young oak trees) were inexplicably closed when I visited.

BUNHILL FIELDS
Between City Road and Bunhill Row EC1. Old Street tube. Open Mon–Fri 7.30am–7pm BST, 7.30am–4pm winter; Sat, Sun and Bank Holidays 9.30am–7pm/dusk. Corporation of London.
A former burial ground, containing the tombs of John Bunyan, Daniel Defoe and William Blake, and relaid in part as a public garden after the Second World War. Ancient London planes and an old mulberry shade the grassy expanses between the tombs, and there are clouds of crocus and daffodils in spring. To my mind, this tranquil place has never looked more beautiful than on Midsummer's Day 2000, when the sculptor Andy Goldsworthy deposited his giant snowballs, frozen from snow that had fallen the previous winter, at selected sites throughout the City. The surreal

sight of this enormous mass of snow, slowly melting and surrounded by puzzled yet captivated Londoners on their way to work, was quite magical.

Around Blackfriars
ST ANDREW'S STREET GARDEN
St Andrew's Street EC4. Holborn or Blackfriars tube. Open daily. Corporation of London.
A neat little modern garden behind a well clipped beech hedge on one side and tamarisks, daisy bushes, berberis and a weeping willow on the others. A small lawn and modern paving has a backdrop of St Andrew's Church, with its pair of sculptural figures set into the wall. The garden bears the trademark original planting style of the Corporation of London, with (for example) cannas and acacias underplanted with different verbenas in a long rectangular bed, and *Vitis coignetiae* and clematis scrambling along the back wall. Continue down St Andrew's Street towards

BLACKFRIARS BRIDGE
New Bridge Street SE1. Blackfriars tube. Open daily. Corporation of London.
There are a few pubs with floral displays along New Bridge Street (the White Swan and Mash Tun for two) but none can compare with the display outside the **Black Friar** down by the bridge. Technically this is not a pub garden but streetside planting (again in best Corporation of London style) that happens to be just outside the pub (which, with its intriguing monastic-meets-Arts-and-Crafts interior, is well worth a visit). A municipal bed some 12 yards long and 3 yards wide is crammed twice a year with a colourful carpet of spring and summer bedding – the display is always particularly eyecatching in late summer. The permanent planting of four spiky palms has spread beneath it a patchwork of colours and textures; last summer the design featured low-growing verbenas in palest pink and mauve, with mid-pink busy lizzies and miniature mauve asters as an edging, and height provided by the lime green fronds of banana palms and the swaying stems and electric violet heads of *Verbena bonariensis*. Planting like this even makes traffic jams worthwhile.

Further north up New Bridge Street, check out a little courtyard garden off **Harp Alley** – a pleasant circular garden popular with office workers, with four benches, low brick walls and evergreen hedging enclosing beds of bamboo and corkscrew hazel.

EAST LONDON

Hackney and the East End

GEFFRYE MUSEUM GARDENS

Kingsland Road E2 (020 7739 9893). Old Street tube. Open Apr–Oct Tues–Sat 10am–5pm, Sun and Bank Holiday Mon 12–5pm. Trustees of the Geffrye Museum. Café and lavatories in museum.

As befits a museum specializing in domestic interiors throughout the centuries, the gardens behind the attractive former almshouses form a series of small gardens illustrating the changes of taste and fashion in garden design over the same period. A **Knot Garden** from the sixteenth century has hedged compartments of santolina and germander infilled with coloured gravels; the **Elizabethan Garden** features herbs for healing, hygiene and food; the **Regency Garden** shows elegant formality in clipped holly, laurel, box and yew, with symmetrical beds of iris, roses and peonies; the **High Victorian Garden** features bright seasonal bedding, tender exotics sourced by plant hunters and a glasshouse in which to overwinter them and the **Edwardian Garden** has a typical period pergola and well stocked herbaceous borders. How long before a Contemporary Garden joins them? The museum's **Herb Garden** is rightly famous and makes a pleasant place to linger beneath its three rose arbours, with the fountain playing softly among beds of culinary, cosmetic, medicinal, dye and honey plants, all clearly labelled.

MUSEUM GARDENS AND LIBRARY GARDENS

Cambridge Heath Road E2. Bethnal Green tube. Open daily 8am–dusk. London Borough of Tower Hamlets.

Pleasant, well tended gardens to the north and south of St John's Church (which, itself, has nice gardens on the Roman Road side). In high summer, the beds are a modern tapestry of unusual bedding options such as castor oil plants with pink and white cleomes towering over red, pink and purple salvias, all edged with spider plants and fluffy mauve ageratums, or *Nicotiana sylvestris*, white hibiscus and banana palms interspersed with reddish cordylines, mauve salvias and smaller tobacco plants. Trees include pines, eucalyptus, catalpas and flowering cherry. Earlier in the year there are equally colourful (though more traditional) displays of tulips and polyanthus.

LONDON BUDDHIST CENTRE GARDEN

Roman Road E2. Bethnal Green tube. Courtyard open Mon–Fri 10am–5pm plus NGS open days in May and November (▶ 263). Wild Cherry restaurant next door.

Plenty of inspiration here for spiritually minded gardeners who have only a small urban space to play with. A very ordinary red door is buzzed open into a tiny courtyard brimming with flowers and features. Straight ahead is a water sculpture in the form of a pyramid that trickles water into three layers of troughs, with benches near by inviting you to pause and enjoy the sound of water and the scent of the plants contained within the high walls. Roses, lilac and a passion flower climb the walls, while a simple arbour takes more roses, clematis, wisteria and mauve-flowering *Solanum crispum* 'Glasnevin' overhead. Raise your eyes still further and you'll see a beautiful mural of lotus flowers in subtle terracottas, pinks and aqua blues – a stunning solution for dealing with an oppressive high wall. In the rest of the garden, other beds and pots are filled with small shrubs and trees, including an acer, oleander, camellias, hydrangeas, bamboos and rhododendrons – all lovingly cared for. The main entrance to the building is a glass-walled conservatory containing a large gilded Buddha surrounded by tender plants, including a strawberry tree, while a gilded crest from the Nelanda University in India adorns the opposite wall.

If you are walking further east down Roman Road to explore **Mile End Park**, check out the little bungalows surrounding a tiny green and sculpture on the left hand side of the road – one of them is an urban gardener's kitsch dream, with window boxes spilling over with busy lizzies and more plastic flowers, windmills and model birds crammed into a few square feet than you'd ever think possible.

MILE END PARK
E1/E2. Mile End tube. Open daily. Mile End Partnership.
This is one of the few truly modern new parks to have been created in the capital in recent years and is well worth a visit, particularly for those interested in incorporating ecology, the arts and self-financing initiatives into public green spaces. The park looks unprepossessing on a map – a thin ribbon of land, only a few yards across in some places, that stretches from Victoria Park in the north (▶ 176) towards Limehouse in the south, intercepted by the busy Mile End Road. In fact, the park's fractured layout has been harnessed to great advantage by its designers to create a series of distinct spaces with different uses and atmospheres. And in the greatest stroke of genius, Piers Gough's popular **Green Bridge** takes a pedestrian walkway and cycle path right over the Mile End Road to link the two main areas. Coming out of Mile End tube and turning left, the surreal sight of silver birches waving on top of the Green Bridge is straight ahead of you. (The nine shop fronts beneath provide the park with income.) Climb the banks to the left to explore the southern side of the park, with its expanses of wild planting and sculptural water gardens between banks of Mediterranean-style (drought-proof) planting – a shifting textural tapestry of senecios, phlomis, eryngiums, ornamental grasses, euphorbias and perovskia. Look south for spectacular views of Canary Wharf rising above the trees (particularly atmospheric at dusk), and continue south for

playgrounds, a go-kart track and stadium. To explore the most innovative part of the park you need to cross the bridge, which is an experience in itself. A modern grove of white-stemmed Himalayan birches (*Betula utilis* var. *jacquemontii*), evergreen black pines (*Pinus nigra*) and finer, silvery Weymouth pines (*P. strobus*) has its roots weighted in the layers of geotextile, lightweight soil, polystyrene and concrete that support this 'mid-air' planting, and contrasts with the ultra-urban views on either side. You have to keep reminding yourself you're on a busy bridge, not a natural hill.

On the other side, paths weave in and out of different areas of water gardens and planting and down to the Grand Union Canal on the east. There's a pseudo hill-fort planted with wild flowers and lavender that buzzes with bees and butterflies in spring and summer, a garden on an island surrounded by water and sculptural metal and timber walls and an ecology park with large expanses of water, a wind-powered pump, pebble 'beach' and a network of bridges and wooden walkways around and over the lake. The high walk around the back of the lake, bounded by tall curved ribs of timber, houses an events building hidden beneath the soil on the far side – this, too, should provide income for maintenance. Attention to detail is superb throughout the park: white lavender and crocosmias are planted in bold stripes rather than dotted about the place, and even the benches and waste bins are beautifully designed in shiny sculptural metal.

At the northern end, dip down to the canalside to reach Victoria Park without crossing the road, taking in an old lock keeper's cottage with a pretty garden on the way.

VICTORIA PARK
Grove Road E2. Bethnal Green tube or Cambridge Heath rail.
Open daily 7am–dusk. London Borough of Tower Hamlets. Café, lavatories,
children's playgrounds.
One of London's oldest and largest parks, Victoria Park dates back to 1848, when a petition of 30,000 signatures was presented to Queen Victoria requesting a large public green space to help counteract the terrible pollution and disease in this densely populated area. These days, particularly since a multi-million pound restoration project in the 1980s, there is no doubt that the park is an asset to East London, but its unwieldy size (290 acres), crisscrossed by busy roads, works against its appreciation by the occasional visitor. The original design, by Sir James Pennethorne, a pupil of the architect John Nash, endeavoured to redeem the flat, featureless site with 40,000 trees and the excavation of several lakes, including a

boating lake, but the impression is one of a series of disjointed features with long walks in between. Many of the park's attractions are concentrated to the north of Grove Road, where large expanses of grass bordered by the canal are dotted with small lakes, a fountain dedicated to Queen Victoria, an open-air theatre and café, tennis courts, games pitches and an adventure playground. The main item of horticultural interest here is the enclosed **Old English Garden**, filled with fragrant and flowering shrubs including roses, lilac and lavender; there is also a fine collection of hollies in the eastern section near Crown Gate East.

The southern section of the park is more intimate in nature, and a brief visit should be concentrated here, strolling around the lake and enjoying the splashing of the jet fountain and the surrounding shrub borders. The rose garden looked sadly depleted on my visit, but plantings of amelanchiers, fuchsias, phormiums, spiraeas, cortaderias and brachyglottis are successful all year round. An avenue of spring-flowering cherry trees runs north towards a children's play area by Royal Gate East, while the bluebell wood is carpeted with blue in May.

BEAUMONT SQUARE GARDENS
E1. Stepney Green tube. Open daily. London Borough of Tower Hamlets.
Pretty and tranquil residential square just off busy Mile End Road. A central standard magnolia presides over an axial scheme in which the radial paths are lined with seasonal bedding and more informal shrubby planting around the edges creates privacy for seating areas.

ALTAB ALI PARK
Pearson St E2 (020 7739 2965). Old Street tube. Open daily.
This one-acre horticultural therapy garden formerly known as St Mary's Garden, run by the charity Thrive (▶ 263), is a training ground for people with learning difficulties or other mental or physical disabilities to learn about and through gardening.

CABLE STREET COMMUNITY GARDENS
Hardinge Street/Cable Street E1 (020 7480 5456). Shadwell tube/DLR.
London Borough of Tower Hamlets.
Community garden established in the 1970s and popular ever since, with locals keen to become key-holders with access to the 50-plus plots, where a colourful jumble of vegetables, fruit, flowers, meadow flowers and oriental salad greens is grown according to strict organic methods. A new communal herb garden has been developed at the front.

CAMERON COMMUNITY GARDENS
Perring Housing Estate, Gale Street E3.
Bromley-by-Bow tube. Not open to the public.
Perring Housing Estate.

An innovative and inspiring community garden created by two former residents, artist Gavin Jones and his late partner Sally Cameron, with the local (largely Bangladeshi) community. The gardens are not open to the public but can be glimpsed through the fence – and, if you ask nicely, one of the locals might let you in. An area the size of a couple of tennis courts, hugged on three sides by 1950s council flats, has been transformed into a beautiful and productive garden. A crazy patchwork of beds edged with box and yew spills over with poppies, huge daisies and familiar and exotic herbs and vegetables. Gravel paths wind in between and the whole is embraced by a living fence of grafted wild pear and crab apple trees – devised to give protection from harsh winds and the midday sun. Retaining walls are made from eighteenth-century roofing slates salvaged from a church whose roof caved in after a fire, and an old herring trawler has been turned upside down and thatched to make a unique shed. (For more on the history of the garden and Gavin Jones's work elsewhere, see pages 12 and 14.)

BROMLEY-BY-BOW CENTRE GARDENS
Bruce Road E3 (020 8709 9735). Bow Road tube. Open daily dawn–dusk.
London Borough of Tower Hamlets.

Inspiring community gardens centred around the Bromley-by-Bow Centre at the church on Bruce Road. The **Paradise Gardens**, featuring potted plants and mosaic portraits by members of the community, are what first catch your eye. But there's also a beautiful modern courtyard garden with a pergola and lily pool outside the new health centre next door, and some intriguing goings-on in **Bob's Park** just around the corner. Formerly the local park and a haven for ne'er-do-wells, the park was bought by the church and transformed with community labour under the direction of the Rev. Andrew Mawson, former vicar of the church, and now sports small community allotment beds surrounded by living willow fences, raised sleeper beds that are accessible to the disabled, and ceramic pathways made by local artists and a children's craft class. The result is a park that is well used and loved by all sectors of the community. Lateral thinking has won out against the vandals: stolen benches are a thing of the past now that new ones weighing several tons each have been carved in stone – in the form of mythical beasts – by a local artist. Gardening classes and a community-based project called Green Dreams are now also run from the centre.

Canary Wharf and Beyond

Redeveloped during the 1980s by the London Docklands Corporation, this stretch of the Thames, once busy with boats and barges bringing their loads in and out of the capital, became a giant building site. The most ambitious scheme was centred around Canary Wharf, where the giant Cesare Pelli tower dominates the skyline; it has recently been joined by two others. Canary Wharf feels curiously un-British: the scale of the architecture, the materials (shiny granite, marble, slate and sandstone and acres of reflecting glass) and the people populating the place (be-suited bankers and journalists or workmen – no mothers with children, no unemployed or self-employed and just a sprinkling of tourists) put one in mind of Chicago or Dallas. The architecture is big, bold and imposing, and demands green parks and open spaces that can hold their own. Works of art are on a similarly impressive scale, and many of the railings, benches and planters were specially commissioned from contemporary artists. A map with information about all the public art to be found around the complex can be picked up in the foyer of the tower at 1 Canada Square.

JUBILEE PARK
E14. Canary Wharf tube/DLR. All gardens open daily. Canary Wharf Group.
At Heron Quays and actually on top of the new Jubilee line Canary Wharf station is this stunning modern park by the renowned Belgian father and son team Jacques and Pieter Wirtz. Six acres of undulating grass, twenty-two interconnecting pools and fountains and a 'forest' of mature dawn redwood trees (*Metasequoia glyptostroboides*) have been deployed to distract attention from the presence of the looming towers. And the scheme works – otherwise, as Pieter Wirtz put it, 'the park would feel like a little doormat at the base of the buildings'. The famous Wirtz curves are here in the humps of the lawns, in the swathes of clipped hedging and in the rough Belgian blue limestone that encases the serpentine water feature. Snaking its way through the site, this is the garden's backbone; the linked pools, raised within their craggy stone walls, have foaming fountains and underwater lighting. Reeds and fountain grass (*Pennisetum setaceum*) follow the flowing lines of the watercourse – the fluffy foxtail heads of the

latter softening the scheme in late summer. The redwood trees, at over 40 feet high, were some of the largest trees ever shipped into this country, and are presumably intended to give the towers a good run for their money as they grow. A few were looking sickly when I visited (one wonders how they have been given enough root run when the station is just beneath), but the evergreen oaks and winter-flowering cherries were in good shape.

CANADA SQUARE
E14. Canary Wharf tube/DLR. Accessible daily. Canary Wharf Group.
Unnerving asymmetrical garden to the west of the Pelli tower, dominated by the huge blue fibreglass sculpture *The Big Blue* by Ron Arad. The sculpture is raised on a transparent Perspex collar that gives it the impression of floating above the grass like a spaceship, while at the same time illuminating the shopping mall below. The surrounding lawn and beds obey a seemingly random geometry, making the garden look like a crazy modern patchwork from the windows of the buildings above. A path on one side meanders through an informal young woodland which will balance the garden better as it matures. Seating and oversize planters are designed by contemporary artists.

CABOT SQUARE
E14. Canary Wharf tube/DLR. Accessible daily. Canary Wharf Group.
To the east of the tower is Cabot Square – town planning rather than gardening, with its imposing central fountain (one of the first in the country to be computer-controlled) and shiny granite seating curved around it. There are a few large pots and shiny metal bowls planted with gaudy spring and summer bedding, but the most successful part of the square is the sunken walk of pleached limes that surrounds it on three sides. Water gushes down a stepped waterfall all the way around, which energizes the air in this otherwise quiet and shady avenue. Shadows of the trunks stripe the grey gravel underfoot, and the benches set against neat yew hedges are popular with workers at lunchtime.

WEST INDIA AVENUE, WESTFERRY CIRCUS AND ESPLANADE
E14. Canary Wharf tube/DLR. Accessible daily. Canary Wharf Group.
From Cabot Square, you can walk north, through a smaller square planted with chestnut trees where there used to be a *pétanque* court, to Fisherman's Walk (with sculptural railings designed by Bruce McLean) and the cleverly designed pedestrian bridge to West India Quay. Or you can follow the main thoroughfare down to Westferry Circus and the pier, where you can catch a

water bus back into town. **West India Avenue** is busy with cars and taxis, but the central reservation is pretty in spring, when snowdrops and daffodils and other small bulbs push through the ground cover of periwinkles beneath the line of mature plane trees. At the end is **Westferry Circus** – in effect a roundabout, but enclosed by walls and planting to create a surprisingly pleasant little circular garden. The octagon of granite-edged grass in the centre is always immaculate, and the four box-hedged beds are bright with spring and summer bedding. Shade-loving plants have been planted in wide borders around the periphery as a barrier against the noise and traffic. Sit and enjoy the surreal view of the glass buildings towering above the trees, as office workers eat sushi and the buses whiz around you. Across the road towards the river is the **Esplanade** of maturing planes set in a swathe between curved sections of grass and paving. Down by the pier, there are pleached limes planted in gravel with the modern tables and chairs of a restaurant set beneath them – it feels a bit like Paris. The upper level offers sweeping views up and down the river, and a recently built path means you can walk – or jog, as many do – a fair distance each way.

Further East

WEST HAM PARK

Upton Lane E7 (020 8472 3584). Plaistow tube. Open daily 7.30am–dusk. Corporation of London. Lavatories, children's play area.

Few people outside the East End have ever been to, or even heard of West Ham Park. Yet this 77-acre oasis is a remarkable place and well worth a visit. Not only is it a haven for ancient trees, including an oak planted to commemorate Queen Victoria's Jubilee and the oldest gingko in the country, planted in 1673, it is also a powerhouse of plant production, supplying seasonal bedding to all the little gardens and churchyards within the City of London and plants and cut flowers to decorate state banquets at Guildhall. In an acre of computer-controlled greenhouses in the north-east corner of the park more than 300,000 plants are raised every year, including the relatively rare varieties of bedding that make the City's bedding displays so distinctive. There's a stunning example of seasonal bedding outside the main office, and also heather beds, a cherry avenue, iris and peony gardens (at their best in May), famous lily beds and a rose garden with seventy varieties in bloom through June and July. Among the impressive trees to be admired are some rare hollies, a magnificent weeping ash, two rare *Quercus* x *hispanica* 'Fulhamensis' and the National Collection of *Liquidambar*, known for its splendid autumn foliage.

GREENWICH PARK
SE10 (020 8858 2608). Open daily dawn–dusk. Royal Parks Agency.
Cafés, children's playground.
Mail order garden design was responsible for the first landscaping scheme
at Greenwich Park – the seventeenth-century French designer Le Nôtre

sent some drawings over by post. A network of avenues, formerly of elms and now of horse chestnuts, was intended to focus attention on the Queen's House and many of these, including Bower Avenue and Great Cross Avenue, still exist. Christopher Wren's Royal Naval Hospital (now College) and Royal Observatory soon followed and these elegant buildings form the focus for some of the best landscaped views in London. Horticulturally, the park has many delights, including London's longest herbaceous border in front of the National Maritime Museum, which is crammed with colour all summer. An aromatic **Herb Garden** near the lower entrance at St Mary's Gate is at its best in June and July, as is a well maintained semi-circular rose garden with 113 neatly labelled varieties near to the Ranger's House. There is also a sunken rhododendron dell beneath a huge beech tree by Blackheath Gate and an exotic **Flower Garden** up near the lake, where majestic cedars and other fine specimen trees are set among more than thirty flowerbeds which are ablaze with colour from small bulbs in early spring through to a firework display of dahlias in late summer. For those who fancy some peace and quiet, the 13-acre wilderness area is often frequented by fallow deer alone.

ISLAND GARDENS
Saunders Ness Road E14. Island Gardens DLR. Open daily. London Borough of Tower Hamlets. Refreshments, lavatories.
This small narrow garden at the very southern tip of the Isle of Dogs peninsula is unremarkable horticulturally but offers by far the best view of Greenwich and the Observatory. Plane trees, grass and seasonal bedding.

UNIVERSITY OF EAST LONDON
University Way E16. Cyprus DLR. Open daily.
Simple geometric landscaping that complements the sculptural blue, white, green and yellow cylindrical student housing blocks. Curvaceous lawns are edged by two-tier black engineering bricks that act as impromptu benches and the views out across the river are exciting – if windswept. More exciting developments are planned.

THAMES BARRIER PARK
North Woolwich Road E16. Silvertown DLR. Open daily dawn–dusk.
London Development Agency.
The shining sculptural masses that make up the Thames Flood Barrier (constructed in 1982) form a surreal backdrop for this bold new park – the first new Thameside park in fifty years. Contaminated land had to be

reclaimed and a suitably modern design dreamed up by Alain Provost, creator of the funky Parc André Citroën in Paris. Its most striking feature is the 'Green Dock' – a sunken channel 13 feet deep that carves through the grassy plateau of the main body of the park. This urban microclimate, hugged in by high walls clothed in clipped *Lonicera nitida* 'Maigrün', is infilled by parallel stripes of yew hedging and bold blocks of perennials, flowering shrubs and swishing grasses that read almost as an abstract painting. Near the main road, a concrete and marble courtyard spurts with thirty-six computer-controlled water jets while, at the river end, a concrete ravine cuts through grassy hillocks to reach a timber deck and memorial to local people who died in the First and Second World Wars. A riverside promenade offers great views of the barrier and the City of London beyond. The linear, graphic design is continued throughout the rest of the park with grid-like plantings of liquidambar, birches, Norwegian maples, black pines and other unusual trees, dissected by straight paths. A children's playground, wildlife area and sports facilities are also popular.

CITY OF LONDON CEMETERY AND CREMATORIUM TREE TRAIL

Aldersbrook Road E12 (020 8530 2151). Manor Park rail. Open daily 9am–5pm; 9am–7pm weekdays in summer. Corporation of London.

One of the largest cemeteries in Europe, this is also one of the most beautiful, laid out by the Victorians with shrubberies, rhododendrons and many notable trees. Seventy trees are featured in the trail, and they are all neatly labelled, making this a good place to go to get to know your trees. An informative guide with photographs and descriptions is available – please ring for further details.

ELTHAM PALACE

Court Road SE9 (020 8294 2548). Eltham rail. Open Wed–Fri, Sun and Bank Holidays, Nov–Mar 10am–4pm; Apr–Sept, 10am–6pm; Oct 10am–5pm. English Heritage. Café, shop, lavatories.

The recently restored Eltham Palace is best known for its splendid Art Deco interiors, but the gardens are also hugely interesting and it is worth scheduling enough time in your visit to enjoy them too. Like the house, the grounds are remarkable for the unique fusion of medieval remains with the fashionable modern aesthetic favoured by Stephen and Virginia Courtauld, the glamorous couple who rescued Eltham from ruin in the 1930s. The Courtaulds entertained lavishly and the garden was often used for parties – one can imagine couples in evening dress strolling beneath the wisteria-clad pergola or wandering in and out of the many garden rooms planned in the manner of Sissinghurst. The garden is structured around the ancient medieval walls and moat – an intact fifteenth-century stone bridge forms part of the approach to the gardens by today's visitors. Enclosed by diamond-pattern walls that once formed part of Elizabeth I's lodgings is a sunken rose garden, made by the Courtaulds and recently replanted with the 1930s cultivars that Virginia would have selected, including hybrid teas and fragrant hybrid musks, such as apricot-pink 'Felicia' and peachy 'Buff Beauty'. Other 1930s features include a rock garden with Japanese trees and shrubs and a series of pools and waterfalls, and an oak bridge crossing the now grassed-over **South Garden**. More recent additions include a clever triangular herb garden near the house, with a lattice parterre infilled with carpet thymes, acaenas and velvety purple sage, and a new 100-yard hot border in the South Garden that explodes with red dahlias, canna lilies, unusual nicotianas and eucomis in late summer. Survivors from the Courtauld days include a number of unusual specimen trees, some of which were gifts from the Royal family and other notables – a large catalpa, tulip tree, walnut and bay, and a strawberry tree that bears clusters of bright fruit in autumn.

NORTH LONDON

King's Cross and Camden

THE CALTHORPE PROJECT
Gray's Inn Road WC1 (020 7837 8019). King's Cross tube/rail.
Open Mon–Fri 10am–6pm. London Borough of Camden. Plants for sale,
lavatories, children's play areas.

An inspiration to Londoners everywhere, these colourful and well designed gardens were created in 1984 by the local community to save a 1.5-acre derelict site from an office development. Marked out from the main road by its big red gates, sculptural sign and tufty turf roof, the project site is entered by a curved bridge that passes over a lower rock garden and past the Walter Segal kit-built community building. Exuberant planting is combined with mosaic paths and walls to create a vibrant feeling and divide the garden into a series of connected areas with different uses and atmospheres. There are secluded areas hedged in by hornbeam, undulating grass for family picnics, a paved area for musical and other organized events, a living willow bower, a wildlife garden, a children's vegetable plot and a beautiful modern pine and Perspex self-built greenhouse. The project describes itself as 'the back garden for the local community' and you'll see local residents hard at work in the flowerbeds

or sunning themselves on the grass. Much of the work in the garden is paid for through fund-raising and carried out by volunteers; courses and workshops on organic gardening and other subjects are offered on site.

ST ANDREW'S GARDENS
Gray's Inn Road WC1. Russell Square or King's Cross tube.
Open daily 7.30am–dusk. London Borough of Camden.
Overlooked by a blue and white 1930s apartment block, Trinity Court, this small neighbourhood park (like nearby St George's Gardens) is a former burial ground – you can still see the gravestones stacked up along the boundaries. It's at its best in early spring, when swathes of crocus are

backlit by the low sun. Otherwise, there are old-fashioned rose beds and a stab at New Perennial-style gardening in the central beds.

ST GEORGE'S GARDENS

Entrances on Handel Street, Heathcote Street and Sidmouth Street WC1. Russell Square or King's Cross tube. Open daily 7.30am–dusk. London Borough of Camden/Friends' Association c/o King's Cross and Brunswick Neighbourhood Association, 62 Marchmont Street WC1.

The atmosphere in this small narrow garden is something rather special, especially if you catch it empty, early on a spring morning. Like nearby St Andrew's Gardens and St John's Wood Church Grounds (▶ 138) this was one of several eighteenth-century burial grounds planned in then open countryside to relieve the pressure on unhealthily crowded inner city churchyards. This one was founded in 1713 for St George the Martyr in Queen Square and St George's Bloomsbury; a small chapel of rest (not open to the public) was added later at the Handel Street end. In the 1880s the churchyard was converted into a much-loved Victorian park, with ornamental bedding displays among the fine chest tombs. A hundred years later, however, it had fallen into grim disrepair, with drug dealers using some of the cracked open tombs to stash their wares; the park was scruffy and no longer felt safe. Thanks to a thorough restoration project overseen by the Friends of St George's Gardens with funding from the new Urban Parks Programme, the garden (reopened in 2001) is once again a pleasant place to sit or stroll beneath the canopies of the huge London planes. Many of the tombs (and the garden's surrounding crumbling brick walls) have been expertly and sensitively repaired (check out that of Anna Gibson, grand-daughter of Richard Cromwell the Protector, and an impressive obelisk pushing through the canopy of an oak tree). The flowerbeds have also been planted in best gaudy Victorian fashion – dahlias, crocosmias and red hot pokers among the banks of lavender and sarcococca. An annual St George's Day event is organized by the Friends.

CAMLEY STREET NATURE PARK

Camley Street NW1 (020 7833 2311). King's Cross tube/rail. Open Mon–Thurs 9am–5pm; Fri closed; Sat/Sun 11am–5pm (10am–4pm in winter). London Wildlife Trust. Disabled access, lavatories.

Hugged on one side by the canal and on the other by the massive King's Cross building works, this long narrow nature park is now twenty years old. Although its peace has been disturbed by the development works, the park is still worth visiting at different times of year to see the wealth of wildflowers and wildlife that flourishes in the heart of this ultra-urban hinterland. The wildflower meadow near the entrance is a picture in April and May when cowslips, bluebells and primroses are in full bloom – and the occasional common spotted orchid. A circular route leads down by the side of the pond, with the bright liveries of canal boats glimpsed through wild flowery borders. At the south end of the park the pond broadens and a decking surround enables visitors to sit in the sunshine and watch the water birds or indulge in a spot of pond-dipping. The path continues up steps to a wooded area that affords a spectacular view of the nearby gasworks and then loops back through trees on the other side of the pond, past a 'log turning area' (where creatures can be glimpsed by moving the logs) to a picnic area outside the picturesque information centre and a striking sculptural log garden hidden behind. The park is popular with local schools, and all manner of workshops, courses and events are held here throughout the year. Hopefully peace will be restored when the building works are finally complete.

Islington and Environs

Islington is not known for its open green spaces. Restaurants, yes, trendy interiors shops, yes – but public gardens are in short supply. **Highbury Fields** north of the tube station is beautiful, but mainly because of the fine Georgian façades that provide a backdrop to the expanse of largely unadorned grass. When the funfair comes to Islington, it crams itself on to the tiny triangle of green between Upper Street and Essex Road. But – as any London gardener knows by now – lack of space can be a springboard for amazing resourcefulness. And behind the main roads there are some private and public examples of creative urban gardening at its best. The gardens below can be enjoyed on a rough circuit leading from Highbury & Islington tube station.

BARNSBURY
N1. Highbury & Islington tube or Caledonian Road & Barnsbury rail. Accessible daily.
Some of the prettiest private gardens are in the area known as Barnsbury, to the west of Thornhill Road. Take a walk around **Barnsbury**

Square and over to the large elliptical Thornhill Square and walk back along **Ripplevale Grove**, which is as charming as its name suggests, with well proportioned Regency villas set behind large (for London) front gardens. The **Albion** pub has a summer display of hanging baskets and window boxes in finest public house style, and a pretty garden behind. Just past the pub you'll come to **Malvern Terrace** on the right – a row of pretty early Victorian cottages in a cobbled cul de sac which are rightly famous for their front gardens. These are open annually in aid of the NGS (▶ 263), but as long as you are discreet, the owners probably won't mind you taking a glimpse over the railings. The diversity of styles reflects the different tastes and temperaments of the owners – some of the gardens are old-fashioned and romantic, with roses flanking an immaculate lawn and wisteria around the front door, while others are more adventurous, with unusual architectural foliage plants and gravel underfoot. Many make use of pots around the front door, swapping them over as different plants come into flower, to give each its moment in the spotlight. Cross Richmond Avenue into **Cloudesley Road** – a terrace of tall Georgian houses with fancy fanlights and decorative ironwork balconies. There are a few pretty front gardens and window boxes here as you stroll down on your way to ▶

CULPEPER COMMUNITY GARDEN
Cloudesley Road N1 (020 7833 3951). Angel tube. 'Generally open during daylight hours.' Ring to check. Plants for sale. No dogs.
This inspired and extremely beautiful community garden is the jewel in Islington's crown. Begun in 1980 as a space to introduce local children to gardening, it has expanded to embrace all the local community, especially those without gardens of their own. Flat-dwellers can join a waiting list for an irregular-shaped plot the size of a large kitchen table in which to grow whatever they like – some choose flowers while others turn their patch into a mini allotment bursting with cabbages, runner beans and red and green lettuces. Some of the forty-six plots are gardened by Mencap, who also run workshops here; other areas, such as the lawn and wildlife ponds, are looked after communally. The cleverness of this garden is that it manages to read as a cohesive whole, rather than a conglomeration of individual interests. In late summer the beds spill out on to paths and a profusion of skyscraping plants such as cardoons, cordylines, giant fennel and macleaya create an air of mystery, inviting exploration. A pergola runs the width of the top end of the garden, festooned with pink and white roses, wisteria, clematis and grapevines that shade the path beneath, and there's a shed, which is the focus for communal activities and barbecues.

Perhaps it's the plants themselves that knit the garden together. For all the different cultures and gardening styles in evidence in the individual plots, the same flowers – valerian, pot marigolds, pink cosmos and creamy sisyrinchiums – self-seed themselves throughout, a potent symbol of the way in which gardening can bring unity and harmony to even the most diverse communities.

Walk back towards Upper Street via **Stonefield Street** (which has some nice basement area gardens) and Victorian Gothick **Lonsdale Square** to Barnsbury Street, where the attractive garden terrace behind the **Draper's Arms** makes a good stop for lunch. Still on Barnsbury Street, on the other side of Liverpool Road, is **The Plant Room**, the headquarters of TV gardener Joe Swift's garden design and construction company (▸ 273). Until recently this was a great little urban garden centre, with groovy accessories on the ground floor and stylish city-friendly plants in a stunning yard out the back. The garden can still be visited by telephoning 020 7700 6766 in advance. From here, walk a short distance south down busy Upper Street, checking out design shops such as twentytwentyone and Dansk Flowers on the way, and left into Cross Street, where a diversion into shops such as Atelier may prove fruitful. Wiggle down Halton Cross Street and Pleasant Place to **Astey's Row** for one of the most surprising and delightful small gardens in London.

ASTEY'S ROW ROCK GARDEN
N1 (020 7263 7800). Angel or Highbury & Islington tube.
Open Mon–Fri 8am–dusk; Sat 9am–dusk; Sun 10am–dusk.
London Borough of Islington/Greenspace.
This narrow strip of shady land has been transformed into an attractive rock garden, with different types of ferns and a few tree ferns sprouting between chunks of rock beneath majestic weeping willows. At the southern end, Mediterranean plantings of *Stachys byzantina*, hebes, phormiums, chusan palms and the curious New Zealand *Pseudopanax ferox* flank a slate path. At the northern end there is a playground with a (sadly empty) pool and paved area. Cross over Canonbury Road to Canonbury Grove for the entrance to ▸

NEW RIVER WALK
Canonbury Grove N1. Highbury & Islington tube. Open Mon–Fri 8am–dusk, Sat 9am–dusk; Sun 10am–dusk. London Borough of Islington.
Another ribbon-thin strip of garden, this one flanking a river – or, rather, the remains of a 38-mile long aqueduct built in the early seventeenth

century to bring fresh drinking water to London from Hampshire. The Islington stretch around Canonbury Grove was restored in 1996–8 by local residents, and is extremely pretty and peaceful. Specimen trees such as *Liquidambar styraciflua* and ornamental viburnums mingle with weeping willows and shrubby elders, while lysimachia and hostas spring up among the self-sown valerian, teasels and flag iris. There's a charming little round tiled house for the linesman who looked after the waterway and ensured that the water remained clean – sad to say, he is much in need again today. Worn rocks like those in the Astey's Row Rock Garden create an almost Japanese atmosphere in places. The gardens get less horticultural in flavour the nearer you get to Balls Pond Road. Check out the gardens of the large villas opposite, many of which back on to the waterside – the large corner plot at 37 Alwyne Road is open through the NGS (▶ 263). Walk back down Alwyne Road and Alwyne Villas to Canonbury Square.

CANONBURY SQUARE
N1. Highbury & Islington tube. Open Mon–Fri 8am–dusk; Sat 9am–dusk; Sun 10am–dusk. London Borough of Islington.
There are quite a few public squares and gardens in Islington – Barnsbury Square, Highbury Fields and Islington Green to name but three – but they are mostly rather uninspired combinations of low stone walls and municipal planting. Canonbury Square provides the exception – a paean to public planting at its gaudiest, Technicolor finest. The low raised beds (identical in style to those in the other squares) are crammed to bursting with spring and summer bedding interspersed with cordylines large enough to give the impression of palm trees and – an unusual and successful touch – multi-coloured maize plants. On my visit in late July I couldn't help but think that the scarlet and crimson pelargoniums, yellow cannas, mauve and magenta busy lizzies and bright purple verbenas must clash awfully with the tasteful interior décor of the surrounding houses.

Walking back up Canonbury Lane to Upper Street and the tube, check out the gorgeous little garden behind the imposing metal railings and gate on **Tyndale Terrace** (behind the furniture shop called Coexistence) – well, if they'd wanted privacy they'd have a hedge or wall instead of railings. This tiny north-facing courtyard is packed with inspiration for gardeners coping with shade: variegated foliage plants to brighten dark corners and an abundance of white flowers, many of them scented (roses, *Nicotiana sylvestris* and lace-cap hydrangeas). Metal steps down from the flat are crammed with potted plants in season, while fragments of stone and sculpture are hidden among the leaves at ground level and a metal spiral staircase leads enigmatically up to the sky.

CLISSOLD PARK
Stoke Newington Church Street N16. Open daily 9am–dusk. London Borough of Hackney. Café and lavatories.
A much-loved family park for north-Londoners, with two lakes and a duck pond, a children's zoo, tennis courts and other sports facilities and a café in the old brick mansion in the centre. Horticulturally there is not much of great note, but a rose garden to the south-east and seasonal planting around the café bring a splash of colour to the expanses of green.

Hampstead and Highgate

Hampstead is a wonderful area in which to wander, and if you make your way between the gardens listed here, you'll have ample opportunity to explore the hilly little roads that scramble, higgledy piggledy, on either side of Heath Street. **Church Row** has been  described as one of the most beautiful pieces of town-scape in the capital – and, though it has no front gardens to speak of, it is worth walking down to **St John's Graveyard** at the far end, where the tilting tombs are romantically mossy and over-grown; see if you can find the painter John Constable's down at the bottom. There are some wonderful front gardens to be found in nearby streets – check out the row of little cottages on **Willow Road** and, tucked away down an alleyway off New End called Streatley Place, the magical **Mansfield Place**, with a central pathway leading between the front gardens of a double row of cottages; as you bend beneath tree branches and bowers of roses that overhang the path, respect the privacy of the owners of these secret city havens. **Flask Walk** has some pretty, if small, front gardens, slightly raised above the street – and even the verge between pavement and road has been planted up like a border. At the pedestrianized Hampstead tube end of Flask Walk is The Flask pub and the extremely pleasant **Judy Green's Garden Store** (▶ 245).

BURGH HOUSE

New End Square NW3 (020 7431 0144). Hampstead tube. Open Wed–Sun 12–5pm (closed some Saturdays for functions). Burgh House Trust. Café.

Less of a garden than a pleasant flower-filled terrace on which to enjoy lunch or tea from the basement Buttery, the little strip of garden to the front and side of the 1704 house is distinguished by having been designed by Gertrude Jekyll. Restored in 1979 by volunteers from the Burgh House Trust, the patterned paved path that leads from the road is flanked by colourful herbaceous borders planted for year-round colour, with spring bulbs and primulas giving way to peonies, irises and then abundant blowzy roses, delphiniums, phlox and foxgloves. An ancient wisteria has wound its way around the railings flanking the steps up to the house and museum – this is stunning in May, when the purple racemes are joined by various types of clematis. Round the corner, on the shadier side of the house, a bay tree, flowering cherry and bamboo are thriving. Tables and chairs are set in trellised enclaves and arbours all along the path and look out on a lower area of grass and the houses of Well Walk.

FENTON HOUSE

Hampstead Grove NW3 (020 7435 3471). Hampstead tube. Open Apr–Oct Wed–Fri 2–5pm; Sat/Sun and Bank Holidays 11am–5pm. Admission to garden £1. National Trust. Some wheelchair access, lavatories available if visiting house. Café. Phone for events, concerts, etc.

Offers Londoners the full country house experience without them having to leave town. Approach from the bottom of Windmill Hill to experience the pleasing view of the perfect Queen Anne doll's house mansion framed by its narrow avenue of robinia trees and neat box and yew hedges. The walled 1½-acre garden behind the house is an unusual treat: the strictly formal design in keeping with the house has some surprisingly off-centre features – variegated holly cones up just one side of the lawn, detailing on the high yew hedge at the far end – that give it a decidedly modern twist. A raised gravel walk with a flower border leads along the right hand side of the lawn, allowing visitors to look down at the hedged garden rooms – an aromatic herb garden and sunken rose garden – behind the yew screen. Steps lead down into these gardens, which would be peaceful hideaways for the lone visitor on a quiet day, surrounded by the heady scents retained within the hedges and walls. Down one more level is an enchanting orchard – a real picture in spring, when anemones, snakeshead fritillaries and narcissi stud the grass beneath the blossom –

and a picturesque vegetable plot where flowers for the house are grown. The house has a collection of historical musical instruments and there are concerts in summer.

THE HILL GARDENS

Inverforth Close NW3. Hampstead or Golders Green tube. Open daily 9am–dusk. Corporation of London.

Hidden away down an unpromising track off North End Way, this is one of London's most magical secret gardens. I first came across the **Pergola** ten years or so ago, when it was in a state of romantic but perilous decay. Since then it has been beautifully restored to its former Edwardian splendour by the Corporation of London, yet it is often completely empty on weekdays. It was the brainchild of Lord Leverhulme who owned the large house now known as Inverforth House (now divided into flats), which he wanted to screen from walkers on the Heath. An incredible 800-foot-long pergola marches at ground level to the house and 30 feet above the gardens below (potting sheds were originally housed in the retaining walls). Smooth white Doric columns of Portland stone bear oak beams, along which wisteria, roses, jasmine and clematis have entwined themselves, and which are periodically crowned by cupolas and arbours. The views out over Hampstead West Heath are breathtaking – and make you long to hold a party here: the whole place, including the Italianate pool garden in front of the house which can be seen through the fence, is still suffused with a sublime Edwardian decadence. To the north side, an unrestored section of pergola where the wisteria trunks are as thick as small trees leads across a bridge to a further section of The Hill gardens – a sunken pool garden with sweeping lawns, stone steps and well planted borders.

GOLDERS HILL PARK

Hampstead Heath NW3 (020 8455 5183). Golders Green tube. Open daily 7.30am–dusk. Corporation of London. Café, lavatories.

Adjacent as it is to the wooded wilds of Hampstead West Heath, Golders Hill Park makes for a complete change of pace. Formerly the grounds of a large eighteenth-century mansion landscaped by Humphry Repton, this popular park is famed for having some of the boldest and brightest annual bedding of any London park. The walled garden (formerly a kitchen garden) is ablaze with exotics such as bananas, fan palms and agaves in summer, interspersed with brugmansias, flaming cannas and dahlias which flower away well into autumn. Elsewhere are water gardens with azaleas, rhododendrons and primulas in spring, an ornamental cherry orchard, zoo, new children's play structures and café on the north-east edge with fabulous views out over the City.

KENWOOD HOUSE AND HAMPSTEAD HEATH
NW3. Hampstead Information Centre (020 7482 7073). Hampstead tube. Kenwood House open 7am–dusk (English Heritage). Hampstead Heath accessible daily (Corporation of London). Café by Kenwood House, lavatories.
The 790 acres of open grass, wild meadows, woods, ponds and marshes that make up Hampstead Heath are almost entirely uncultivated – and that is the charm of this unenclosed wilderness, beloved by dog walkers, Sunday strollers, horse riders, families and wildlife alike. Among the few gardened areas are the surrounds of Kenwood House on the northernmost boundary, originally designed by Humphry Repton. The **Flower Garden** to the west of the house is part of his original design, where sinuous paths and an ivy-clad tunnel weave among trees and shrubberies, opening to reveal sculptures by Barbara Hepworth and Henry Moore in sunny grassy glades. A promenade leads back between the elegant **Orangery** and the grass slopes leading down to the lake and Sham Bridge, where concerts are held in summer, and on to the café and restaurant where you can enjoy good food in a pretty walled garden with roses, lavender and other aromatic plants growing up and around trellis supports. Further east, past the little belvedere offering splendid views out over London, is a secluded and little-visited walled garden. Known as the **Kitchen Garden**, it now contains mainly flowers and an engaging 'human sundial' where your own shadow tells the time.

WATERLOW PARK
Highgate High Street N19. Archway tube. Open daily 7.30am–dusk. London Borough of Camden. Lavatories, café, children's playground.
Named after Sir Sydney Waterlow, who bequeathed the 26 acres between Highgate Cemetery and the High Street as 'a garden for the gardenless' in 1889, this is a popular local park with loads of horticultural – and other – interest. Stunning views over the City can be enjoyed from the summit, and grassy slopes with curving paths sweep down towards the lower reaches. Three lakes and a stream are surrounded by weeping willows, acers, swamp cypresses and rhododendrons, and carved logs have been made into sculptural seats. Other notable trees in the park include limes, oaks, gingkos, cedars of Lebanon and a large weeping birch – many of which are survivors from the original estate – and there's also a popular wishing tree with copper tags bearing wishes. Year-round horticultural interest begins

with spring flowers on the hillside and continues with iris and azaleas around the lakes, rose beds and herbaceous borders in high summer and splendid autumn colour from the acers in particular. A small aviary features exotic birds, while wild species have colonized the lower ponds. On the High Street side is the lovely Grade II-listed Lauderdale House, which has its own walled garden containing a large tulip and gingko trees, a honey locust, huge copper beech and a pair of beautiful magnolias. While you're here, check out the excellent garden centre (▶ 243).

Northern Outskirts

CROUCH HILL FOREST GARDEN
Crouch Hill Recreation Centre N8. Crouch Hill rail. Open by arrangement only, ring 08454 584697. Naturewise.
An enterprising attempt to create a 'Forest Garden' (a sustainable edible landscape, with fruit trees, perennial vegetables and herbs – part of the sustainable gardening system known as Permaculture) on a slope behind a housing estate.

ELTHORNE PARK
Hazelville Road N19. Crouch Hill rail. Open Mon–Fri 8am–dusk, Sat 9am–dusk, Sun 10am–dusk. London Borough of Islington.
Popular local park, with laurel-lined walkways and areas of woodland. The **Noel Baker Peace Garden** – named after the 1959 winner of the Nobel Peace Prize – is well worth a visit as an interesting example of late-twentieth-century garden design. Centred around a water feature and striking bronze sculpture, the design uses brick and York stone paving, with raised beds and grassed areas. The hard landscaping is softened by the excellent planting, in shades of green, grey and white with splashes of brighter colour here and there. There are several secluded sitting areas, which are usually taken by loyal local residents.

ALEXANDRA PALACE
Alexandra Palace Way N22 (020 8365 2671). Alexandra Palace rail. Gardens open daily; Palm Court sometimes closed for events. Alexandra Palace Trust. Café, lavatories.
High on the ridge of the Northern Heights, the Victorian palace is visible for miles and made a bleak sight after the last fire in 1980 (the first came shortly

after its opening in 1873). On a fine day you can see from the park as far as Kent and the North Downs. The original flowerbeds have been turfed over and the 220-acre parkland consists mainly of grassy slopes where dog walking and kite flying are popular, but there are some fine specimen trees (including hollies, copper beech, nothofagus and silvery poplars), a boating pond and a compact yet thriving nature reserve. At the top of the hill, the secluded grounds of a former aristocratic summer residence called The Grove is rich in historical associations (an avenue of trees is known as Dr Johnson's Walk) and is the venue for jazz concerts and other summer events. There is also a large garden centre (▶ 231).

CAPEL MANOR GARDENS

Bullsmoor Lane, Enfield (020 8366 4442). Turkey Street rail. Open daily Apr–Sept 10am–6pm, Oct–Mar 10am–5pm. Admission £5/concessions; season tickets available; £4 in winter. Capel Manor College.
Good wheelchair access. Refreshments, lavatories.

There is a lot going on in the 30-acre grounds of the attractive Georgian house, home to the well known horticultural college (▶ 277). Historical themed gardens close to the house follow gardening styles through the centuries, and an **Italian Holly Maze** and **Tropical House** are great in winter. Then there are the sponsored demonstration gardens in a variety of styles, exploring (and inevitably sometimes promoting) different materials and plants – some, such as the **Japanese Garden**, are more successful than others. One of the most fascinating areas is the trial ground run by *Gardening Which?* magazine. One area shows many different types of clipped hedging, with an unclipped specimen for comparison at the end, while another compares pruning methods, with the same plants grown in similar conditions shown after various different types and degrees of pruning. Other beds are given over to trials of new cultivars, an A–Z of shrubs and the national collection of achilleas, while a **Low-Allergen Garden**, with no wind-pollinated plants, will be interesting to hayfever sufferers. The large water lily lake is beautiful, as is a wilderness area with folly, while the woodland walk is carpeted with bulbs in early spring. Rare breeds of animals are a draw for those less interested in gardening, and a programme of festivals and other events is laid on over the summer. Equip yourself with a map from the information centre so you can plan your time here – perhaps over refreshments in the restaurant. You may well decide to come back here to attend one of Capel Manor's excellent gardening or horticultural courses.

MYDDLETON HOUSE GARDENS
Bulls Cross, Enfield (01992 702200). Turkey Street rail. Open Apr–Sept
Mon–Fri 10am–4.30pm, Sun and Bank Holidays 12–4pm; Oct–Mar
Mon–Fri 10am–3pm. Also open through the NGS (▶ 263). Entrance £2.10.
Lee Valley Regional Park Authority.
This is the garden created by the famous plantsman and author E. A. Bowles
(1865–1954), who lived in the main house. These 4 acres were home to his
phenomenal plant collection and are slowly being restored to their former
glory. Planted with year-round interest in mind, the garden boasts an alpine
meadow and rock garden that are ablaze with early spring bulbs; abundant
irises and tulips, with roses and lilies following later in summer; and a vast
number of nerines and naturalized autumn crocuses and cyclamen as winter
approaches. Even in the depths of winter the hellebore collection and
unusual evergreens hold their appeal. Other interesting features created by
Bowles include a 'lunatic asylum' of plants that grow irrationally (such as
corkscrew willow and green roses), and 'Tom Tiddler's Ground' planted with
golden, variegated and coloured-leaved plants. The National Collection of
irises contains more than three hundred varieties, while the rose garden has
been replanted with many of Bowles' original favourites, plus tree peonies
and camellias around the old Enfield Town Market Cross. The terraced lake
with its water lilies, gunnera and elegant reeds and grasses is worth
exploring, as is a new conservatory crammed with tropical, Mediterranean
and desert plants and an exhibition on Bowles' achievements. But nothing
can compare to the old Victorian tiled conservatory with its life-size ostrich
statues hiding among the exotic palms and cacti.

 **SOUTH LONDON**

Battersea and Clapham
BATTERSEA PARK
Prince of Wales Drive SW11 (020 8871 7530). Battersea Park rail.
Open daily dawn–10pm. London Borough of Wandsworth. Café, lavatories,
children's playgrounds and zoo. Thrive (020 7720 2212).
Battersea Park on a sunny Sunday afternoon reminds me somehow of
Central Park in New York. It is much smaller, of course, and much more
intimate in scale (and you don't get the views of the skyscrapers), but there
is that same feeling that everyone is out enjoying themselves – families
with young children, dog walkers with charges of every shape and size, old
couples taking the air, cyclists and skateboarders, roller-bladers and

joggers. Popular features include the landscaped serpentine lakes, the enclosed **Old English Garden** with its pergolas clad in roses, wisteria and honeysuckle and the quaint children's zoo. The **Herb Garden**, hidden behind what looks like a van depot, is one of the best in London. Laid out in 1846 and restyled as the Festival of Britain Gardens in 1951 by a team that included Russell Page, John Piper and Osbert Lancaster, Battersea Park is currently in the throes of a dramatic restoration project that includes plans to revive the subtropical garden and rose gardens of the original design. The pale stone Peace Pagoda, built as a gift from a Buddhist order in 1985, has become a landmark from across the river, and people also travel from far and wide to attend the Battersea Garden Project run by Thrive, the national charity that works to help disabled and disadvantaged people through gardening (▶ 263).

TRINITY HOSPICE
Clapham Common North Side SW4 (020 7787 1000). Clapham Common tube. Only open by appointment and three weekends a year through the NGS (▶ 263). Admission £1 for public open days, children free. Trustees of the Hospice. Refreshments available on open days.
A 2-acre garden, well stocked with shrubs and perennials, which is a great solace to the residents of the hospice and their visitors. Designed by John Medhurst and restored in the 1980s by the American designer Lanning Roper (after whom it is now named, as he died before the restoration was complete), it features expanses of lawn, spring and summer herbaceous borders, a hidden wild garden containing a lily pond and a wildflower area, as well as some beautiful mature trees. The healing nature of this garden is highlighted by a 'blessing tree' hung with personalized blessings on copper tags, and a 'sitting circle' enclosed by soft pastel plantings of roses, lavender, nepeta, salvias and buddleia. The gardens are excellently maintained by a keen team of volunteers.

Brixton, Dulwich and Peckham
BROCKWELL PARK
Norwood Road SE24. Brixton tube or Herne Hill rail. Open daily dawn–dusk. London Borough of Lambeth. Café, lavatories, children's playground.
A large 128-acre park that stretches between Brixton Water Lane and Herne Hill. Hilly and wild areas make it appear even larger. The secret walled garden is a great attraction, with mature yew hedges, pretty pergolas, formal beds planted with a good range of herbaceous plants and seats round a central pond. On top of the hill, the former Brockwell House is now a

friendly café surrounded by tables and seating, a nineteenth-century clock tower, formal gardens and lawns for picnicking. The park also has some ancient oak trees, ornamental water gardens and a lively community garden project and forest garden around the park's old greenhouses. There's another café at the fabulous 1930s lido on the Dulwich Road side.

CRYSTAL PALACE PARK
Thicket Road SE20 (020 8778 9496). Crystal Palace rail.
Open daily 7.30am–dusk. London Borough of Bromley.
'The Crystal Palace Gardens will do more to encourage a taste for gardening and a love of flowers among the lower classes, than even the London Parks' – or so it was asserted at the time of the park's creation, to house Joseph Paxton's spectacular conservatory, relocated from Hyde Park after the Great Exhibition of 1851. Since the glasshouse burnt down in 1936, the 200-acre park has become more famous for its giant dinosaurs, also relics from the Great Exhibition. Placed in realistic poses among facsimiles of natural rock formations, they still look dramatic lurking in the trees around the boating lake or appearing to emerge from the waters. Paxton's bright Italianate gardens in front of the palace have long since gone, but the walled garden with its seasonal bedding and azalea beds still has a Victorian flavour. The park was seriously in need of a facelift when the designer Kathryn Gustafson won the competition to revamp it, and the results of her projects, which include a new network of paths and mixed perennial beds, are eagerly anticipated. Paxton's collection of rhododendrons has also been recreated, using varieties that would have been available in 1850, and another area has been planted with only modern cultivars.

BELAIR PARK
Gallery Road SE21 (020 8693 5737). West Dulwich rail. Open daily
8am–9pm BST, 8am–dusk in winter. London Borough of Southwark.
A 10-acre park laid out as a suitably grand setting for Belair House (now a restaurant) and now Grade II listed. Informal sloping lawns in the English landscape tradition, with ancient trees, shrubberies and some rose beds, sweeping down to a long serpentine lake.

DULWICH PARK
College Road SE21 (020 8693 5737). North Dulwich rail 10 mins.
Open daily 8am–9pm BST, 8am–4.30pm winter. London Borough of
Southwark. Café, lavatories, children's play area.
Traditional Victorian family park of 70 acres that makes a good place for a

stroll after a visit to the excellent Dulwich Picture Gallery over the road or lunch at Belair House (see above). Technicolor banks of rhododendrons and azaleas are a great attraction in May, and the park can also boast some unusual specimen trees, including a Japanese pagoda tree, Kentucky coffee tree and Cappadocian maple, alongside fine examples of Turkey oak, Atlantic cedar, copper beech and ancient oaks. A 3-acre boating lake is home to all manner of ducks and wildlife (and a Barbara Hepworth sculpture) and there are two ecological sites and a nature trail for children. The **Drought Tolerant Garden** is a great introduction, planted with Mediterranean-style plants that need no watering at all – silver-leaved plants such as lavender and santolina; evergreen euphorbias, cistus and rosemary; and succulents such as sedums, sempervivums and crassulas that store their own water supplies in fleshy leaves. Following in the footsteps of Beth Chatto's famous Gravel Garden in Essex, which has not been watered since it was first planted, this should inspire eco-minded Londoners to conserve water in their own back gardens. The main drawback of this park is that it is crisscrossed by roads, and the rows of parked cars interfere with the views. Various unusual types of bicycle, including recumbent ones, are available for hire at weekends.

DULWICH UPPER WOOD NATURE PARK
Farquhar Road SE19 (020 8761 6230). Gipsy Hill rail.
Open Mon–Fri 10am–4pm. Woods open daily. The Trust for Urban Ecology.
One of the few examples of Ancient Woodland preserved within an urban environment, this 5-acre wood is made up of mixed oak and other native species, and includes some oak trees that are more than four hundred years old. The site is managed as a nature reserve, and local schools and colleges make good use of it for nature studies. There is a pond and bog garden created by puddling the underlying London clay, and a herb garden, with fern and fungi gardens under way. Carpets of wood anemones, primroses and bluebells make this a great place to visit in spring.

SYDENHAM HILL WOOD
Dulwich Common/Crescent Wood Road SE26 (020 8699 5698).
West Dulwich or Sydenham Hill rail. Open daily. London Wildlife Trust.
Well established broadleaf woodland teeming with birds and wildlife – early morning walks are held here to witness the dawn chorus. Wood anemones and bluebells flower in spring, before the tree canopy grows dense and green. Good autumn colour, especially along Cox's Walk, where you might see a nuthatch or green woodpecker in the old oak trees, and

can also peer over the layered hedge to the allotment site behind. One of the most picturesque allotment sites in London, however, lies on the other side of the woods. This is ▶

GRANGE LANE ALLOTMENTS
Grange Lane SE21. West Dulwich or Sydenham Hill rail. Private.
Drive up College Lane – the nearest London has to a country lane – to the car park for the woods and you'll see a huge allotment site on your right.

Lucky members with plots at the top of the hill can enjoy one of the best views out over London as they work. If the gate is open and you ask someone nicely, they might let you in for a wander, but you can still see a certain amount from the road.

PECKHAM RYE PARK

SE5 (020 8693 3791). Peckham Rye rail. Open daily 7am–dusk. London Borough of Southwark. Some wheelchair access, lavatories, visitors' centre.

The ancient common at Peckham Rye has had a chequered history – recorded as a site for one of Boudicca's battles, England's oldest stag hunting ground, one of the places where William Blake saw visions of angels, and a prisoner of war camp in between long periods when it was used as common grazing land. The Rye is still a pleasant open space, but the horticultural interest lies in the adjacent 50-acre park, which was added in 1894. A recent much-needed restoration project (funded by the Heritage Lottery Fund) is refocusing the park on its Victorian roots, with its **Rock Garden**, **Japanese Garden** and **American Garden** all due for a timely facelift. The tone is set with some great gaudy bedding displays as you enter the enclosed part of the park – wilder areas on the other side have been set aside for a wildlife meadow, and there is a secluded **Woodland Walk** (beautiful in winter and early spring) up near the children's adventure playground towards the northern boundary. One of the stars of the park is the **Sexby Garden** – a rose garden enclosed by 100-year-old yew hedges and dissected by a pergola clad in climbing roses and wisteria, and restoration work is already under way here. **The Clockhouse** pub opposite the eastern entrance to the common on Peckham Rye has won awards for its exuberant hanging baskets and window boxes, and is a good place to stop for a drink.

CHOUMERT SQUARE

SE15. Peckham Rye rail. Private gardens open under the NGS (▶ 263), but front gardens can be seen from the path.

An iron gate off Choumert Grove (just north of Choumert Road) leads into a narrow path between two rows of small cottages so full of flowers that it has been described as 'a floral canyon'. There is no room for back gardens, so all the residents' gardening energies are concentrated in the front – the plots are only a few feet deep, but often jump the walls or fence to line the path in pots, troughs and other containers brimming with plants. There are forty-six houses in all, and the gardens are as varied as their creators' tastes and interests. Some are neat and elegant,

with fashionable garden furniture, canvas parasols and tubs of lavender; others are gloriously romantic with a tangle of rambling roses round the front door; a few go down the kitsch road with rows of china ornaments and coloured fairy lights. Almost all make room for a table and a few chairs or benches – the residents must be sociable people as there is little or no privacy from the neighbours just a few feet away. Following the central path, from time to time you have to duck beneath a leaning tree or pass beneath a charming arch of roses or white solanum; a gate at the far end leads into a communal seating and barbecue area. The gardens of Choumert Square can be visited at any time – respecting the privacy of the residents, of course – but for a real carnival atmosphere, when everyone pulls out all the stops and there's a chance to meet the gardeners themselves, try to make it to one of the NGS open days (▶ 263).

CENTRE FOR WILDLIFE GARDENING
Marsden Road, Peckham SE15 (020 7252 9186). East Dulwich rail.
Open Tues, Wed, Thurs, Sun 10.30am–4.30pm. (Closed for three weeks over Christmas, ring for details.) London Wildlife Trust. Picnic area, lavatories.
A wildlife garden, attractive community park, information centre and plant nursery all in one, this hidden treasure is well worth a visit for anyone interested in wildlife gardening and green issues. From a residential side-street it is clear something interesting is going on: wrought iron gates with a bold flower design offer glimpses down a path lined with bright flowers, murals and mosaics to a timber building with a 'green' plant-covered roof beyond. The centre is friendly and accessible, with an information centre in the main building where you can pick up a map and leaflets and advice about virtually any aspect of wildlife gardening. To the right of the building a series of reed beds collect water running off the roof and 'grey water' from the kitchen and filter it into a pond. 'Bird island' rustles and cheeps with birds of many kinds, and the various other wildlife habitats (among them a miniature meadow, wildflower and butterfly borders, a moth garden and log garden) are as attractive to humans as they clearly are to wildlife. Several areas, a living willow bower and 'kids' corner' among them, have been designed with younger visitors in mind, and dipping nets and magnifying glasses for the curious are available from staff. Right down to the smallest details – violas planted in a pair of old boots, jolly ceramic tiles decorating the vegetable beds and home-made scarecrows with flower pot heads – effort has been made to ensure this place looks as good as its intentions (an area where many wildlife gardens fall down). To the left of the main path are raised beds for vegetables, flowers and grasses, and a plant nursery selling many herbs, wildflowers and small trees in season. An annual 'free tree' scheme offers one small tree per family in the winter months. Day courses and workshops in aspects of wildlife gardening are offered throughout the year (▶ 262), and there is a Wildlife Watch club for children.

HORNIMAN GARDENS
Horniman Museum, Horniman Drive SE23 (020 8699 1872). Forest Hill
rail. Open Mon–Sat 7.15am–dusk; Sun and Bank Holidays 8am–dusk
(closed 25 Dec). Café in museum, lavatories.
The main attraction may be the museum of anthropological artefacts
brought back by John Horniman MP, a Victorian tea merchant and
traveller, but the 16-acre grounds are also of great interest to garden lovers.
Standards of planting and upkeep are impressively high here, and many of
the plants are raised on site in a nursery at the top of the hill. Much of this
stock must be packed into the **Sunken Garden**, which is a Technicolor riot
from summer through to autumn with glowing dahlias, zinnias, coleus
and fluffy celmisias in every colour of the rainbow set against the darker
foliage of castor oil plants, furry amaranthus and purply-black chard,
orach and basil. The pattern of concentric squares set against bright green
grass looks great when viewed from above – the garden is set on a steep
hillside and affords great views out across London from near the
bandstand and Dutch Barn. There are some other stunning borders near
the top that have a great mix of colour, height and texture all year round,
but the most recent developments are centred around the new museum
entrance, with mixed borders near the newly restored Victorian glasshouse
and tropical-style planting beneath the turf roof of the new educational
building. The only price to pay for such high standards is that this is a
strictly patrolled park, where children and dogs have to be kept under
control. There are twice-annual plant sales, and gardening classes are also
given here.

Kennington and the Elephant

CHUMLEIGH MULTICULTURAL GARDENS
Burgess Park, Albany Road SE5 (020 7525 1065). Elephant and Castle tube.
Open daily dawn–dusk. London Borough of Southwark. Friends of Burgess
Park (020 7639 9755). Café, lavatories, good wheelchair access.
This is one of the most impressive and unexpected gardens in the whole
of London – and all the more so for being found in the middle of the rather
uninspiring Burgess Park, just south of Elephant and Castle. As part of the
Abercrombie Plan to create new 'green lungs' for London after the Second
World War, 135 acres of bomb-torn and overcrowded Southwark were
bulldozed to make way for Burgess Park. Tower blocks replaced the
narrow terraced houses but some of the older buildings were retai~
including the attractive Gothick almshouses built in 1821 by the Frie~.ai\
Female Society as an 'asylum' for elderly women. These are now the

headquarters of the Multicultural Gardens, created with a view to illustrate different garden styles from around the world and to show how plants adapt to different environments and are used by different cultures. If it all sounds too worthy to be true, don't be put off! The gardens are delightful – design and sensory impact comes first, and signs (apart from plant names) are kept to an informative minimum. The **English Gardens**, contained within the alms building walls, are a traditional mix of lawns, stone walkways and borders, with generously planted lead-look planters. There are some exquisite plant combinations here, including, in late summer, crocosmias and dark red day lilies interplanted with blue echinops thistles and spires of Russian sage against a backdrop of the smoke bush (*Cotinus coggygria*). Wander through into the peaceful **Oriental Garden**, designed in the Japanese fashion as a miniature landscape of mountains (rocks and gravel), woods (bamboos and grasses) and water (central pond) and through to the **Afro-Caribbean Garden** beyond, which has dry areas with cacti and succulents and jungly planting suggested by tree ferns and bamboos, hardy Japanese bananas, dark red canna leaves and red hot pokers. Blue benches are backed by banks of blue agapanthus (African lilies), salvias and olive trees. The **Islamic Garden** is, perhaps, the star of the show, with a blue-tiled pool in the centre, a huge fanning jelly palm (*Butia capitata*) and a Persian ironwood tree (*Parrotia persica*) with its multi-coloured autumn foliage. Last but not least is the sunny **Mediterranean Garden**, where the scent of herbs and other aromatic plants is retained within the high brick walls and shade is provided by a pergola clad with grapevines. There is also a **Vegetable Garden**, with raised beds tended organically to demonstrate the ways different food plants and herbs are used and grown by specific cultures. Butterflies incorporated into the walls and fences refer to the Camberwell Beauty, brought here with imported wood by canal.

ROOTS & SHOOTS
Walnut Tree Walk SE11 (020 7735 0602). Lambeth North tube.
Open Mon–Fri 9.30am–5pm. London Borough of Lambeth/Friends of
Roots & Shoots. Plants for sale.
Diverse, lively and attractive wildlife garden created in the early 1980s on a derelict, overgrown and polluted Civil Defence site. The colourful lush garden that now greets visitors is testimony to the power of plants – and hardworking, visionary people – to transform even the most unprepossessing places. At its peak in high summer when it buzzes with bees, birds and butterflies, the garden provides a range of different wildlife

habitats, with a pond with timber dipping deck, a large wildflower meadow, hazel coppice, hop hedge, thyme circle and abundantly self-seeding flower borders. Beehives and butterfly borders are popular with local children, who are encouraged to spot other beneficial insects – local schools often use the garden as a 'living classroom' and artists work with visitors to create colourful mosaics and other artworks. A **Kitchen Garden** has cordoned apples, strawberry beds, herbs and raised vegetable beds, while the **Paradise Garden** is home to exotic delicacies such as bananas, pineapple guavas and Chinese gooseberries. Practical courses in horticulture and gardening are held here for the local community, with the focus on training for young people with learning difficulties. Roots & Shoots is now the base for the London Beekeepers Association, and a programme of beekeeping courses is planned. Long term plans include expanding the garden centre (which is a good source of cheap, well grown plants in summer) and replacing the old wartime building with modern staff, community and seminar rooms.

Further South

THE ROOKERY
Streatham High Road SW16. Streatham rail. Open dawn–dusk. Closed 25 Dec. London Borough of Lambeth. Café, lavatories.
A real surprise up on the hill from traffic-laden Streatham High Road, this peaceful garden, once attached to a private house, has a lot packed into a relatively small area. There's a walled **English Garden** with abundant fragrant planting; a secluded rock garden and stream; a small yew-hedged pond garden and wisteria-clad pergola; shrubbery-lined paths and a fine **White Garden** (at its peak in June and July) that has been said 'to rival Sissinghurst'. Further down the hill is a quiet orchard, often used for picnics.

SOUTH LONDON BOTANICAL INSTITUTE
Norwood Road SE24 (020 8674 5787). Tulse Hill rail. Open Thursdays 10am–4pm and by appointment; also through the NGS (▶ 263).
London's smallest botanic garden, founded in 1911 and densely planted with more than five hundred labelled species from around the world – many of them rare and interesting. The layout is formal, with paved paths between the banks of packed planting. British plants are a speciality, as are medicinal and carnivorous plants and ferns.

HALL PLACE
Bourne Road, Bexley, Kent DA5 1PQ (01322 526574). Bexley rail.
Garden open Apr–Oct Mon–Sat 10am–5pm, Sun and Bank Holidays
11am–5pm. Bexley Heritage Trust.
Named 'the most interesting and best-kept public garden in south-east
London', the gardens of Hall Place surround a splendid Tudor mansion built
in 1537 and extended a century later. The 16 acres are planned with the
public in mind, with a strong emphasis on imaginative spring and summer
bedding, and a variety of smaller themed gardens. The Elizabethan-style rose
garden and splendid double herbaceous borders are some of the best of their
type, while several well stocked shrubberies, a beautifully designed and
patterned herb garden (with labels in Braille), rock and heather gardens,
wildlife sanctuary and working nursery are all worth exploring. It is the
topiary though, that sticks in the memory: abstract cones and concentric
discs near the chequered flint-and-stone wall of the house, and a surreal
regiment of the Queen's Beasts, planted to commemorate the coronation in
1953, that marches across the immaculate lawn.

 # WEST LONDON

Notting Hill

Notting Hill is a great area for garden-
spotting – there are some pretty public
squares and gardens, but you'll also find
plenty of inspiration strolling up and down the
residential streets, from the grand houses to the
west of Ladbroke Grove to chic roof gardens
and trendy window boxes around Portobello.
Arriving by tube, the best advice for garden
lovers is to head straight off busy Notting Hill
Gate – either up Campden Hill Road to the
south and on towards Holland Park or
Kensington, or down Pembridge Road to
the north and into the heart of Portobello.

PORTOBELLO
W11. Notting Hill Gate tube.
The funky, junky shops on Pembridge
Road are good for antique knick-knacks or

unconventional garden ornaments or containers. More of this ilk can be found at **Portobello Market**, which is open Fridays (quieter, and the best day to go) and Saturdays. The top end of **Portobello Road**, before you get to the market, has some pretty front gardens. With the turnover of residential property being so rapid in this area it is not fair to mention individual examples – but the **Gate Hotel** at No. 6 is usually festooned with hanging baskets in summer while, just a few doors down, the front path of one of the tiny terraced houses is so covered with plants, windchimes and ornaments you would have a job getting to the door. As you walk down towards the market, check out the front gardens of the brightly painted houses on the right – there are some delightful touches, from the contrast of a dark red climbing rose against an aqua blue wall to a romantic Gothick arch clothed in honeysuckle and jasmine. Don't forget to look upwards, too – well trained wisteria pours over balconies while the tiniest rooftop terraces are fringed with green. Where the market starts in earnest, you could always turn right down wide, tree-lined **Chepstow Villas** for a glimpse of the front gardens of the large stucco-fronted houses there – or down **Westbourne Grove** for London's grooviest florist, **Wild at Heart**, and the chic little roof gardens that crown the string of fashionable shops and restaurants. Back on to Portobello Road, the Friday and Saturday antiques market is not a bad place to pick up an unusual addition for your garden, be it a stone Buddha, an ancient cast iron bench or a boot-load of old galvanized baths and buckets to use as containers. Further down, in among the fruit and vegetable stands, there are often cheap houseplants and clipped box plants for sale around the junction with Elgin Crescent. It's hard not to be waylaid by shops here, and among those of interest to gardeners are **Graham & Green** on Elgin Crescent (▶ 244), source of some of the smartest modern and traditional garden furniture and lighting around, and the wonderful **Garden Books** (or Blenheim Books incorporating Garden Books, as it is now known) at 11 Blenheim Crescent (020 7792 0777). **Harper and Tom's** (020 7792 8510) is another great florist (on the corner of Blenheim Crescent and Kensington Park Road) – they often sell interesting succulents and other less conventional window box options. While you're there, look up at the potted garden above the launderette opposite for a good example of resourceful and creative urban gardening in the most confined of spaces.

COMMUNAL GARDENS AND SQUARES
W11. Notting Hill Gate or Ladbrooke Grove tube. Private squares.
Cross Ladbroke Grove and head up **Elgin Crescent**, **Lansdowne Crescent** or **Lansdowne Road**, where the splendid town houses, many of them

painted in bright colours, back on to the much-coveted communal gardens. This must be the ideal way to garden in the city – each house has its own small back garden with gates leading in to large leafy communal gardens. The whole point of the shared gardens is privacy, and access is strictly guarded, but you can catch a glimpse of some of them from Ladbroke Grove, Kensington Park Road and Lansdowne Rise – see if you can spot the one where Julia Roberts and Hugh Grant canoodled on a bench in the film *Notting Hill*. Your best chance of getting inside one of these gardens is on London Squares Day (▶ 262) or visiting lucky friends. Heading down towards Holland Park, **Norland Square** is pretty (home of the famous nanny-training school), as is **St James's Gardens**, with its central church – some nice examples of chic window boxes, small balcony and basement gardens here. Some of the best front gardens in the area are in **Addison Avenue**, a wide, tree-lined street of pastel-painted Regency houses which leads from the church to Holland Park – you'll find every style here, from traditional roses, lavender and hydrangeas to abstract evergreen hedges and cloud-pruned box.

VIRGINIA
98 Portland Road W11 (020 7727 9908). Holland Park tube.
Open Mon–Fri 11am–6pm; Saturday by appointment.
The tiny yard behind Virginia Bates' antique clothes shop is an exercise in over-the-top, romantic gardening. Pink and white hydrangeas, petunias, pelargoniums and busy lizzies are crammed into scrolling wirework *étagères* or on the shelves surrounding a huge overmantel mirror that reflects more light into the diminutive space. The walls are painted bubblegum pink and are covered with the signatures of famous friends and clients; antique shawls adorn tables and chairs, while beaded bustiers and other delights are hung from the shelves like rare exotic blooms.

Holland Park and Environs
CAMPDEN HILL SQUARE
W8. Notting Hill Gate tube. Private square.
Just off busy Holland Park (see below), this is the quieter, more elegant side of Notting Hill – a large hillside square surrounded by beautiful houses, many of which (here and in surrounding streets) have well kept and interesting front gardens. The central square is accessible only to residents and subscribers, but glimpses over the low (and beautifully old) black railings show an enviably peaceful space, with close-mown lawns, well stocked shrubby borders and shady walks beneath the

mature trees on the periphery. Carefully sited benches and some good stone planters and terracotta urns filled with lavender and other low-key plants all add to the air of understated, well-bred charm. Continue south for St Mary Abbots Gardens (▶ 148) and Kensington Roof Gardens (▶ 147).

HOLLAND PARK
Ilchester Place, Holland Park W8 (020 7471 9813). Holland Park tube 10 mins. Open 7.30am–dusk. Royal Borough of Kensington and Chelsea. Lavatories, café and restaurant, children's adventure playground.

Holland Park is a life-saver for west-Londoners but, at just 55 acres, can often seem overcrowded at weekends and tired at the end of a long hot summer. Enter from Holland Park Avenue to the north for a striking contrast between the naturalistic landscape and the grand stucco villas of the surrounding streets. There are many treats for gardeners concentrated here: a Dutch garden, peaceful woodland enclosure, iris and azalea gardens that are both at their peak in late spring, dahlia and sub-tropical beds for late summer, stately avenues and many rare specimen trees such as the lovely snowdrop tree that flowers in May, the Chinese sweet gum, Pyrean oak and Himalayan birch. The formal gardens around the remains of Holland Park House (damaged in the Second World War) have been well maintained, and the lovely old Orangery is a good place for a rest and a drink. (The opulent Belvedere restaurant (020 7602 1238) is now in the hands of Marco Pierre White.) One of the most popular areas is the one-acre **Kyoto Garden** – a Japanese garden with acers of many different kinds planted around a peaceful pool with a waterfall and carefully placed rocks, stepping stones and ornaments in faithful Japanese style. Wildlife is another valued feature of the park and the **Ecology Centre** organizes an impressive programme of events throughout the year. Various habitats including the ponds, woodlands and tree stump area encourage many forms of wildlife including sixty different bird species such as the tawny owl and sparrowhawk, both rare in the capital.

LEIGHTON HOUSE GARDEN
Holland Park Road W14 (020 7602 3316). Open every day except Tues 11am–5pm. Royal Borough of Kensington & Chelsea.

Many visitors do not realize that the opulent and colourful house belonging to the Victorian painter Frederick Leighton has a beautiful garden too. The large shady lawn, giant trees and herbaceous borders come as a quiet breather after the dazzling interiors, and there is lots to admire, from the spring blossom of the fruit trees to rambling roses scrambling up a pergola and borders spilling over with irises, geraniums, foxgloves and chrysanthemums. Trailing ivies clothe the surrounding walls to create a suitably sombre Victorian backdrop, while a sculpture entitled *Moment of Peril* features a horse and a python in a death-defying struggle.

EMSLIE HORNIMAN PLEASANCE PARK
Bosworth Road W10. Westbourne Park tube. Open daily 8.30am–dusk.
North Kensington Council. Children's play areas.
This remarkable Arts and Crafts garden hidden away in North Kensington deserves to be better known, especially in the wake of recent renovation work. Designed in 1913–14 as a Spanish garden by the architect Charles Voysey, it is named after a local MP who, realizing there was no park for children in the area, gave the land in perpetuity 'for the people of London as a recreation ground'. The walled flower garden is screened from the road by a high white wall with turrets and circular viewing holes; inside, a chunky pergola with a slim moat of water beneath frames the central beds which spill over with roses, lavender and late-flowering perennials all summer long. Next door, a popular children's playground has been created in a contrasting modern style, with a brightly coloured undulating floor surface made from recycled car tyres, and gates and fencing fashioned from panels of perforated sheet metal.

MEANWHILE COMMUNITY GARDENS
Kensal Road W10 (020 8960 4600). Westbourne Park tube. Open daily.
Meanwhile Gardens Community Association. Children's playground.
This ribbon-like park in the shadow of the newly fashionable Trellick Tower is a popular community garden, originally made in the 1970s but given a welcome revamp a few years ago. There are several distinct areas: a grassed area beside the Grand Union Canal has a gentle atmosphere and is popular with families with young children, while the woodland walk with its timber boardwalks invites exploration as well as wildlife. One of the most popular attractions is the bike and skateboard bowl, its bold and colourful graffiti contrasting with the surrounding greenery to make a vibrant inner city landscape. A sparkling spiral path made from glass chippings set in resin links all the parts of the garden, and salvaged railway sleepers, set at leaning angles in the soil, are used to divide the spaces.

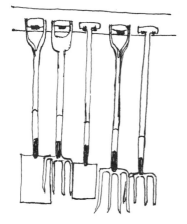

LONDON LIGHTHOUSE
Lancaster Road W11. Ladbroke Grove
tube. Open Mon–Fri 9am–9pm, Sat
10am–5pm and through the NGS (▸ 263).
Small courtyard garden on three levels,
created in 1988 and the winner of
several awards. Rose-covered walls and
trellis provide privacy as well as a warm
microclimate in which many tender and
unusual plants flourish, in mixed
borders and in pots. The Italianate
topiary is impressive, and there's also an
established pond.

EDWARDES SQUARE
W8. High Street Kensington or Earls' Court tube. Open through the
NGS (▸ 263) and London Squares Day (▸ 262). Edwardes Square
Garden Committee.
Often described as one of London's most beautiful and secluded garden
squares. The 3-acre private residents' garden is worth visiting on an open
day to explore its serpentine paths leading through shrubberies, lawns,
flowerbeds, a rose pergola and past a croquet lawn, tennis court and
children's playground. A Greek revival style temple is used as the
gardener's headquarters. The square was built in 1811–19 and the garden
laid out in 1820 by the Italian artist Agostino Agliothe who lived at No. 15.
An Act of Parliament was passed for 'paving, cleansing, lighting, watching,
watering, planting and improving' Edwardes Square and a fine of £5
imposed on anyone allowing swine to wander into the gardens and
carriageways. Near by is **Rassell's Garden Centre** (▸ 237).

Fulham, Hammersmith and Barnes
FULHAM PALACE PARK
Bishop's Avenue SW6 (020 7736 5821). Putney Bridge tube 10 mins walk.
Open daily dawn–dusk; closed 25 Dec and 1 Jan. London Borough of
Hammersmith & Fulham. Children's playground. Braille in walled garden.
This garden is a timeless treasure that seems set apart from the rest of
London. The summer home of the Bishops of London from the eleventh
century to 1973, the Palace's ornamental garden was created by Bishop
Henry Compton in the late seventeenth to early eighteenth century. This
keen plantsman was responsible for introducing many rare plants, and

visitors came from all over the country to see them growing in his garden. To this day, the park has retained a fine collection of 'foreign' trees, including an ancient evergreen oak and black walnut, a Judas tree on the Great Lawn and newer Indian bean tree (catalpa), Atlas cedar and Chinese paper bark maple. But it is for the wisteria in April and May that Fulham Palace Park is most loved: fragrant blooms cover the south side of the Palace, while a magnificent specimen is trained over an old pergola that flanks the **Victorian Knot Garden**. Here also is a picturesque collection of old greenhouses, neat aromatic herb gardens and botanic 'order' beds, while an orchard has recently been replanted with historic varieties of fruit trees. Just opposite is **Fulham Palace Garden Centre** (▶ 233).

BISHOP'S PARK
Bishop's Park Road SW6 (020 8748 3020). Putney Bridge tube.
Open daily dawn–dusk. London Borough of Hammersmith & Fulham.
Café, lavatories, children's playgrounds.
After visiting Fulham Palace Garden Centre, walk down Bishop's Park Road to admire the impressive allotment site to the left and the old world charm of the half-timbered tennis pavilion to the right and enter Bishop's Park at the far end. Very much the poor relation to Fulham Palace Park (see above), its most notable feature is a pretty ornamental lake that formed part of the original layout in 1893, when there was an artificial beach with sand imported from the Kent coast (now a bog standard paddling pool). The original Victorian terracotta walls and balustrading remain in parts, and there are peaceful benches for watching the ducks. The riverside promenade continues in the shade of mature London planes to ▶

THE RIVER CAFÉ
Thames Wharf, Rainville Road W6 (020 7386 4200). Hammersmith tube 10 mins. Visible from the Thames Walk.
The simple modern garden on the river side of the restaurant is perfectly in tune with the building and the style of cooking for which the River Café has become famous. A square courtyard is lined with beech trees and edged with blue engineering bricks, while a sunken bank of grass protects outdoor diners from the winds blowing in off the river. Architectural plants such as ornamental grasses, artichokes, figs and angelica form a stunning, ever-changing border – most plants are edible, including, of course, the herbs, salad greens and other vegetables growing in large raised beds and metal containers flanking the entrance path. Plenty of inspiration for the modern urban kitchen garden.

FURNIVAL GARDENS
Great West Road W6. Ravenscourt Park tube. Open daily.
London Borough of Hammersmith & Fulham.
Part of the Thames Walk leading along the banks of the river, these gardens owe much of their charm to the stunning views down to Hammersmith Bridge.

RAVENSCOURT PARK
Ravenscourt Road W6. Ravenscourt Park tube. Open daily dawn–dusk. London Borough of Hammersmith & Fulham. Café, lavatories, children's playground.
Worth a stroll or a picnic lunch after a visit to the excellent **Gingko Garden Centre** that is situated under the railway arches at the southern end (▶ 234), Ravenscourt Park is a well frequented community park providing sports grounds, children's play areas and other popular facilities within a comparatively small space. Its main attraction for gardeners is the **Old English Scented Garden** with its old-fashioned pergola laden with rambling roses, wisteria, passion flowers and jasmine, and corner rose beds. The garden was specially designed for the visually impaired, and it is a pleasant place to sit and enjoy the heady perfumes that are concentrated within the walls, which are also covered in scented climbers. Back in the main body of the park, an avenue of cherries dissects the main grassy area, and this is quite glorious in blossom-time; a sweet gum, sweet chestnut, mulberry and catalpa are among the many other fine trees that ensure some good autumn colour. Weeping willows, cedars, acers, rhododendrons and pampas grass can be found around the lake, where wildfowl enjoy their own private island. A nature conservation area on the northern boundary looks full of potential with a pond with decking jetty, layered hedging and planting for different wildlife habitats, but was sadly full of rubbish when I visited. The cream stucco villas in **Ravenscourt Gardens** (on the west side) have some pretty front gardens.

LONDON WETLANDS CENTRE
Queen Elizabeth Walk SW13 (020 8409 4400). Barnes rail or Hammersmith tube plus 253 bus. Open daily 9.30am–5pm. Admission (adults) £6.75.
Barnes Wildfowl and Wetlands Trust.
An extremely urban and stylish nature reserve which is unlike any other open space in London. Covering 105 acres on the site of four disused Victorian reservoirs, the site now boasts a 25-acre lake where you can watch 130 species of ducks, geese, gulls, waders and other birds (some quite rare, particularly in the city) against an unlikely distant backdrop of

modern office blocks and Fulham Football Stadium. The London Wetlands Centre was opened in 2000, and bears witness to the variety of designers involved in all aspects from the broader landscape layout to the information signs and interactive computer screens that punctuate the network of themed walks. The Waterlife section explores the natural marshland habitat with a fritillary meadow and an area explaining how marshlands can eventually evolve into oak woodland, while World Wetlands comprises an ambitious series of miniature habitats created to imitate wildlife conditions from all over the globe from Iceland to New Zealand. The planting may look wonderfully natural, but has to be carefully managed to prevent the entire area from reverting to a watery jungle, with the large expanses of water closing over. Three contemporary garden design teams have created modern wildlife gardens here – eschewing lawns and pesticides in favour of sustainable, non-toxic ingredients, while incorporating the best of modern design. Isabelle van Groeningen and Gabriella Pape of Land Art have created a spiralling path made from shards of slate that glow purple under the open skies and contrast with the bleached miscanthus grasses and massed perennials that surround it, while Cleve West and Johnny Woodford are responsible for a water-preservation garden with square planting of drought-resistant plants, a reed-bed filter and a 'bouncing' sculpture that skims the surface of a long pool. Inspired by the ripples a pebble makes when dropped into a pond, Arne Maynard made curving concentric walls of split oak logs topped with wildflower turf that weave around an existing stream and pond and are interplanted with silver birches. As the logs slowly rot down they are colonized by hibernating amphibians, insects and fungi. Whether your main interest is wildlife, conservation or garden design, there is a lot to enjoy at this remarkable new amenity.

Western Outskirts

The sweep of west London encompassing Twickenham, Chiswick, Richmond, Kew and Wimbledon has so many great gardens that one could write a book just on these. Many, like those at Hampton Court Palace and Chiswick Park, are of great historical importance; others, like York House sculpture garden, are curiosities, while Gunnersbury Triangle and the Terrace Gardens in Richmond are open spaces much loved by locals. Some, as at Ham House and Marble Hill and Gunnersbury Park, are in the throes of ambitious restoration projects. Most of the larger gardens publish their own guide books, so the following sketchy outlines are merely to whet the appetite for further exploration.

BUSHY PARK

Hampton Court Road TW12 (020 8979 1586). Hampton Wick or Teddington
rail. Open daily. Vehicular access 6.30am–7pm, pedestrians 5am–10.30pm
(later opening during culls in autumn, check for details). Royal Parks Agency.

I still remember the thrill of passing deer around the fountain in the early morning mist as I pootled through this park on a scooter *en route* to work in Teddington many years ago. The wide mile-long avenue of horse chestnut trees that flanks the road is ravishing when in flower in May, and the deer strip the undersides of the branches to a uniform height, making for wonderful shadows on the bright green grass below. What the drive-through visitor doesn't see, however, are the beautiful **Waterhouse Woodland Gardens** in the western reaches of the 1,100-acre estate – a romantic glade enclosed by trees, with some unusual specimens such as Persian ironwoods and dawn redwoods, rhododendrons, camellias and other flowering shrubs.

MARBLE HILL PARK

Richmond Road TW1 (020 8892 5115). St Margarets or Twickenham rail.
Open daily 7.30am–dusk (house closed Mon/Tues). English Heritage.
Café (seasonal).

Marble Hill House, a perfectly compact Palladian mansion on the banks of the Thames, was built by Lady Henrietta Howard (later Countess of Suffolk) in the 1720s. The gardens, laid out by her neighbour Alexander

Pope (whose famous grotto, 'finished with shells interspersed with pieces of looking glass in angular forms' still just about exists in the grounds of a convent school) and Charles Bridgeman, landscaper to the King, are currently undergoing restoration by English Heritage. Excavation has revealed one of the two grottoes known to have been constructed here – the extant one affords a wonderful view (particularly in winter) across the river to Richmond Hill. There is also an ice house (a throwback to the eighteenth century, when ice had to be kept wrapped in straw in as cold a place as possible), some wonderful avenues of stately horse chestnut and lime trees, and a majestic black walnut tree that survives from Lady Henrietta's time. Until the restoration is complete, however, the grounds continue to be largely taken up by sports pitches and are a popular venue for music concerts in summer. Afterwards, take the frequent ferry service to Ham House (▶ 225) over the water or combine with a specially arranged visit to Strawberry Hill.

STRAWBERRY HILL
TW1. Strawberry Hill rail. Open for groups by appointment only from
Easter to October on Sunday afternoons – ring 020 8892 0051 for details.
St Mary's College.
It would be well worth rounding up a group of aesthetes and garden-lovers to visit Horace Walpole's 'little Gothick castle' and Grade II* listed garden.

YORK HOUSE
Champions Wharf Gate TW9. Richmond tube. Open daily 8am–dusk.
London Borough of Richmond-upon-Thames.
This extraordinary and unlikely garden on the banks of the Thames is remarkably under-visited, and well worth exploring. A contemporary **Sculpture Garden** greets visitors on arrival, so that the Italianate **Water Garden**, with its massive fountain and marble nymph sculptures, comes as a complete contrast. It is the creation of a former owner, an Indian merchant prince called Sir Ratan Tata, who bought the late-seventeenth-century house in 1906. Water lilies bloom in the pool below in summer, and the garden is surrounded by yews and laurels and overhung by mature willows. Victorian-style gardens with mixed shrub and herbaceous borders lie nearer the house, where a sunken lawn is the venue for performances of Shakespeare in summer. The little footbridge overlooks a tidy rock garden (not open to the public) with a lily pond, bamboos, palms, flag irises and ferns.

ORLEANS HOUSE GALLERY GARDEN
Riverside TW1 (020 8892 0221). St Margarets or Twickenham rail. Open
Mon–Sat 7.30am–dusk, Sun and Bank Holidays 9am–dusk. London Borough
of Richmond upon Thames.
All that remains of Orleans House is two wings and the elegant eighteenth-century Octagon Room, which have been converted into a gallery. An attractive woodland garden surrounds the building, and the large catalpa tree and views out over the Thames mean that a visit here (particularly for a private view) brings art and nature together in an extremely pleasant experience.

HAMPTON COURT PALACE

KT8 (020 8781 9500). Hampton Court rail. Gardens open 7am–dusk.
Admission to grounds free except charges for Maze, Privy Garden, Great
Fountain Garden, South Gardens and Great Vine (which close at 5.30pm
BST, 4.30pm in winter). Historic Royal Palaces Agency. Restaurant,
lavatories, no children's playground, but child-friendly.

Another of the capital's gardens that is an absolute must for visitors. Leave
as much time for the 66-acre gardens as for the interior of the Palace,
especially on a fine day in spring or summer when the many different areas
will be at their sparkling best. One of the main attractions, which can be
glimpsed from the riverbank through the splendid gilded Tijou Screen, is
the **Privy Garden**, recently restored to its William and Mary splendour with
elaborate parterres, topiary and exquisite spring and summer planting
schemes. Its layout, as intricate as a piece of embroidery, can be admired
from above from the splendid hornbeam allée, also recently restored, just to
one side. Other popular attractions are the famous **Maze** (by no means as
straightforward as it looks), a pretty walled rose garden and, to the east of
the Palace, the longest herbaceous border in the country and the fan-
shaped **Great Fountain Garden** with its radiating paths and brightly
planted flowerbeds between lime allées, huge yew cones and neatly
trimmed hollies. Less frequented but none the less lovely is the series of
sunken gardens on the south front, which are packed with colourful plants
in summer, and the exotic plantings in front of the Orangery. The ancient
vine in the glasshouse near by was planted by 'Capability' Brown in 1768
and yields an average of 500–700 bunches of grapes every year. There are
also some splendid herbaceous borders in the **Tiltyard Gardens** (near the
café) that are at their peak in July, and some gorgeous woodland paths *en
route* to the Maze. Easiest to miss are the **Twentieth-Century Gardens**, on
the edge of the garden and **Home Park**, where a mix of wilder planting and
contemporary design holds sway. Hornbeam topiary hedges with cut out
'windows' enclose hidden gardens, specimen trees and ornamental grasses,
and there is a lovely trellised herb garden with carpets of thyme. This is a
great spot for a picnic. In early July each year, the lawns flanking the Grand
Canal and a large chunk of Home Park (currently under restoration) are
taken over by the **Hampton Court Palace Flower Show** (▶ 260).

GUNNERSBURY PARK

Popes Lane W3 (020 8992 1612). Acton Town tube. Open daily 8am–dusk.
London Boroughs of Hounslow & Ealing. Café, lavatories, picnic areas,
children's playground.

More than 186 acres of old parkland, thought to have been laid out by William Kent and currently under restoration with the help of the Friends of Gunnersbury. Kent is thought to have designed the circular pond and elegant classical temple that stands reflected in the water; a formal rose garden is just near by. There was once another pond on the lower slopes beside the orangery, where rolling lawns are planted with beautiful and rare trees including a fern-leafed beech (*Fagus sylvatica* var. *heterophylla* 'Aspleniifolia'), catalpas, a tulip tree, gingko and metasequoia. Another lake, now hidden in the woods and popular with anglers, was originally a clay pit and the folly on the banks has been converted from a former kiln. The estate only became a public park in the 1920s, when it was purchased by the local authority from the Rothschild family – the two neo-classical mansions at the top of the lawns at the north-east corner of the park that were once the main residence now contain a museum, Victorian kitchens and an arts centre. A large part of the former gardens is now a sports centre and children's playground. Information boards explain the original layout, its alteration over the centuries, and the programme of restoration, including the rebuilding of the eighteenth-century bathhouse and a former Japanese garden created in 1901.

GUNNERSBURY TRIANGLE NATURE RESERVE

Bollo Lane W4 (020 8747 3881). Chiswick Park tube. Open Apr–Sept Tues–Sun, winter Tues, Fri and Sun (telephone for details). London Wildlife Trust.

A hidden 6-acre interlude sandwiched between three railway lines and rescued from redevelopment in 1981. A nature trail leads through birch and willow woodland, past a pond and marshland as well as wet woodland to an open meadow that is carpeted with wildflowers in summer. Bluebells, cow parsley, geraniums and anemones abound, and there are flag irises and reeds around the pond. Seats provide an opportunity to rest and enjoy the sight of nearly fifty bird species and many butterflies. Train noise can be a problem, but is offset by birdsong on summer days.

CHISWICK HOUSE GARDEN

Burlington Lane W4 (020 8995 0508). Turnham Green tube 15 mins, Chiswick rail 10 mins. Gardens open daily dawn–dusk. London Borough of Hounslow/English Heritage. Café (seasonal), lavatories.

A piece of Palladian Italy marooned in suburban Chiswick, this perfect Renaissance house (remodelled in 1725 after Palladio's Villa Rotonda) is surrounded by handsome eighteenth-century gardens with a lake, beautiful statuary, fine bridges and monuments (including a pagan temple) and magnificent trees. Its creator Lord Burlington employed both Alexander Pope and Charles Bridgeman in the layout, but by far the greatest part was played by William Kent, whose concept of a classical Arcadia is divided by radiating paths and breathtaking vistas, and dotted with statues purloined from Hadrian's Villa in Italy. Kent's long serpentine lake was intended to end in a cascade that never worked but which has recently been activated by English Heritage with the aid of excavation work and original archives. In the nineteenth-century Italian garden a conservatory designed by Joseph Paxton to house the famous camellia collection, which was begun by the 8th Duke, is still spectacular from March to May; the massed bedding displays in front of it are renewed from March through till early autumn. Banks of rhododendrons surrounding the lawn burst into gaudy bloom around May, while the many majestic trees can usually be relied on for a wonderful display of autumn colour. Though the garden is at its most idyllic in summer, don't rule out a visit in the depths of winter, when the villa and its landscape loom atmospherically out of the mist.

CHISWICK MALL
W4. Turnham Green or Stamford Brook tube. Accessible daily.
This must be one of the most glorious places to live in London. A pleasant walk along the riverbank passes a number of impressive villas, many of which habitually open their gardens through the NGS in April and June (▶ 263). The houses, dating back to the seventeenth century or earlier, are interesting at any time, though many have newer façades, and some have front gardens worth discreetly spying into.

ROYAL BOTANIC GARDENS, KEW
Kew Green, TW9 (020 8332 5655/www.kew.org). Kew Gardens tube or Kew Bridge rail. Open daily 9.30am–dusk (glass houses and galleries close earlier). Closed 24–25 Dec. Admission £5, concessions £3.30/£2.50, family ticket £13. The Trustees of the Royal Botanic Gardens, Kew. Guided tours daily from Victoria Gate at 11am and 2pm. Cafés, gift shop, lavatories.
How to describe and explore a London institution that is deemed the greatest botanic garden in the world and is (since 2003) a World Heritage Site? If you live within reasonable striking distance of Kew, the best way to appreciate it is to treat yourself to a season ticket and keep coming back at different times of the year. It is impossible to take in all the delights of its 300 acres and 70,000 different plants in a single visit, and the joy of a

season ticket means that, like dropping in to the National Gallery to contemplate just one painting, you can visit without the pressure of trying to pack too much in. Just an hour walking around the steamy glass houses in January is enough to cure the winter blues. Having said that, a one-day tour of the gardens can provide an excellent introduction, and there are two conducted tours daily (see above). If you prefer to explore at your own pace, a circular walk starting at the Main Gate can take in the newly

restored Kew Palace and **Queen's Garden**, the **Azalea Garden**, **Rhododendron Dell**, **Bamboo Garden**, **Lake** and ha-ha before progressing on to the wilder areas around Queen Charlotte's Cottage and the **Redwood Glade**, the **Japanese Garden** and the famous **Pagoda**. From here it is a short stroll through the **Heather Garden** and along the path parallel to Kew Road to the Decimus Burton **Temperate House** (with plants from around the world arranged geographically) and on to the famous Victorian **Palm House** and smaller **Waterlily House**, where the spectacular pond and bedding displays in front are not to be missed. The **Woodland Garden** and **Rock Garden** are also worth exploring on your way to the elegant modern **Princess of Wales Conservatory**, with its computer-controlled microclimates and excellent succulent displays – and don't forget the **Student Beds**, hidden away behind the laboratory block on your way out – little allotment-type plots in which the year's intake of horticultural students experiment in style. Annual displays and events throughout the year (such as the Orchid Festival in February and Autumn Cornucopia) are advertised on the information line.

RICHMOND PARK AND ISABELLA PLANTATION
TW10 (020 8948 3209). Richmond tube/rail. Open daily 7am–dusk in summer, 7-30am–half an hour before dusk in winter. Royal Parks Agency. Café, lavatories.

At 2,500 acres, this is the largest park in London, and its ancient oaks and antlered stags seem to keep it in perpetual Tudor mode – it is almost offensive to see modern cars passing through its wild expanses. Though there are wonderful views down the river to Windsor Castle and inland to the city of London itself, the horticultural hot spots are few and far between. The café at Pembroke Lodge, perched high above the river, affords some of the finest views and is also surrounded by lawns, terraced rose beds and bedding displays, but the real attraction is the **Isabella Plantation**. This steep wooded garden of nearly 42 acres, found on the Kingston Hill side of the park (enter via Broomfield Hill Gate), was enclosed in 1831 and is home to many fine old oaks and beeches, more showy camellias, magnolias, witchhazels and spindles and – of course – the famous rhododendron and azalea collection. From April to June these create a brilliant display which tempts thousands of visitors down the hill from the rest of the park. But the Plantation is attractive at other times of the year, too, with flag iris, candelabra primulas and other waterside plants flowering on the banks of the stream in spring, followed by Japanese iris, day lilies and spires of foxgloves in the shade. Strong autumn colour is provided by the many Japanese maples, while the earliest rhododendron, 'Christmas Cheer', is usually in bloom by the New Year.

HAM HOUSE

TW10 (020 8940 1950). Richmond tube/train. Gardens open Sat–Wed 11am–dusk (house open Apr–Oct only, Sat–Wed). Admission to grounds £2. National Trust. Café and shop during house opening hours only. Lavatories. Guide dogs only.

A wonderful example of seventeenth-century formal gardening which may give you inspiration for something at home – the clipped balls of santolina and lavender set among parterres of box and edged with yew look smart and contemporary while being obviously in keeping with the house's glorious Jacobean façade. On the raised south terrace, historic pots and planting are backed by pomegranate trees, and the grass plats (a simple rectangular grid of lawns) lie beyond. The National Trust is in its final stage of restoring the gardens to their original 1670s appearance, and work on the **Wilderness** is recreating one of the original highlights. Don't expect wild nature: this is a seventeenth-century version of wilderness, with hornbeam hedges and radiating paths creating private garden 'rooms' containing naturalistic plantings of spring bulbs and summer flowers, replicas of seventeenth-century seats and statues. The walled kitchen garden is planted with period herbs, fruit and vegetables, and the orangery (now home to a café) is the earliest surviving one in the UK. A frequent ferry service links Ham House with **Marble Hill House** and its gardens (▶ 218) across the river. And just down the road, don't miss the chance to visit the **Palm Centre** (▶ 236) and the newly revamped **Petersham Nurseries** (▶ 237).

TERRACE GARDENS, RICHMOND

Petersham Road TW10. Richmond tube/rail. Open Mon–Sat 7.30am–dusk, Sun and Bank Holidays 9am–dusk. London Borough of Richmond-upon-Thames. Lavatories in Riverside Park.

Well kept and much-loved terraced gardens rising steeply from Petersham Road up to Richmond Hill. The formal areas have lawns and a fine display of seasonal bedding, while the surrounding woodland gardens have shade-loving shrubs and herbaceous plants beneath the trees. Amelanchier, prunus and spiraea are attractive in the spring, and the autumn colour tends to be good. A Coade stone statue of a river god faces the Petersham Road entrance, while an underground passage comes out in a flinty grotto overlooking the Thames. A large rustic summerhouse adds to the eccentric attractions and a conservatory (not often open) is packed with tender ornamental plants.

CANNIZARO PARK
Cannizaro Road SW19 (020 8946 7349). Wimbledon tube/rail 10 mins.
Open Mon–Fri 8am–dusk; Sat, Sun and Bank Holidays 9am–dusk.
London Borough of Merton. Lavatories, picnic area, café.
In contrast to the wilds of Wimbledon Common next door, Cannizaro Park has highly manicured gardens that are packed with horticultural treats at any time of year. A grand entrance flanked by neat and colourful flowerbeds leads to the elegant house, which now houses a conference centre and café. From here, lawns sweep down towards an impressive variety of trees, including unusual Chilean firebush, sassafras, cork oak, loquat, mulberry and pomegranate, and a lovely laburnum walk. Snowdrops and crocuses are in bloom at the very start of the year, and a daffodil walk is worth the trip in April, when the azalea dell will be sparking into its annual blaze of colour. The rose garden and an abundance of summer bedding follow on until the autumn colour takes up the baton. The spring bulbs and summer bedding schemes in the sunken garden and walled garden beside the house are usually well thought out and cleverly colour-schemed. There are performances for children by the Polka Theatre in the Italian Garden, while Wimbledon Art College stages a sculpture show each year.

SYON HOUSE AND PARK
TW8 (020 8560 0881). Kew Bridge or Gunnersbury rail and 237 or 276
bus. Open daily 10.30am–5.30pm/dusk. Closed 25–26 Dec. The Duke of
Northumberland. Café, lavatories.
One of the oldest landscape gardens in the country, this 55-acre park, modelled by 'Capability' Brown, shows British gardening on a grand scale. A walk around the long lake and its surrounds will take in some of the 200 fine tree species (including ancient oaks, swamp cypresses and a huge weeping Caucasian wingnut), splendid avenues, water meadows, a wilderness garden and a rose garden that has recently been replanted with lovely old roses. The sublime domed conservatory near the house is filled with scented flowers, succulents, vines and palms, with a fern-covered waterfall. One of the glories of Syon is the view from the ha-ha across water meadows towards the Thames and the palm house at Kew. A continuing restoration programme is working to improve these views and

also includes work in the woodland garden and a new gravel garden with grasses and perennials. While you are here, you might as well visit the adjoining garden centre (▶ 240) and have unusual butterflies perch on your person in the rather wonderful Butterfly World.

OSTERLEY PARK

TW7 (01494 755566). Osterley tube 10 mins. Open daily dawn–dusk. The National Trust. Café and shop (seasonal), lavatories.

Nearby Osterley Park is much larger, with 650 acres of Regency pleasure grounds and serpentine lakes surrounding the neo-classical Robert Adam villa. A long walk along the west side of the Garden Lake and through the West Woods will take in many of the ancient trees (including the spectacular cedars of Lebanon), the Temple of Pan and elegant semi-circular Garden House (1780) before stopping for refreshment in the stable tea rooms. The arboretum and pinetum, Jubilee Avenue, Middle Lake and Chinese Pavilion can then be explored on the outward journey.

Part Three

DIRECTORY

MARKETS

COLUMBIA ROAD

Between Gosset Street and the Royal Oak pub E2. Shoreditch tube. Sun 8am–2pm.
It's worth setting the alarm clock early for a trip to Columbia Road flower market – especially in summer, when the street and its surrounds can be thronged with crowds by 9.30am. The market hits its peak at around midday, when the central street becomes a moving forest of yuccas, palms and trays of pansies and pelargoniums held high above their new owners' heads. By one or two the whole place is winding down, and this is when the best bargains are to be had, if you can stick it out that long. If you're after cheap and cheerful bedding plants, or trays of pelargoniums in bright colours, head up to the Gosset Street end, where bulk buys are sold off at ever-decreasing prices, depending on demand. The main drag is also a good source for shrubs and herbaceous plants, flower bulbs (in season), palms and indoor plants and cheap potted herbs (good if you're starting a herb garden). And of course there are the flower stalls, where huge bunches of glorious (and often unusual) blooms can be picked up for a fraction of what you'd pay at a central London florist (the only trouble being that you'll be tempted by so many you'll spend twice as much anyway). The best one is about half way down the market, outside **Christian Christopher's Rare Plants** (07958 299914), which is where the gardening *cognoscenti* go for less run-of-the-mill fare. There are two entrances – at 61 Columbia Road and tucked away in The Courtyard, off Ezra

Street; plants are all meticulously identified with hand-written labels, and advice is freely and patiently given. **S&B Evans** (also in The Courtyard) is a great source for pots, as is **Red Mud Hut** (at 92 Columbia Road) for more unusual containers. A number of other pot shops and garden accessories stores are to be found on Shipton Street and Ravenscroft Street, and the artists' studios in the area are also often open for all sorts of innovative bargains.

The impromptu, itinerant nature of Columbia Road on a Sunday makes it difficult to compile a definitive list of all that's on offer – but that is also a major part of its charm, so the best thing to do is head off and explore, arming yourself with one of the custom-made nylon plant carriers if you're in serious buying mode, and stopping for frequent rests, coffee and bagels at the many great little cafés in the area (Green Door on Ropley Street and Jones Dairy Café on Ezra Street are my favourites, and you can pick up fresh-baked bread and pastries at the stall near by). Remember that Columbia Road is not just a summer thing: the market continues through autumn and winter, when it is a lot less crowded, and makes a great place to do some alternative Christmas shopping. Behind the plant and flower stalls on Columbia Road a series of colourful shop fronts announce a great range of small design businesses (big players such as Ralph Lauren and Terence Conran regularly send buyers to the area to scout for talent). Check out Pot Luck at No. 82 for modern china, Angela Flanders at

No. 96 for prettily bottled scents, Fred Bare at No. 118 for great hats, Wild, Wild, Wild at No. 120 for funky presents and Idonia Van Der Bijl at No. 122 for cute gadgets and quirky toys. Open House at No. 152 has some stylish furniture and accessories for inside and outside the house.

Back on the gardening trail, the shops and stalls at the Hackney Road end have an inspiring mixture of new and old junky and reconditioned garden pots and furniture piled up in the street and crammed into tiny courtyard gardens behind. If you've still got the energy, head for **Brick Lane** and **Spitalfields Markets** (where the odd eccentric container or piece of antique garden furniture may be picked up for a song), stopping at Brick Lane Beigel Bake for the cheapest and best bagels in town and **Labour and Wait** at 18 Cheshire Street (▶ 245) for great gardening tools and down-to-earth sundries. **Plaster Paraphernalia** at 3 Fournier Street (ring 020 7375 2757 for erratic opening hours) does casts of antique heads and architectural fragments that could be of use in the right kind of garden, while Story at 4 Wilkes Street (open daily 3–7pm, ring 020 7377 0313 to check) is another real find in this area – a tall Huguenot house crammed with an eccentric, ever-changing array of finds for house and home, mostly for sale.

NEW COVENT GARDEN
FLOWER MARKET
Nine Elms Lane SW8. Vauxhall tube.
Open Mon–Sat 5am–10am. £3 entrance
for private cars.
Another early morning start will take you to the capital's one and only

wholesale flower market and one of its real institutions. Part of the fun, on entering the huge aircraft hangar-like space, is spotting some of London's top florists haggling for the best roses and eavesdropping on the warm witty banter of the stall holders. Have a good stroll around to see what's what before buying (remembering the gate number you came in through is a good way to keep your bearings). Cut flowers are the main draw, of course, and the best selections (in my opinion) are to be found at **John Austin** and **Baker and Duguid**. A friend and I bought all the flowers for my wedding there at a fraction of the price I would have paid elsewhere. The market is also a great place to pick up horticultural bargains – a couple of stalls sell large potted orchids for as little as £15 and it's easy to find cheap trays of seasonal bulbs such as hyacinths in winter and stargazer lilies in summer; just remember that 17.5 per cent VAT will be added to all your purchases here. **Quality Plants** is an excellent source of smart clipped evergreen trees and topiary bushes for very competitive prices – I've bought 5-foot bay pyramids for as little as £30 and there are small fruiting orange trees, 10-foot fir trees trimmed into spirals and fragrant jasmines trained up 8-foot obelisks. Other unusual bargains can be found in the sundries shops around the periphery of the market, such as **Something Special** and **C Best** – chunky glass bowls and containers for growing 'Paper White' narcissi bulbs on pebbles, hyacinth forcing jars, all manner of pots and vases, candles for table decorations and bundles of raffia and bright ribbons. The market is a great place to come if you are planning a big party and want to deck the place out in style. I love it, too, in the weeks leading up to Christmas, when potted Christmas trees and bunches of mistletoe can be had for a song, and the foliage merchants around the outside of the market have huge bundles of holly and ivy and sprayed silver and

sparkling twigs. Inside, trays of bulbs or other plants can be paired with pretty containers and tied up with ribbon to create cheap, cheerful and totally unique presents. I love arriving in the dark, when the bustling bright interior is instantly cheering, and leaving an hour or two later, the car crammed with goodies, just as the sun is coming up.

NURSERIES AND GARDEN CENTRES

ADRIAN HALL HAMPSTEAD GARDEN CENTRE
161–163 Iverson Road NW6 (020 7328 3208). Kilburn or West Hampstead tube. Open Mon–Sat 10am–6pm, Sun 11am–5pm.
Popular local garden centre which has embraced the urban culture with some good display ideas – a Mediterranean area with citrus trees, olives, large unusual shrubs and out-of-the-ordinary trees such as mimosas, while a contemporary section has bold topiary shapes and modern water features. The garden furniture on sale is mostly on the contemporary side, though some equally fashionable traditional wirework pieces sit well alongside.

ALEXANDRA PALACE GARDEN CENTRE
Alexandra Palace Way N22 (020 8444 2555/ www.capitalgardens.co.uk). Wood Green tube/Alexandra Palace rail/W3 bus. Open Mon–Sat 9am–6pm, Sun 10.30am–4.30pm.
One of London's largest garden centres, but with a more personal service and thoughtful selection of plants than its size might imply. Run by Capital

Gardens, who pride themselves on forging links with good British nurseries, it has a better selection of plants than the average garden centre, including an impressive number of unusual clematis. The indoor section of tools, accessories and other gardening sundries is massive, and includes houseplants and gardening-themed gifts. Prices are reasonable and there are often special offers. An on-site gallery offers art and craft workshops and a framing service.

CAMDEN GARDEN CENTRE
2 Barker Drive NW1 (020 7387 7080/www.camdengardencentre.co.uk). Camden Town tube. Open summer Mon, Tues, Fri, Sat 9am–5.30pm, Wed, Thurs 9am–7pm, Sun 11am–4pm; winter Mon–Sat 9am–5pm, Sun 11am–4pm.
Much improved in recent years, this is a very serviceable garden centre for north Londoners, with a large yard set out according to types of plant, conditions, etc. Trees are well represented, with a good range in impressive sizes including olives, acers and eucalyptus; climbers are also well stocked, with many varieties of clematis in particular. Hard landscape supplies include trellis,

paving, pots and pond-making materials. In summer there is a good display of bedding plants outside at reasonable prices. The equally spacious and well-ordered inside section has a great display of cactus (some really large ones for more than £100), other succulents and indoor plants, alongside the usual tools, pesticides, seeds, books and accessories. Garden DIY is particularly well catered for here. A notice board on the way out is packed with useful contacts.

CENTRE FOR
WILDLIFE GARDENING
28 Marsden Road, Peckham SE15 (020 7252 9186). East Dulwich rail. Open Tues, Wed, Thurs, Sun 10.30am– 4.30pm (closed for three weeks over Christmas, ring for details.) Picnic area, lavatories.
Small nursery selling wildflowers, herbs, indigenous trees and other plants for creating wildlife habitats, attached to the information centre and attractive wildlife garden (▶ 205).

THE CHELSEA GARDENER
125 Sydney Street, Chelsea SW3 (020 7352 5656/www.chelseagardener.com). Sloane Square or South Kensington tube. Open Mon–Fri 10am–6pm, Sat 9am–6pm, Sun 12–6pm.
One of the capital's ritziest garden centres, this is the place to come if you need some smart window boxes to keep you up with the Joneses – or Fforbes-Fitzjoneses – next door. The site is large for central London, with an attractively designed yard full of well-ordered herbaceous plants, climbers, shrubs and small trees suitable for London gardens. The

undercover section is also spacious, with all the indoor plants, stylish tools and accessories and a great new book section – plus a gorgeous mirrored conservatory full of orchids, palms, citrus trees, succulents and bonsai. Topiary and (tasteful) bedding plants are well represented here, together with a wide range of elegant pots and planters, some great modern garden furniture, and not-too-naff statuary and water features. There is a concession on **R. K. Alliston** goods (▶ 242) in the main shop and, just next door, **Le Prince Jardinier** (▶ 245) has tools, tool belts, clothes and accessories that are almost *too* good for gardening in. Prices are inevitably a little higher than average. Ask about the excellent in-house design and maintenance service.

CLIFTON NURSERIES
5A Clifton Villas, Little Venice W9 (020 7289 6851/www. clifton.co.uk). Warwick Avenue tube. Open Mon–Sat 8.30am–6pm (winter till 5.30pm), Wed 8.30am–8pm, Sun 10.30am–4.30pm.
The crème de la crème of London garden centres, and a good starting point (or finishing point, if you are buying plants) for a walking tour of the canalside gardens of Little Venice (▶ 140). The narrow entrance between two imposing stucco villas is lined with olive trees and large shrubs in elegant planters – a taste of what is to follow. This is the place to come when money is no object: huge zinc containers planted with acanthus, silvery astelias or swishing grasses with a mulch of black pebbles are priced at £245, while some of the cacti near the £1000 mark. 'Large plants for an instant garden: why

wait years for your plants to grow?' urges a sign, and some of the climbers and flowering shrubs are particularly well established. But Clifton is full of inspiration for gardeners of every budget, favouring 'good taste' colour schemes rather than screaming bright colours. Plants are arranged in stripes of sultry colour on raised brick beds, and even their hanging baskets are tasteful. A 'conservatory' area is crammed with indoor plants and accessories, while a fernery contains dicksonias as well as smaller tender ferns. An excellent range of pots, furniture and lighting includes traditional and state-of-the-art modern styles, while there is also a good replicas service, creating copies of antiques. Staff are knowledgeable and friendly; there's an in-house design and maintenance service and, for the DIY approach, helpful free information sheets on many aspects of urban gardening, from lawns to containers.

CROXTED ROAD GARDEN CENTRE
Croxted Road, Herne Hill SE24 (020 8674 4366). Herne Hill rail. Usually open Wed–Sun 9.30am–6pm, daily May and June. Best to ring first.
One of south London's little secrets: a family business established more than thirty years ago and now run by friendly and knowledgeable brothers Kevin and Steve Abbotts. You can't miss it as you come down Croxted Road, as the tiny site spills out on to the pavement and a good way down the street. Stock caters for trendy urban gardeners and old-fashioned allotmenteers alike – everything from bamboos and tree ferns to herbaceous and bedding plants and

(unusual for a garden centre) an impressive range of vegetable seedlings in season, all grown to order. Also a good selection of sundries and accessories: if you can't see what you want, ask – chances are it will be hidden away somewhere, or can be ordered in.

DULWICH GARDEN CENTRE
20–22 Grove Vale SE22 (020 8299 1089/ www.dulwichgardencentre.co.uk). East Dulwich rail. Open Mon–Sat 9am–5.30pm, Sun 10am–3pm.
A less personal service than at Croxted Road just a couple of miles away, but larger, and with a good stock of plants displayed supermarket style in the open yard out back. A good place to find mature climbers such as wisteria and clematis in good condition, and some of the more unusual options for window boxes and summer bedding. The shop is well stocked with supplies and sundries, and worth a good browse. Gardeners relying on vicious chemicals are particularly well catered for – but there is usually a good supply of bagged-up organic horse manure. You might also find some stylish birdfeeders, lanterns and outdoor candles that are a little out of the ordinary.

FULHAM PALACE GARDEN CENTRE
Bishop's Avenue SW6 (020 7736 2640/www.fulhamgardencentre.com). Putney Bridge tube. Open Mon–Thurs 9.30am–5.30pm, Fri, Sat 9.30am–6pm, Sun 9.30am–5pm.
All profits from this excellent urban garden centre go to Fairbridge, the charity that works with disadvantaged young people in inner

cities. The inside space is like a giant greenhouse, packed with houseplants, including some beautiful orchids, books, tools and sundries, candle lanterns and well-chosen garden-themed gifts. Outside, a good selection of plants is arranged according to type in a series of 'outdoor rooms' defined by trellis walls with roses, clematis and other climbers knitting them all together and clambering over the interconnecting arches. There is a good sense of community around this garden centre: people pop in from the allotments just down the road, or from the stucco-fronted villas in surrounding streets. Many may not be aware that the Fairbridge Garden Society (▶ 265) organizes talks and countrywide visits. Bring your own tubs or window boxes to be planted up by one of the staff (£5 per pot or tub; free service if you buy the pot here). No mail order, delivery is charged by postcode.

GINGKO GARDEN CENTRE
Ravenscourt Avenue, off King Street W6 (020 8563 7112/ www.gingkogardens.co.uk). Ravenscourt Park tube. Open Mon–Fri 9am–6pm, Sun 10am–6pm (summer late opening Thurs and Sat, 8pm). Parking is easier on the west side of Ravenscourt Park.
Tucked away on the southern boundary of Ravenscourt Park, beneath the arches of the tube line with District Line trains rumbling overhead, Gingko is a hidden treasure. The railway arches house a selection of good quality modern garden furniture, a vast range of terracotta and metal pots (check out the smart dark matt metal ones), houseplants, tools and sundries. The open part of the site is divided into trellis 'rooms' draped in

clematis, roses and other climbers, with water-loving plants grouped around a working water feature, and hostas and ferns in shady enclaves. Catering for urban nomads who haven't got time to sit and watch their gardens grow, and can afford to pay for a bit of 'instant gardening', Gingko is good for large-size shrubs and standards – the standard lavenders and wisteria are particularly impressive. There's also a good selection of trees – semi-mature figs, olive trees and magnolias and huge umbrella palms. Gingko can also design, build and maintain your garden for you; their landscape design division based in Battersea can be contacted on 020 7498 2021.

GROWING CONCERNS GARDEN CENTRE
2 Wick Lane (on corner with Cadogan Terrace) E3 (020 8985 3222/ www.growingconcerns.org). Bow Road tube and S2 bus. Open Tues–Sun 10am–6pm; 9am–dusk winter.
Community organization run by knowledgeable locals on a British Waterways site close to the canal. An impressive and expanding range of exotic plants is cultivated for sale at affordable prices, including palms, bananas, cannas, bamboos and ornamental shrubs. Worth checking out if you are into this style of gardening.

HIGHGATE GARDEN CENTRE
1 Townsend Yard N6 (020 8340 1041). Highgate or Archway tube. Open Mon–Sat 9am–6pm, Sun 9.30am–6pm.
Hidden away down a little lane behind the High Street, the steeply sloping site, surrounded by trees and overhung by weeping willows, is part of the appeal

of this excellent local garden centre. The headquarters of the chain Capital Gardens, which owns several other garden centres in the capital and prides itself on stocking more than the usual suspects, the place has a good selection of trees, shrubs and other garden plants, displayed on terraced beds as you travel down the hill. There are some stylish townie touches: topiary holly, bay, camellia and wisteria standards are all of a good size, while trailing ivies are trained around a range of modern metal arches, and a good range of (mostly glazed terracotta) pots will gladden the courtyard gardener. The sundries section, housed in a greenhouse, has all the usual supplies, along with seeds and bulbs in season and an impressive collection of healthy houseplants and orchids.

JOHN'S GARDEN CENTRE
175 Stoke Newington Church Street N16 (020 7275 9494/ www.johnsgardencentre.co.uk). Stoke Newington rail/73 bus. Open Mon–Sat 8.30am–6pm, Sun 10am–4pm (10am–5pm BST).
Great little garden centre right on the busy high street – hard to miss in summer owing to the trays of bright bedding plants stacked up high outside. Out back is a long narrow yard packed with plants: small trees, shrubs, border plants, herbs and bedding, with some climbers in impressive sizes. The small indoor section is packed with more products than you'd imagine possible in the space, and cheerful help is usually on hand. Good supply of bulbs in season.

THE KEW GARDENER
18 Station Parade TW9 (020 8948 1422) and 366 Merton Road SW18 (020 8874 9962/www.kewgardener.com). Kew Gardens tube and Southfields tube respectively. Open daily 10am–6pm (closed Jan).
The exterior of Kew Gardens station is suitably decked out with palms and hanging baskets – the pots on the pavement outside the Kew Gardener (which is almost the first shop you pass on your way to Kew Gardens) only add to the greenery. The Kew shop has an attractive back yard with gravel and sleeper paths underfoot, well-stocked with trees, shrubs and other plants, including a good selection of topiary specimens for smart urban gardens. There is also a fair amount of semi-exotic stuff – large palms, bamboos and yuccas, and some nice potted cycads inside. The shop front and interior cater for impulse buyers on their way back from Kew Gardens, with small portable potted plants, a good range of orchids in pots, and unusual presents such as 'grow your own' exotic and rainforest plant kits. The Wandsworth shop has a similar range, but concentrates on more established plants. Both shops operate a successful landscape design and maintenance business, geared to west London gardens.

NEAL'S NURSERIES
Heathfield Road SW18 (020 8874 2037/www.capitalgardens.co.uk). Open Mon–Sat 9am–6pm, Sun 10.30am–4.30pm.
Recently taken over by the chain Capital Gardens, the much-loved Neal's nursery offers one of the largest plant sales areas in London. An extensive

range of trees, specimen plants (including bamboos and olives of various sizes), herbs, climbers, alpines, herbaceous, water and marginal plants, attractively and clearly laid out. Also, a good collection of houseplants in the large traditional glass house, traditional and contemporary outdoor furniture, state-of-the-art barbecues and lighting and the usual tools, composts and other supplies. Capital also offer an in-house design and maintenance service (▸ 275) and on-line 'Ask Sage' after-care service.

NORTH ONE GARDEN CENTRE
25A Englefield Road N1 (020 7923 3553). Dalston Kingsland rail.
Open Fri–Wed 9.30am–6pm,
Thurs 9.30am–7pm.
Popular and friendly local garden centre for north Londoners, with its own café selling homemade cakes and playing classical music. The exterior area displays the usual shrubs and trees, rose bushes, perennials and lots of bedding plants in summer, and indoors there's funky garden furniture, including some great pink sun loungers, and a brilliant gift section selling everything from garden flares and scented candles to handcream and bath lotions, as well as the basic composts, seeds and slug pellets.

THE PALM CENTRE
Ham Central Nursery, Ham Street, Ham, Richmond, Surrey TW10 7HA
(020 8255 6191/ www.palmcentre.co.uk).
Richmond tube/rail then 371 bus.
Open daily 9am–5pm.
Bananas and tropical palms of all types, shapes and sizes are among the exotic delights to be found at this wonderful specialist nursery just down the road from Ham House (▸ 225). Owner Martin Gibbons is a real expert on palms and how to grow them in the London microclimate – new deliveries arrive from all corners of the world every week. Atmospheric gardens and greenhouses are part of the charm of this place. Allow more time than you would to visit a normal garden centre – and be prepared to catch the bug and come home with a tropical treasure in tow. Sculptures are half-hidden among the greenery and there are often exotic flowers to be admired, too. Since the Palm Centre was founded, its remit has widened to include bamboos and Mediterranean-type plants as well as palms. Prices range from just £1.50 for a small palm seedling to around £3000 for an ancient olive tree.

PARK FARM NURSERY
Sewardstone Road E4 (020 8529 2708).
Chingford rail then 505 bus.
Open daily Apr–Oct 9.30am–5pm,
Nov–Mar 10am–4pm (Jan/Feb weekends closes at 1pm).
Great collection of seasonal and bedding plants grown on site and housed in five greenhouses and around the gardens. Also, a very good source of houseplants. This is a small family-run business and the staff are friendly and full of knowledgeable advice.

PATIO GARDEN CENTRE
100 Tooting Bec Road SW17 (020 8672 2251). Tooting Bec tube.
Open daily 9.30am–5.30pm.
Claims to be the capital's oldest garden centre (established more than two hundred years ago), but is best known

for its great line in terracotta pots, mainly from Italy and Crete. Good range of Mediterranean-style plants, palms and ferns as well to complement the containers. All trees, including olives, have been grown outside in Tooting for at least two years so that hardiness is pretty much guaranteed.

PETERSHAM NURSERIES
Petersham Road, Petersham, Richmond TW10 7AG (020 8940 5230). Open Mon–Sun 9am–5.30pm.
This previously old-fashioned nursery down a little lane near the water meadows has recently changed hands and has been completely revamped under the expert eyes of garden designers James and Helen Dooley. As part of their plan to 'change the aesthetic of the garden centre', plastic has been banished, the glorious greenhouses have all been renovated and one of them filled with gorgeous eighteenth-century French and Indian garden antiques and unusual metal pots and planters. Plants are by no means forgotten: the Dooleys have brought in 'the best of everything' including a thousand roses, hundreds of water lilies, peonies and unusual perennials not often found in London: visiting 'guest nurseries' from around the country will also be invited to stage a display every month. A café and series of horticultural evening lectures is also planned.

PLANET GARDEN
116 Peckham Park Road SE15 6UV (07900 823374). Peckham Rye rail. Open Thurs and Fri 9am–5pm.
A unique new venture on a recently reclaimed patch of land behind the owner's house in Peckham. An impressive selection of unusual perennials, many raised from seed on the premises, of a rarity, desirability and quality that you'd normally have to travel miles outside London to find. Walk through a 120 x 80 foot back garden spilling over with old roses, violet buddleia, *Verbena bonariensis* and swishing angel hair grasses (*Stipa tenuissima*) to find the nursery, where the nursery beds are crammed with full-sized plants displayed in stunning combinations – a 'living catalogue' from which you can decide which plants to buy. Unusual vegetable seedlings are also available in season. The owner, photographer Jilly Sharpe, is on hand to offer expert planting advice (and fresh mint tea), and all plants have attractive eye-level laminated labels bearing photographs and cultivation tips. Well worth a trip, even if you're one of those pathetic north Londoners who panic south of the river.

RASSELL'S GARDEN CENTRE
80 Earls Court Road W8 6EQ (020 7937 0481). Earls Court or High Street Kensington tube. Open Mon–Wed, Fri, Sat 9am–5.30pm, Thurs 9am–6.30pm; additionally (Apr–Jun, mid-Oct–Dec only) Sun 11am–5.30pm.
Rassell's exterior is gloriously old-fashioned, and must have changed very little since it was founded by the Rassell family in 1904. An old painted sign declares all the 'Jobs to do this Month', while a roadside display of seasonal plants and terracotta pots tempts you in off the street. Rassell's is an enchanting and inspiring place, hugged in on three sides by smart

residential streets and towered over by enormous trees. Good-quality plants are neatly displayed – many of the larger trees, shrubs and roses have detailed handwritten labels full of useful advice – but the overriding atmosphere is one of picturesque ramshackle charm, with a cascade of trailing fuchsias and pelargoniums spilling down from an upstairs balcony, and a grapevine ramping over the outdoor sales area. You're spoiled for choice with bedding and herbaceous plants in summer; in autumn look out for some unusual spring bulbs – fritillaries, species tulips and narcissi are all sold loose, like a horticultural 'pick 'n' mix', rather than in pre-packed bags. Garden design, maintenance and installation of irrigation systems is also on offer; deliveries are free when you spend £25 or more (normal delivery charges are based on postcode). Staff are extremely helpful – the original Miss Rassell was a staunch socialist of the old school, and introduced one of the country's earliest profit-sharing schemes. Neighbouring Pembroke Square and Pembroke Villas have some pretty front gardens to spy into.

SECRET GARDEN
Coxwell Road (off Westow Street) SE19 (020 8771 8200). Crystal Palace or Gipsy Hill rail. Open Mon–Sat 9am–6pm, Sun 10am–5pm (slightly shorter hours in winter).
Closed over Christmas.
A true secret, hidden away in Gipsy Hill, a corner of the capital that even hardened south Londoners may not know. It's well worth a visit, particularly if you are exploring nearby Crystal Palace Park (▶ 200)

or Dulwich Upper Wood Nature Park (▶ 201). Approach along Westow Street from Church Road (it is one way in this direction) and follow the sign, immediately on your left, down a twisting hill where you can park in Safeway's car park if you are prepared to do some shopping there. The garden centre is a real find, attractively laid out on a sloping site, with clematis and other climbers beneath a pergola on the right and shrubs and trees on terraces below the church. Lots of unusual bedding options in summer (different lobelias, convolvulus and bacopas) and potted bulbs in the winter months. Owner Roger Cox specializes in things that are a little out of the ordinary as well as what you would find in a regular garden centre – lots of unusual hardy perennials and annual climbers. On my first visit I found three things I'd had a hard job tracking down elsewhere in London – small seedlings of *Cobaea scandens*, the rare(ish) and beautiful texensis clematis 'Etoile Rose' and good-sized daturas (brugmansias). There's also a comprehensive, neatly displayed range of composts and sundries.

SHEEN GARDEN CENTRE
181–189 Upper Richmond Road West SW14 (020 8876 3648). Open Mon–Sat 9am–6pm, Sun 10am–4pm.
Surviving sister of the now defunct Putney Garden Centre, this is a good general garden centre which (rare these days) concentrates on plants rather than other accessories. A wider than average selection of trees, shrubs, grasses, perennials and seasonal bedding – 'If we ain't got it, you don't need it' is their cheerful

motto, but staff are happy to source and order more unusual items.

SYON PARK GARDEN CENTRE

Wyevale Garden Centre, Syon Park, Brentford TW8 8JG (020 8568 0134/ www.wyevale.co.uk). Gunnersbury tube or Syon Lane rail, 235 and 237 buses. Open Mon–Sat 9am–6pm, Sun 10am–4pm.

Good all-round garden centre which is worth a visit if you are in the area or visiting the neighbouring house and gardens (▶ 226). The cactus and succulent section is particularly impressive, and there is a good range of houseplants and hanging baskets in summer. Colourful bedding is a speciality – as part of the Wyevale chain, this is not the place to come for anything rare or unusual, but everyday gardening needs are well met. The horticultural sundries section is huge, and includes everything from wellies and watering cans to every gardening chemical known to humankind.

TEMPLE FORTUNE GARDEN CENTRE

788A Finchley Road NW11 (020 8455 5363). Golders Green tube 15 mins, lots of buses. Open Mon–Sat 9am–6pm, Sun 9.30am–6pm. Closed over Christmas.

Small friendly local garden centre, owned and managed by Capital Gardens and, like their other outlets in London, well stocked with good, healthy plants. Bedding plants are the principal concern (as befits their proximity to Golders Hill Park, with its spectacular seasonal displays), and there is also a good selection of shrubs and herbaceous perennials (no trees). The indoor section features an impressive display of orchids, the usual tools and sundries, plus a small selection of garden-themed gifts and cards.

WORLD'S END NURSERIES

441–457 King's Road SW10 (020 7351 3343). Open Mon–Sat 9am–6pm, Sun 10am–5pm.

Slap bang on the King's Road (near the World's End pub at the western end), this small garden centre is well equipped for London gardening, with impressive ranks of smart topiaried box, bay and holly near the front entrance and a good range of trees and shrubs suited to small, shady gardens. The site is attractive, dominated by a huge weeping willow and a curious tower on a folly-like shed. There are spring bulbs and summer bedding in season, plus a small sundries section. Local maintenance teams are available for hire.

SPECIALIST GARDEN CENTRES

CONCRETE JUNGLE BONSAI
124 South Ealing Road W5
(020 8840 7886/
www.bonsai2bonsai.co.uk).
South Ealing tube.
Open Mon, Tue, Thurs–Sat 10am–6pm,
Wed 10am–1.30pm.
A bonsai-lover's heaven, with pine, oak
and beech trees, some up to sixty-five
years old – prices range from
£17.50–£2500. Also, everything you
need to do it yourself – tools, books,
courses. There is even a tree hospital
and maintenance tips for when you're
on holiday.

EAST HAM AQUATICS
146 High Street South E6 (020 8470
3600). East Ham tube. Open Mon– Wed,
Fri–Sat 9.30am–6pm, Sun 10am–2pm.
Closed all day Thurs.
All manner of pond-making
equipment including liners, pumps
and fountains, etc., plus a good range
of aquatic plants including water
lilies. Koi carp and goldfish are the
real attraction.

GREENHOUSE GARDEN AND PLANT CENTRE AND MAIDENHEAD AQUATICS
Birchen Grove NW9. Wembley Park
tube. The Greenhouse (020 8905 9189),
Maidenhead Aquatics (020 8200 3545).
Open Mon–Sat 9am–5.30pm, Sun
10am–4.30pm.
The setting, amid the lush Welsh
Harp reservoir, is attractive, and
both operations are well run. The
Greenhouse has a good plant selection,
composts, etc. and gardening
accessories, while the attached branch
of Maidenhead Aquatics is a good
water gardening centre, with plenty of
pond and aquarium equipment and fish
of all kinds and sizes including some
giant koi.

JUNGLE FEVER
85–87 Lee High Road SE13 (020
8318 9919). Lewisham rail/DLR.
Open Tues 9.30am–7pm, Wed–Fri
9.30am–5pm, Sat 9.30am–4.30pm.
Hydroponic gardening in all its
technical glory – all you need to create
an artificial, soilless environment where
all plants, including tropical species
(and whatever else you might fancy)
grow super-fast and healthy. Many
different systems can be inspected, and
the owners can offer advice on getting
started – whatever the scale and nature
of your project.

ONE-STOP AQUARIUM AND POND COMPANY
Wyevale Garden Centre, 89 Waddon Way,
Croydon, Surrey CR0 4HY (020 8681
3132/www.onestopaquatics.co.uk).
East Croydon rail. Open Mon–Sat
9am–5.30pm, Sun 10.30–4.30pm.
You could fit in a visit to this excellent
water garden nursery alongside a trip
to Ikea (▶ 244). It sells everything you
need to make a pond or water feature
of any size – the majority of deliveries
are apparently for small-to-medium
ponds in and around London.
Particularly good source of different
types of pebbles for pond and fountain
surrounds, and stock a good range of
all types of aquatic and marginal

plants. Staff are knowledgeable and enthusiastic, so it's a good place to start if you've never made a pond or water feature before. Also mail order.

TACHBROOK TROPICALS
244 Vauxhall Bridge Road SW1 (020 7834 5179). Pimlico/Victoria tube. Open Mon–Sat 9am–7pm, Sun 12–5.30pm.
Small but enthusiastic shop specializing in aqautic plants and supplies for tropical and unusual coldwater fish. Pond-making equipment can be ordered.

WILDWOODS WATER GARDENS
Theobalds Park Road, Crews Hill, Enfield, Middlesex EN2 9BP (020 8366 0243/ www.wildwoods.co.uk). Crews Hill rail. Open daily 9am–5.30pm.
Another good general water garden supplier, with pond-making equipment, pumps and filters for all types of water features, a good range of aquatic and marginal plants, and coldwater and tropical fish.

GARDENING SUPPLIES AND ACCESSORIES

R. K. ALLISTON
173 New King's Road, London SW6 4SW (0845 1305577/ www.rkalliston.com). Parson's Green tube. Also at The Chelsea Gardener (▶ 232). Open Mon–Fri 9am–5pm, Sat 10am–6pm.
One of just a handful of London garden shops that make you wish you could buy absolutely everything, from the immaculate potted olive trees and box balls on the pavement to the old-fashioned wooden-handled tools, perfectly designed bird houses and tartan-lined wellies within. The sort of place that makes you feel you really can't do without a suede gardening apron, leather-trimmed leaf carrier and oilskin kneeler. There's also a young gardeners' range, lots of garden candles and other equipment for outdoor entertaining, some great gift sets and the inevitable post-gardening pampering supplies. Owner Harriet Scott's garden design business is also based here (▶ 273). Also mail order.

AMPHORA
340 Fulham Road SW10 (020 7376 4808). Fulham Broadway tube. Open 10am–5.30pm daily.
Two floors chock-a-block with pots of all styles, shapes and sizes from all over the world. Lots of other bits and pieces that could be used to good effect in the right sort of garden: Mexican figurines, ceramic candleholders, various busts, etc. Prices are very reasonable – usually half what is marked. (Don't ask; just be pleased you've bagged a bargain.)

THE CONRAN SHOP
The Michelin Building, 81 Fulham Road SW3 (020 7589 7401) and 55 Marylebone High Street W1 (020 7723 2223/www.conran.com). Open Mon, Tues, Fri 10am–6pm, Wed, Thurs 10am–7pm, Sat 10am–6.30pm,

Sun 12–6pm (Marylebone branch Wed 10am–6pm, Sun 11am–5pm).
The 'outdoor living' department is one of the most stylish around, and well worth checking out at different times of the year. The clever buyers will always have something unusual to surprise you, from pretty old terracotta pots to Mexican tin trays to striking ideas for lighting and eating outside. The attractive displays will give you further ideas. A good book section geared to fashion-conscious urban gardening often includes some unusual titles from America and elsewhere.

CROWTHER OF SYON LODGE
77–79 Pimlico Road SW1W 8PH (020 77308668/ www.crowthersyonlodge.com). Sloane Square tube. Open Mon–Fri 10am–6pm, Sat 11am–3pm.
Antique statuary and other outdoor ornaments for the garden of your dreams. Prices start at £1000 and climb to around £20,000 for seventeenth-century stone cherubs, antique chimneypieces and other one-off finds.

H. CROWTHER
5 Chiswick High Road W4 (020 8994 2326/www.hcrowther.com). Stamford Brook tube. Open Mon–Fri 7.30am–4.30pm.
Handmade lead garden ornaments made by this business since 1908. The look tends to be traditional: planters, statues, plaques, fountains and jardinières can be ordered from hundreds of master patterns, and there are lots in stock to look at in the simply landscaped garden of this Victorian house. Pumps and systems for fountains are also sold here.

DESIGNERS GUILD
267–271 King's Road SW3 (020 7351 5775/www.designersguild.com). Sloane Square or South Kensington tube. Open Mon–Sat 10am–6pm, Sun 12–5pm.
The tiny courtyard behind this gorgeous interiors shop is crammed with unusual metal and terracotta pots in stylish sizes and dimensions. Owner Tricia Guild is a keen gardener and her buyers are always on the lookout for new ideas and eye-catching ways to display them – the high brick walls were painted bright blue on my last visit, and banners of fabric in the DG trademark bright colours make great impromptu awnings.

GARDENS AND BEYOND
47 Highgate High Street N6 (020 8340 3409/www.gardensbeyond.com). Highgate tube. Open Mon–Wed 10am–5pm, Thurs–Sat 10am–6pm.
Chic garden shop specializing in garden-related furniture and accessories. Styles stocked tend towards the contemporary. The range of garden furniture is impressive, featuring aluminium, steel and wood; the eco-minded can take solace from tables, chairs and benches made from teak from sustainable forests. Garden sculpture, all forms of lighting and irrigation are also well represented. A small selection of plants includes urban favourites such as palms and shaped topiary, planted in elegant pots. The in-house design team can plan a makeover of your garden (initial consultation £95).

GRAHAM & GREEN
10 Elgin Crescent W11 (020 7727 4594).
Latimer Road or Holland Park tube.
Open Mon–Sat 10am–6pm,
Sun 11.30am–5.30pm.
Super-good-taste home accessories
shop, which stocks a great range of
garden furniture (traditional and
modern) in the summer months, plus
rugs, cushions and picnic sets galore.

GRAND ILLUSIONS
41 Crown Road, St Margarets,
Twickenham TW1 3EJ (020 8607 9446/
www.grandillusions.co.uk). St Margarets
rail. Open Mon–Fri 9am–6pm,
Sat 10am–5pm.
Some of the most stylish (and
sometimes quirky) garden accessories
around – great galvanized and wirework
pots, lanterns and other outdoor
lighting, and ornaments you won't be
ashamed of. Great garden furniture, too,
and an ever-changing selection of
orchids, box and other plants for inside
and out, ready-potted in interesting
containers. Also mail order.

HABITAT
Branches in Finchley Road,
Hammersmith, High Street Kensington,
King's Road and Tottenham Court Road.
Ring 0870 4115501 for details of your
nearest branch.
The buying teams at Habitat are quick
to latch on to contemporary design
trends, but not always so hot on
practicalities – so check that those
wonderful-looking pots in the window
actually have drainage holes in the
bottom before you rush to buy. Stock
changes seasonally, but spring and
summer are good times to stock up on
cheap and cheerful garden furniture,

lanterns, pots and other accessories.
Their galvanized mini-greenhouses
were a hit with urban balcony owners,
and they can usually be relied on for
some clever and stylish solutions for
containers, seating and lighting for
small spaces.

HORTUS
26 Blackheath Village SE3 (020 8297
9439/www.hortus-blackheath.co.uk).
Blackheath rail. Open Mon–Sat
9.30am–5.45pm, Sun 11am–4pm.
An ultra-chic shop for garden-lovers
that works as a shop front for owner
Joanna Herald's garden design business
(▸ 271). Tasteful pots for inside and
out, beautiful glass and stone vases,
driftwood sculptures, orchids and
succulents in stylish metal or ceramic
pots, the best-looking barbecues and
garden-inspired gifts including bath
oils and skin lotions. The yard at the
back (bamboo screens with stone and
gravel underfoot) has some fantastic
large pots, stylish carved stone
sculptures and fountains and a good
selection of small trees (including
olives), bamboos, tree ferns and border
plants as well as watering cans, hoses
and other more prosaic wares.

IKEA
Branches in Brent Park and Croydon,
ring 0845 355 1141 for details.
Sometimes I buy plants from Ikea just
to rescue them from the hideous
lightless environment to which they are
subjected – and they have usually done
me proud, probably out of gratitude.
Houseplants are the thing – in good
large sizes and at rock bottom prices –
and there's usually also a pretty good
selection of well-priced pots and items

of furniture that would serve just as well outside as in. Don't go just for plants, however. They are your reward after negotiating the car park and trooping past miles of ugly sofa beds only to find the flat-pack shelving you want is out of stock.

JUDY GREEN'S GARDEN STORE
11 Flask Walk NW3 (020 7435 3832). Hampstead tube. Open Mon–Sat 10am–6pm, Sun 11.30am–6pm.
A lovely little shop, geared to the style-conscious terrace, courtyard or balcony gardener, which is well worth a visit after a tour of Hampstead gardens. The eye-catching display on the alleyway pavement always has something attractive, from small pots of bulbs in spring to little fig and olive trees and unusual succulents in pots. Inside, there's a tempting range of gardening equipment and accessories, all on the stylish side of functional, from old restored tools and terracotta barbecues to storm lanterns, twig birdhouses and Cath Kidston tablecloths.

LABOUR AND WAIT
18 Cheshire Street E2 (020 7729 6253). Aldgate East tube. Open Fri by appointment only, Sat 1–5pm, Sun 10am–5pm.
Well worth checking out after a visit to Columbia Road flower market (▶ 229), this quaint and eclectic shop offers the sort of good, old-fashioned tools and accessories that are harder and harder to find as traditional hardware shops close down and plastic prevails. A great range of garden ware includes hefty spades and forks (a bargain at under £50), wooden rakes, French steel compost buckets and old enamel water pitchers.

LASSCO HOUSE AND GARDEN
St Michael's Church, Mark Street EC2 (020 7749 9944/www.lassco.co.uk). Open Mon–Sat 10am–5pm.
You never know what you'll find at this inner city architectural salvage centre – it could be a beautiful but rusting wrought iron gate or archway, an old spiral staircase leading nowhere, old pews to use as outdoor benches or fragments of stone columns or architrave to scatter about your garden for an air of ancient abandon. Walking round the place is enough to fire your imagination as to what you might do, particularly if you had more space – many of the items are on the large side. Smaller treasures are also to be found here, though – I've picked up piles of Victorian terracotta pots for less than you'd pay for ugly new ones, and some lovely old glass specimen jars from Kew Gardens, complete with their original, slightly browning, type-written labels.

LE PRINCE JARDINIER
at The Chelsea Gardener, 125 Sydney Street, Chelsea SW3 (020 7352 5656/www.chelseagardener.com). Sloane Square or South Kensington tube. Open Mon–Fri 10am–6pm, Sat 9am–6pm, Sun 12–6pm.
Beautiful old-fashioned (but new) tools, suede gardening aprons, clothing, bags and garden-inspired china and other gifts that are all in the best possible taste. Indeed, many of the elegant linen 'gardening clothes' may strike you as much too smart for kneeling in the border. Connected to the excellent Chelsea Gardener garden centre (▶ 232).

PATIO GARDEN CENTRE (▶ 236)

SNAPDRAGON
*266–268 Lee High Road, Lewisham
SE13 (020 8463 0503/
www.snapdragonpots.co.uk). Lewisham
rail/DLR. Open Mon–Sat 10am–6pm,
Sun 10am–4pm.*
Slightly ramshackle shop on a corner of
scruffy Lee High Road, but a treasure
trove if you're looking for cheap large
pots and other garden ornaments. The
lead look-a-like planters (made from
stained cement) are pretty convincing
and a snip at £20 for quite large sizes;
large terracotta and glazed pots also
available, along with windchimes,
garden-themed cards and gifts, bulbs in
autumn and other seasonal stuff.

THE WEDGE
*11–13 Norwood High Street SE27 (020
8655 9628). West Norwood rail. Open
Mon–Fri 9am–4.30pm.*
Cast concrete garden pots, plaques,
balustrading, bird baths and other
ornaments in deliciously simple
designs – all the more remarkable for
the fact that they are made by people
with learning difficulties who live in
the L'Arche communities near by.

WOODHAMS' FLOWER AND
GARDEN STORE
*45 Elizabeth Street SW1 (020 7730
3353). Victoria tube/rail.
Also at One Aldwych WC2 (020 7300
0777/www.woodhams.co.uk).
Open Mon–Fri 10am–6pm; Elizabeth
Street also open Sat 9.30am–4.30pm.*
Huge magnolias in steel drums and
bright blue hydrangeas in shocking
pink window boxes made Stephen
Woodhams' Knightsbridge shop hard to
miss on the day I last passed by, and the
Aldwych branch is similarly fashionably
dressed. Chic central showcases for his
flower consultancy and landscape
design business (▶ 274), the shops sell
Woodhams' trademark avant garde cut
flowers and potted plants – orchids in
clear glass vases and pebbles, mother-
in-law's tongues set in purple sand, etc.
Good for stylish modern presents, such
as scented candles or dried roses
packed into square glass pots, if you
like that sort of thing.

ARTS AND CRAFTS IN GARDENS

THE CRAFTS COUNCIL
*44A Pentonville Road N1 4BY
(020 7278 7700).*
Good place to look for a contemporary
craftsperson to commission to create
something for your garden. As well as
a gallery shop (also at the V&A
Museum) and regular exhibitions,
some of which have a garden or
outdoor theme, the resource centre
holds the national Register of Makers
(extensive files of designers' work), and
staff can help you make a selection.

JOHN PITT
*44 Marsala Road SE13 (020 8690
2245/www.incisiveart.com).*
A sculptor and letter cutter who can be
commissioned to carve words on slate
or stone.

LUCY SMITH CERAMIC GARDEN SCULPTURE

2a Richmond Road E11 (020 8558 4734/ www.lucysmith.org).

Artist who works in ceramics to create a wonderful range of garden plaques and water features, often incorporating lizards, snakes and animal heads. One-off pieces can also be commissioned. Entire systems together with plaque/ spout, basin and pump are supplied.

THE NEW ART CENTRE

Roche Court, East Winterslow, Salisbury, Wiltshire SP5 1BG (01980 862244/ www.sculpture.uk.com).
Open daily 11am–4pm. Admission free.

This outdoor art gallery is well worth the trip and features work by well- and lesser-known artists set in the landscape (from huge Barbara Hepworths to smaller sculptural bird baths and benches for upwards of £1000). A walled former vegetable garden contains many beautiful works by letter-cutters, and the work of Gary Breeze, who translates well-known popular songs such as 'Singing in the Rain' into Latin, is featured in a smaller courtyard.

WOLSELEY FINE ARTS

12 Needham Road W11 (020 7792 2788). Open Wed–Fri 11am–6pm, Sat 11am–5pm.

Small mainly twentieth-century art gallery with a particular interest in letter cutting. A tiny courtyard garden at the back is crammed with stone and slate inscriptions and other pieces suitable for even very small gardens, and an annual Garden Art show in June has even more to offer.

GARDEN ARCHITECTURE, GLASSHOUSES, ETC.

ANTHONY DE GREY TRELLISES

Broadhinton Yard, 77A North Street SW4 (020 7738 8866/ www.anthonydegrey.com). Clapham Common tube. Open Mon–Fri 8am–5pm.

The shop on North Street is a showroom displaying the range of garden trellises, arches, pergolas, summerhouses and other structures which can be made, customized or designed to measure for a range of purposes. Choose from one small piece as a focus or a fully designed scheme to give your garden year-round structure.

ASH SAKULA ARCHITECTS

24 Rosebery Avenue EC1R 4SX (020 7837 9735/www.ashsak.com).

Young innovative team who have created some wonderful spaces that connect inside and out – their graceful 'Birdswing Conservatory' in north London won a RIBA Award in 1997.

GARDEN ARCHITECTURE

259 Munster Road SW6 (020 7385 1020/ www.gardenarchitecture.com). Parsons Green tube. Open Mon–Wed, Fri 8am–5pm, Thurs 8am–7.30pm, Sat 9am–5pm.

Interesting and ambitious shop geared to well-off urban gardeners who are after something a little different. Garden sculpture, trellises and unusual ceramic plant pots, either off-the-peg or tailor-made to commission. A set of pots costs from £80; sculptures start at £200.

GLASS HOUSES
41C Barnsbury Street N1 (020 7607 6071/www.glasshouses.com).
No shop front – ring for an appointment.
Company that specializes in designing and installing period-style conservatories – mainly Victorian and Edwardian. All sizes of work are undertaken, from small lean-to conservatories on the back of London terraced houses to grand orangeries in the country. Also sells blinds, lanterns and related fixtures and fittings.

LLOYD CHRISTIE
15 Langton Street, off New King's Road SW10 (020 7351 2108).

Fulham Broadway tube.
Open Mon–Fri 9am–5pm.
Designers and manufacturers of one-off conservatories in all styles. Also good for garden structures such as trellises, arches, troughs and containers: 'anything made from timber for the garden'.

MARSTON & LANGINGER
192 Ebury Street SW1 (020 7881 5717).
Sloane Square or Victoria tube. Open Mon–Fri 10am–6pm, Sat 10am–4pm.
Specializes in glasshouses and conservatories – standard designs and custom-built – and everything to put in them. The elegant shop is also a great source of garden and conservatory furniture, wirework accessories, blinds, flooring and lighting, with shabby chic style prevailing.

ROOM IN THE GARDEN (▶ 257)

COMPOST, TOPSOIL AND LAWN SUPPLIES

FENLAND COUNTRY SOILS
(020 7607 0689 or 07932 917339/ www.soil-compost.co.uk).
A variety of soil conditioners and composts delivered bagged or loose. From £60 per ton (loose) to £4.50–£7 per bag, depending on quantity; spread on garden for £10 extra. Deep black two-year-old horse manure, organic mushroom compost, multi-purpose compost, pine bark, topsoil and potting soil; also horticultural sands, grits and gravels and a 'Clay Breaker' soil conditioner composed of river

sand, chicken manure, peat and gypsum. Also turf at £4 per square yard. Free delivery anywhere within the M25.

GREENACRES HORTICULTURAL SUPPLIES
PO Box 1228, Iver SL0 OEH (01895 835235/www.greenacres.eu.com).
All you ever needed – and more – to do with lawns and lawn care. Many different types of grass seed, geared to specific needs and situations, including pre-germinated seed (for faster growth

– only five weeks till the lawn is ready to use) and a DIY pre-germinated seed Lawn Repair Kit; lawn feeds, moss-killers and soil improvers, including a natural organic feed. Free and friendly expert advice is offered over the telephone on all aspects, including choice of seed, site preparation, application and aftercare.

THOMPSONS OF CREWS HILL
(020 8363 1383/
www.thompsonsofcrewshill.com).
Phone lines manned daily 8am–6pm.
Efficient service offering a wide range of soils and soil-based composts, peat- and manure-based composts, soil conditioners including blood fish and bone, bark, gravels, chippings and aggregates. Also turf and grass seed. All delivered to your door for a charge of £3–£40 depending on proximity.

HARD LANDSCAPING SUPPLIES

THE SUPERSTORES
Large garden centres and DIY superstores such as **B&Q** (0845 609 6688) and **Homebase** (0870 900 8098) – ring for local stores – are usually good cheap sources of commonly found materials in smallish quantities. If you are after something unusual, however, or want large quantities at cheaper prices, the following specialist suppliers may be able to help.

BORDER STONE
(01938 570375)
Supplies all manner of stone, cobbles and gravel products to garden centres and landscapers nationwide. They do not normally deliver direct to private clients but can advise you of a good local supplier of their products.

THE CAST IRON SHOP
394 Caledonian Road N1 (020 7609 0934/www.thecastironshop.co.uk).
Caledonian Road tube. Open Mon– Thurs 10am–5pm, Fri 10am–4pm.
Glorious long-established company specializing in the casting of

reproduction antique ironwork such as gates, railings, grates, etc., and particularly proud of their filigree work. Ready-made balustrades, balconies and spiral staircases are on display and for sale – or commission your own.

CED (CIVIL ENGINEERING DEVELOPMENTS)
728 London Road, West Thurrock, Grays, Essex RM20 3LU (01708 867237).
Suppliers of all kinds of stone products, from cobbles, gravel, slate and paving flags to one-off chunks of stone to use as seats or monoliths. Will deliver to private customers nationwide.

DECKOR TIMBER
(01423 527505).
Nationwide suppliers of specialist garden decking and timber structures.

FARROW & BALL
249 Fulham Road SW6 (020 7351 0273/mail order and colour cards 01202 876141).
Emulsion paints for exterior walls and fences in a wide range of beautiful

colours and in both gloss and exterior eggshell finishes (as used and approved by the National Trust). Also available from Homebase stores (0870 900 8098 for local outlet).

FRETCO
(020 8533 7979).
Family business founded in 1920 that offers a unique service in all kinds of metal-cutting or architectural ironmongery. Metal grilles, staircases, window grilles or balcony railings, metal pot stands or legs for custom-built furniture, etc.

JOHN CULLEN LIGHTING
585 King's Road SW6 2EH
(020 7371 5400).
Experienced specialist garden lighting consultants who can devise and install lighting systems of all styles and levels of complexity.

LEWIS DUCTWORKS
450 Rathgar Road SW9
(020 7737 4435).
Manufacturers of excellent galvanized metal planters, custom-made and reasonably priced.

NORTON ENGINEERING
Norton Grove Industrial Estate, Norton, Malton, N. Yorks (01653 695721).
Suppliers of aluminium grille for use as decking, pond covers or steps.

OUTDOOR DECK COMPANY
Mortimer House, 46 Sheen Lane SW14 8LP (020 8876 8464).
Suppliers, designers and installers of outdoor decking. Can supply you with the materials to lay yourself or will design and fit everything from decking to steps and pergolas.

SALOP SAND AND GRAVEL
(01952 254101).
Stock a wide range of gravel-based products such as stone chippings and pebbles in a number of sizes and colours and will deliver to private customers nationwide.

WWW.KELLYSEARCH.COM
A search engine that sources all kinds of home and garden DIY materials at trade prices. 150,000 companies and 110,000 products, split into categories that you can list by distance from your postcode.

MAIL ORDER PLANTS, SEEDS, ETC.

Mail order suppliers will offer a larger range of varieties, and at more competitive prices than your average garden centre. These days most have websites and orders can be made by email or phone and sent out in a couple of days. Or ring for a catalogue (usually sent out free) and browse at your leisure.

THE BETH CHATTO GARDENS
Elmstead Market, Colchester, Essex CO7 7DB (01206 822007/ www.bethchatto.co.uk).
The inspiring Beth Chatto Gardens are a must for gardeners of all levels of expertise: her mantra of 'the right plant for the right place' is crucial to remember. The excellent *Handbook* (descriptive catalogue, £3) is an

essential reference book as well as a great source of unusual mail order plants for tricky situations: dry shade, dry sun and boggy areas, as featured in the display gardens, are a speciality. Mail order Sept to March only.

BLOMS BULBS
Primrose Nurseries, Melchbourne, Bedfordshire MK44 1ZZ (01234 709099/www.blomsbulbs.com).
Great catalogues (two a year) of spring- and summer-flowering bulbs, with some border and rockery plants also. Bloms are the absolute tops for tulips; their list includes more than 100 species, striped, streaked, fringed and double varieties (many photographed in colour) – plus clouds of daffodils, hyacinths and crocus, and lots of lovely lilies for summer.

CLAIRE AUSTIN
HARDY PLANTS
The Stone House, Coppice Green Lane, Cramp, Shifnal, Shropshire TF11 8PE (01952 463700/ www.claireaustin-hardyplants.co.uk).
Daughter of David Austin (below), Claire Austin has one of the most beautiful catalogues around, specializing in hardy perennials – most plants are photographed in colour, which is great for those not familiar with them all. Only the best varieties get past her great eye – bearded iris and peonies are particularly well represented.

DAVID AUSTIN ROSES
Bowling Green Lane, Albrighton, Wolverhampton WV7 3HB (01902 376300 or 376307/ www.davidaustinroses.com).

One of *the* main sources in the country (and indeed world) for roses of all kinds. The huge range includes most of the favourite old shrub and species roses, climbers and ramblers and modern 'patio' varieties and hybrid teas. Specialist breeders of English roses, developed to keep all the fragrance and beautiful appearance of old roses, but with a greatly extended flowering period.

DE JAGER
The Nurseries, Marden, Kent TN12 9BP (01622 840229).
I buy every year from this extensive catalogue, which features especially good ranges of rare species tulips, spring- and autumn-flowering crocus, early-flowering iris and fritillaries. Also a good source for prepared hyacinth bulbs, amaryllis and 'Paper White' narcissi for winter blooming inside the house.

DOWNDERRY NURSERY
Pillar Box Lane, Hadlow, Tonbridge, Kent TN11 9SW (01732 810081/ www.downderry-nursery.co.uk).
Lavender specialists, offering every type of lavender you can imagine, from the traditional English varieties to the French and Spanish types with their butterfly 'ears', silver and cut-leaved varieties, and blooms in every colour from white through pinks and mauves to electric violet and deepest indigo. Also a good range of rosemaries. Worth visiting in June and July if you can to see the plants growing in the show garden.

FUTURE FOODS
Luckleigh Cottage, Hockworthy,
Wellington, Somerset TA21 ONN
(01398 361347/ www.futurefoods.com).
Quirky catalogue for vegetable
enthusiasts offering one of the most
unusual ranges of seed around – weird
and wonderful varieties of squash, root
vegetables, peppers, tomatoes and
tomatillos from all around the world –
plus mushroom growing kits, ferments,
saffron crocus and a small range of
sundries and gift packs (including a
tempting 'Salsa Sensation' set).

JACQUES AMAND
The Nurseries, Clamp Hill, Stanmore,
Middlesex HA7 3JS (020 8420 7110).
A great selection of some of the more
unusual bulbs alongside the old
favourites: twenty-five varieties of
allium, thirty-one crocus, ten eremurus,
nearly a hundred narcissi and even more
tulips, including rare historical tulips
much prized in the seventeenth century.

JOHN CHAMBERS
15 Westleigh Road, Barton, Seagrave,
Kettering, Northants NN15 5AJ
(01933 652562).
Suppliers of wildflower and grass seed,
including many mixes for specific areas
and even a 'wildflower window box'
mixture. Plugs of wildflowers to plant
in your lawn as an easier shortcut to a
wildflower meadow are also available.

THE ORGANIC GARDENING
CATALOGUE
Riverdene Business Park, Molesey Road,
Hersham, Surrey KT12 4RG
(0845 130 1304/
www.organiccatalogue.com).
The mail order arm of the excellent

organic association HDRA (▶ 266), this
catalogue is *the* source for all those
serious about organic gardening. Not
all the seed and plant material listed is
organic, but much is, including lots of
unusual lettuce varieties and a good
range of seed potatoes. The twenty-odd
pages of sundries include organic feeds
and soil conditioners, composting
equipment, organic and biological pest
control and all manner of growing aids,
from root trainers to full-size
polytunnels. HDRA members receive a
10 per cent discount.

PETER NYSSEN
124 Flixton Road, Urmston, Manchester
M41 5BG (0161 747 4000).
Offers all the usual suspects, but with
hefty discounts for customers ordering
more than twenty-five of each variety
(and mega discounts on 250 and over).
Most of the other companies only offer
such discounts to trade buyers.

SARAH RAVEN'S
CUTTING GARDEN
Hill Farm, Brightling, Robertsbridge,
East Sussex TN32 5HP
(01424 838181/
www.thecuttinggarden.com).
Sarah Raven's heavenly catalogue goes
from strength to strength, selling all
you need to create a modern cutting
garden in your own plot (however
small), from seeds and young seedlings
of the most sumptuously coloured and
textured varieties (plus unusual
vegetables, too), to pretty vases and
jugs in which to arrange them once
grown, and assorted gardening
accessories. A range of courses is also
taught on site.

SEEDS OF ITALY

260 West Hendon Broadway NW9 (020 8930 2516/www.seedsofitaly.com).

A must for those who combine a love of gardening with a taste for Mediterranean cooking. Seeds for the ingredients of all your favourite dishes – wild rocket, gourmet tomatoes, basil, borlotti beans, crinkly dark green 'Cavolo Nero', striped 'Romanesco' courgettes, hot chilli peppers and endless varieties of lettuce and radicchio – all in their original Italian 'Franchi' packaging. Plus a range of accessories including a food drier.

SIMPSON'S SEEDS

The Walled Garden Nursery, Horningsham, Warminster, Wiltshire BA12 7NQ (01985 845004/ www.simpsonsseeds.co.uk).

Family-run business specializing in seed for unusual tomato varieties (more than a hundred on offer), chillis and other peppers and all sorts of other unusual and oriental vegetables. For those without a greenhouse, young plantlets of many varieties are sent out at the appropriate time (see the excellent catalogue for details). Flower seed and a small range of growing accessories and books are also available.

SUFFOLK HERBS

Monks Farm, Coggeshall Road, Kelvedon, Essex CO5 9PG (01376 572456).

Another great source for organic gardeners – particularly strong on organic seed for herbs, wildflowers and unusual vegetable varieties (plantlets of some herb varieties also available). Alongside helpful planting tips and recipes, the catalogue also offers tools, organic pesticides and feeds and a great range of alternative health products, dried herbs and spices, herb teas, books, gifts and organic wines.

THOMPSON AND MORGAN

Poplar Lane, Ipswich, Suffolk IP8 3PU (01473 688821/ www.thompson-morgan.com).

All-round seed catalogue stocking seed for most of the commonly grown garden plants and flowers – plus a vegetable section too. They pride themselves on offering the very latest novelties each year – but you'll have to use your own taste and eye to weed out the desirable stuff from the garish over-bred horrors. There is a separate catalogue of garden plants sent out in season.

TREES DIRECT

(01588 680280/www.treesdirect.co.uk).

'To give and to grow' is the motto of this small family-run company that specializes in sending trees as presents (with a message or commemorative plaque attached to its trunk). Many different varieties of garden tree are listed in the brochure, and more can be sourced on request – there's also a 'mail order knot garden' that would make a fantastic wedding present with a group of people contributing.

UNWIN'S

Wisbech, Cambridgeshire PE13 2BR (01945 588522).

Another all-round catalogue, specializing in flowers, but with a good kitchen garden section. New varieties are again sometimes prized for novelty above all else. Unwin's are one of the very few sources of sweet pea seedlings in named varieties – collections of six different scented or showbench varieties are sent out in March for very competitive prices.

OTHER GARDENING MAIL ORDER

FOREVER FLOWERING
(020 8392 9929/
www.foreverflowering.com).
Great if you're searching for an instant gift for a keen gardener. A wide range of pot-grown outdoor and indoor plants and beautiful hand-tied bouquets and baskets are sent out, beautifully packaged, to arrive by post the next day. The flowers are particularly beautiful – old roses, sweet peas and bright parrot tulips (from £25) that look as if they had been hand-picked that morning from some wonderful garden.

GARDEN BIRD SUPPLIES
Wem, Shrewsbury SY4 5BF (01939
232233/www.gardenbird.com).
The largest range of bird feeds and feeders around. Different feed mixes geared to different types of birds, feeders in all styles and sizes (including squirrel-proof models that might prove useful to Londoners), nesting houses and accessories to attract other types of beneficial wildlife to your garden. The catalogue is more of a magazine, full of useful articles and information.

GLUTTONOUS GARDENER
Vitis House, 50 Dickens Street SW8 3EQ
(020 7627 0800/ www.glut.co.uk).
Fun company offering 'gifts that grow': attractively packaged gift sets for those who like eating and drinking as much as getting their hands dirty. The 'Wedding Day' crate contains a 'Wedding Day' rambling rose, pair of Felco secateurs and bottle of champagne, while other

ideas include an 'Olive Enthusiast's Kit' (with olive tree, olive oil and jar of olives), an 'Under the Gooseberry Bush' package and 'Moroccan Mint Tea' crate.

GRASSROOTS GARDENING
(01189 712085).
Makers and mail order suppliers of the 'Potta System' that enables you to make the eco-equivalent of plastic cells for sowing seeds – from strips of newspaper. A clever template system enables you to make batches of twenty-four or so at once, directly in a seed tray.

GREEN GARDENER
41 Strumpshaw Road, Brundall, Norfolk
NR13 5PG (01603 715096/
www.greengardener.co.uk). Worm
products (01394 420087).
There's not much that owners Annie and John Manners don't know about biological pest control, and via their excellent telephone helpline they spread their expertise with great good humour and patience. Natural nematodes and other organisms that prey on pests such as slugs, vine weevil, aphids, chafer grubs and more are sent out at the right time of year – in annual planned programmes if required. (See pages 79–84 for more on how biological controls work.) An innovative selection of harmless barrier controls is also illustrated in the fact-packed catalogue, together with wildlife shelters to encourage beneficial insects such as ladybirds and lacewings to live and breed in your garden – and even a ladybird breeding kit. Also, a range of worm composting kits and

accessories, including a 'Wormery Rescue Kit' for when it all goes wrong.

LWS (LANDSCAPE WATERING SYSTEMS) LTD

(01722 716969/www.lws.uk.com). Irrigation systems of all types, to cater for everything from a few hanging baskets to a large garden and greenhouse. A simple 'Dripper Kit' and 'Spray Kit' are the two most straightforward products to get you started, but the design team are able to advise and help with installation. Automatic and remote control systems also available. Ring for a brochure or consult the website to get an idea of the range of products available.

REAL FLOWERS

(0870 403 6548/ www.realflowers.co.uk). Absolutely no danger of stiff old yellow carnations and gypsophila here. This is a great company to use if you're sending flowers to a keen gardener – traditional, blowzy, scented English roses in more than thirty varieties and a wide range of colours can be sent out to the object of your affections for as little as £39 including delivery.

WATERWELL LTD

The Barley Mow Business Centre, 10 Barley Mow Passage W4 (020 8742 8855) Professional installers of all types of irrigation systems – will advise on a scheme to suit your space and needs.

WIGGLY WIGGLERS

Lower Blakemere Farm, Blakemere, Herefordshire HR2 9PX (01981 500391/ www.wigglywigglers.co.uk). All you need to make your own compost – and much more besides. Composting bins and kits including worm bins (some of which, like the popular 'Can-O-Worms', are constructed from connecting trays so that you never have to handle the worms). Worms in abundance, plus organic and peat-free gardening products, insect and bird houses, mealworms and other 'live' bird foods and feeders. Also, a good selection of books on natural gardening and special products for children. Advice on composting and worm bins available over the phone.

MAIL ORDER ACCESSORIES

R. K. ALLISTON (▶ 242)

ARABELLA LENNOX-BOYD PRODUCTS

Gresgarth Hall, Caton, Lancashire LA2 9NB (01524 770313 or 771838). Small but perfectly formed range of garden tools and accessories, many of which have been designed by the famous garden designer herself.

Victorian-style glass cloches, long-handled bulb-planters, an asparagus knife, beautifully designed rain gauges and thermometers and a lovely plant-labelling kit where the names are permanently acid-etched on to zinc labels. Not cheap, but unusual products that are hard (if not impossible) to find elsewhere, and make great presents.

BUY GREEN BY MAIL
(01654 705959/www.cat.org.uk).
The mail order offshoot of the excellent Centre for Alternative Technology in Wales (▶ 265) with all sorts of products for the eco-minded. Ideas for the garden include solar-powered lights and fountains, wildlife-friendly slug traps, butterfly houses, worm bins and root trainers. Plus a great selection of unusual books on everything from building a shed and gardening by the moon to storing garden produce.

THE COTSWOLD COMPANY
(0870 550 2233/ www.cotswoldco.com).
Quite a few stylish and practical items including brushwood and willow screening sold cheaply by the roll; folding woven willow screens; a nifty wooden doormat with built-in foot-scraper and double-headed brush; 'boulder' candle holders and sack-shaped woven planters.

CROCUS
(0870 000 1057/www.crocus.co.uk).
Selected plants and products are interspersed through this award-winning catalogue and website, created with the style-conscious urban gardener in mind. Some of the sculptures may not be to everyone's taste, but the spiral pyramid supports, galvanized planters and small lean-to greenhouse are great. Plants are sent out in good sizes and in good condition – some well-known garden designers regularly use this site.

DIBOR
(0870 013 3666/www.dibor.co.uk).
Very stylish, very desirable garden accessories, mixed up with similarly good general home products. Lovely wirework shelves for outside and in, tasteful picnicware and outdoor lighting, containers, striped square floor cushions and extremely good-looking (and reasonably priced) garden furniture.

GRAND ILLUSIONS
(01747 858300/ www.grandillusions.co.uk).
Stylish and sometimes quirky range of garden furniture and accessories (▶ 244).

GREENFIBRES
(01803 868001/www.greenfibres.com).
Eco-friendly clothing company – the place to order your organically grown, bleach-free gardening socks and long-johns. Read the heart-breaking testimonies about the effects of pesticides in cotton-growing communities in Africa – not to mention the effects of chemicals on the skin – and you'll think twice about wearing any old fabrics again. Also a great range of organic skin and bath products for after-gardening pampering.

GREENFINGERS TRADING LTD
(0845 345 0728/ www.greenfingers.com)
The huge range of products ranges from twee fairy sculptures to good reproduction Victorian cloches, great garden furniture, including a metal seat to fit around a tree trunk and lots of fun garden games. Also offers a few plants, tools (including larger items such as shredders and pressure washers, etc.) and pet equipment.

MANNERS
(0870 6000 662/
www.mannersmailorder.co.uk)
In between the grim reproduction furniture and reconstituted stone dogs and cherubs are some real gems at very reasonable prices – the last catalogue featured an elegant distressed white-painted wooden bench, original galvanized tin baths to use as planters, chunky hazel plant protectors and an attractive 'Twigwam' playhouse for children.

OCEAN
(0870 242 6283/www.oceanuk.com).
Mostly offers pared-down furniture for indoors, but some seriously stylish slatted loungers, including one that doubles up as a coffee table. Some great minimalist indoor/outdoor containers made from brushed aluminium and galvanized metal, and even some wheels to scoot the heaviest pots about. Solar-powered garden lighting, the smartest stainless steel portable barbecue, and the most stylish 'patio heater' around, which has a blue canvas sack to hide the gas cylinder – also an unusual wall-mounted version for those who'd prefer their garden not to look like a French café.

THE ORGANIC GARDENING
CATALOGUE (▶ 252).

ROOM IN THE GARDEN
(01403 823958/
www.roominthegarden.co.uk).
Stylish range of plant supports, sweet pea tepees, arches and obelisks in rusted iron. Also a romantic range of Gothick openwork summerhouses just waiting to have roses and honeysuckle planted up the sides.

SECRET GARDENS FURNITURE
(020 8464 5327/
www.secretgardensfurniture.com).
Artistic and innovative designs for plant supports and garden furniture, mostly in metal. Can also work to commission.

TRADITIONAL GARDEN SUPPLY
COMPANY
(0870 600 3366/
www.stowgrange.co.uk).
Traditional-style, quality products, ranging from sculpture, garden furniture and tools to a full-scale pergola and deck (plus a very reasonably priced one to attach to the side of a house). A limited range of plants, including banana palms, is also offered. The lead-look planters are good-looking, as are the natural split bamboo, heather and coppiced willow screens.

TREE OF LIFE
(0870 6066314/
www.treeoflifeshop.co.uk).
Supported by the HDRA and the Wildlife Trusts, this company offers 'gifts inspired by nature' including a set of three useful garden trugs made from recycled polythene, bird feeders, nesting houses and bug boxes (for encouraging beneficial insects).

ASSOCIATIONS

THE ROYAL HORTICULTURAL SOCIETY

Administrative Offices, Lindley Library and Exhibition Halls, 80 Vincent Square SW1P 2PE (020 7834 4333).
Membership enquiries and Lindley Library 020 7821 3050. Office hours Mon–Fri 9.30am–5.30pm. Members only horticultural advice service 01483 224234.

Founded in 1804, the RHS is Britain's largest gardening charity and is 'committed to being the leading organization demonstrating excellence in horticulture and promoting gardening'. Renowned for its outstanding gardens and inspirational flower shows, the RHS is a key source of advice and information for gardeners of all levels. It produces its own publications, holds lectures, and carries out trials, education programmes and scientific research – there are also many other activities on a local level: RHS events are run in partnership with gardens, colleges, horticultural clubs and societies, nurseries and garden centres. Annual membership is a rite of passage for those whose curiosity about gardening has extended beyond the local garden centre. It costs £31 per year for individual membership plus a one-off £7 enrolment fee, and this entitles you to free entry to the London RHS Flower Shows, a free copy of the excellent monthly *The Garden* magazine, and free entry with a guest to the RHS gardens in Wisley in Surrey, Rosemoor in Devon, Hyde Hall in Essex and Harlow Carr in North Yorkshire, plus many other inspirational partner gardens across the country. Members also enjoy privileged entry on allocated days and special rate tickets to national RHS flower shows including those at Chelsea, Hampton Court Palace and Tatton Park, plus reduced admission to BBC Gardeners' World Live and the Malvern Spring and Autumn Garden and Country Shows. Free seeds harvested from RHS gardens are another perk, as is the excellent free advice service, where plants can be identified and other information gleaned from the RHS experts either by letter, fax, email or face to face. Phone 01483 224234 for details.

London Shows

These shows fast become a way of life for gardening Londoners – you will know it is that time of the month again when you see people lugging the characteristic green and white carrier bags, bristling with plants, around the environs of Vincent Square. The shows are held from January to April and from September to November inclusive at the RHS Horticultural Halls in Westminster, in Greycoat Street, just around the corner from Vincent Square. There is also an annual Orchid Conference and Show in March and a Great Autumn Show spreading into both halls in October. Walking into the high-ceilinged halls is a treat for all the senses: the heady scent of so many plants in one room is quite something, as is the sight of the immaculate table displays from some of the best specialist nurseries in the country. Awards are given for the best displays, and browsing your way around is a great way to see and buy a far wider range of plants than you'd ever find in any London nursery. As you admire, it's a good idea to take a notebook and write down the names and descriptions of the plants that most take your fancy. (This is how none other than Rosemary Verey began her gardening career, thanks to a present of RHS membership from her family.) Second-hand books and horticultural sundries are usually on sale too, and there may be exhibitions of botanical paintings or garden photography. The plant competitions are also a big draw, particularly the vegetable displays in autumn and the alpine plants in spring. These competitions are open to members and non-members alike – ring 01483 224234 for details. The other great perk of the shows is that free expert horticultural advice is on hand from the advisory bureau in the Lawrence Hall.

The Lindley Library

Recently revamped in a smart modern wing of the main building, the Lindley Library holds the most comprehensive collection of horticultural books in the world – more than 50,000 volumes covering all areas of horticulture, gardening and garden history, from the sixteenth century to the present day. More than 18,000 botanical drawings – many of great historical importance and heart-stopping beauty – are also stored here. The ground-floor Upper Reading Room houses a portion of the book stock, current periodicals and nursery and trade catalogues, while the Lower Reading Room has the catalogues and offers plenty of room for readers engaged in research; the Rare Books, Drawings Collections and conservation studio are housed separately. Access is open to everyone, and members can borrow books by post as well as in person. Visitors wishing to look at the Drawings Collection are requested to make an appointment by telephoning 020 7821 3050 or emailing library_enquiries@rhs.org.uk. Opening hours are Mon–Fri 9.30am–5.30pm.

The Chelsea Flower Show

Love it or loathe it, this most famous of RHS shows takes place over five days towards the end of May and has been held in the grounds of the Royal Hospital, Chelsea, since 1913. The first day is for press only, followed by the Royal Family and gala evening; the second and third days are for RHS members only, and the general public gets the remaining days, including the final Friday, when plants and other components from show gardens and display stands are sold off at bargain prices and the streets of Chelsea resemble a walking forest, with people balancing shrubs and tree palms on their heads. Arrive as early as you can to avoid the crowds – or chance it and come towards the end of the day when they should have thinned out again (sadly there is no readmission, though members can return for the Friday 'sell-off' after 4.30pm on presentation of a valid membership card). The large show gardens in the main avenue are the main attraction and gain the most press attention, but the recently introduced smaller city and courtyard gardens spread throughout the site are proving increasingly popular. The nursery displays in the Floral Pavilions are not only stunning, they are a good place to get to know new plants, ask advice straight from the growers and place orders for your garden; there are spectacular flower arrangements and vegetable displays. (It's also a useful retreat when the inevitable rain pours down.) Outside the pavilions, the full range of greenhouses, garden furniture and every type of gardening tool and sundry under the sun is available for inspection and demonstration. Go with a clear aim in view: to choose a new greenhouse, or plants for a new border – and you should come back with useful information; the rest of us usually end up with a carrier bag full of brochures that never see the light of day. All tickets must be booked in advance on ticket hotline 0870 906 3780.

Hampton Court Palace Flower Show
Many people enjoy this early July show more than Chelsea, as the exhibits are spread over so much larger an area and the crowds are dispersed. Held in 25 acres of Royal parkland, beside the Long Water and overlooked by the Palace, it's a much more leisurely and elegant affair, with most of the main gardens in a line on either side of the canal. The floral marquees are, again, a huge attraction – especially the British Rose Festival – and the *Daily Mail* (the main sponsor) usually pulls out all the stops for an innovative display in its Pavilion. Unlike at Chelsea, plants are available for sale all through the show – it's much more of a shopping experience overall. Behind the show gardens and pavilions, acres of stalls selling greenhouses, garden furniture, tools, sundries and garden-themed gifts stretch almost to the river. There is also a *Country Living* Pavilion selling food, clothes and other items with little or nothing to do with gardening, and a variety of cafés and restaurants. If you end up too tired and laden to make your way on foot to the station, exit via the river and treat yourself to a boat trip to the opposite bank. Members-rate tickets must be booked in advance on 0870 906 3790; full-price tickets are available on the gate.

Other London Societies and Organizations

BRITISH TRUST FOR CONSERVATION VOLUNTEERS (BTCV) (▶ 265)

BRITISH WATERWAYS LONDON
The Toll House, Delamere Terrace W2 6ND (020 7286 6101/ www.britishwaterwayslondon.co.uk).
For more information about London's 90 miles of waterways and 110 acres of docks: canalside walks and landscaping, boat trips, museums and riverside pubs.

THE LONDON HONEY COMPANY
(020 7771 9152).
Runs regular courses on urban beekeeping. Londoners who aren't able or inclined to keep bees can enjoy local honey by joining the Cropsharers scheme at the London Honey Company. An annual subscription of £250 entitles you to visit the capital's beehives and receive 12½ pounds and three frames of honey and ten beeswax candles. Beekeeping courses are also held at Roots & Shoots in Kennington (▶ 207).

LONDON IN BLOOM
Vernon House, Fourth Floor, 23 Sicilian Avenue WC1A 2QQ (020 7831 2543).
Founded in 1966 to promote the development of floral displays in public places for the benefit of people who

live, work or visit London. Every year, the thirty-one boroughs and the two Cities of Westminster and London can enter a fiercely fought competition designed to encourage the planting and displaying of flowers, shrubs, trees and landscaping visible to the public. The wide range of eighteen categories includes Best Pub, Best Restaurant and Best Front Garden as well as awards for Parks Departments and the Environment, and judging takes place in July within the boroughs, with the finals in August. Once the results are announced, a list of the winners can be obtained from the above address – it could be fun to visit some of the award-winning displays and see if you agree with the judges. If you are interested in taking part in London in Bloom in some way, the first step is to contact your local council, which should have a London in Bloom representative.

THE LONDON PARKS AND GARDENS TRUST
Duck Island Cottage,
St James's Park, London
SW1A 2BJ (020 7839 3969/
www.londongardenstrust.org).
An admirable independent charitable organization whose objectives are 'to promote education about historic parks and gardens in London and to seek to conserve these gardens for the education and enjoyment of the public'. Knowledge and expertise about the protection and management of such spaces is garnered under the auspices of the trust – providing a real source of information and inspiration for anyone seriously interested in the history and future of London's green environment. Membership costs from £16 (standard)

to £100 (corporate) and £250-plus (life). Members are entitled to a real treat in the form of the trust's annual journal, *The London Gardener*, edited by Todd Longstaffe-Gowan, and packed with esoteric, scholarly and often extremely witty articles about the history and development of London's public and private gardens. The newsletter *London Landscapes* has details of the trust's programme of talks, walks and other events all focused on aspects of London parks and gardens. There are also opportunities for interested members to volunteer in aspects of the trust's work. The trust is also behind the excellent London Squares Day (see below).

THE LONDON PARKS AND GREEN SPACES FORUM
City Hall, The Queen's Walk SE1 2AA
(0118 946 9060/www.green-space.org.uk).
London arm of National Greenspace (▶ 267), which has its headquarters in Reading. It is a not-for-profit organization that lobbies to protect open spaces in the capital and to secure resources for management. Members of the public can join, or simply alert the Forum to their own concerns.

LONDON OPEN HOUSE
PO Box 25361 NW5 1GY
(09001 600061/
www.londonopenhouse.org).
For just one day each year in mid to late September, free entry is offered to more than five hundred of the capital's private and public buildings, most of which are rarely otherwise opened to the public. Some stunning little-seen gardens may be viewed in this way, including Pope's Grotto in Twickenham

(part of St James's Independent School), the Winter Garden at the University of Greenwich and a modern eco-house with courtyard garden and green roof in N7 – see individual entries in the guide. An updated annual list of properties open is usually published free with the *Evening Standard* the week before the event, and is also available from participating council libraries, tourist and information centres, and, from a week or so before the Open House day, from City Hall Information Point, The Queen's Walk SE1, open Mon–Fri 9am–6pm. Or you can send an SAE with a 60p stamp and a cheque for £2 payable to London Open House to the PO Box address above. There are also associated walking tours, events and lectures.

LONDON SQUARES DAY
c/o The London Parks and Gardens Trust (see above) (www.opensquares.org).
Have you ever envied the lucky key-holders who enjoy access to London's finest private residential squares? Once a year, usually around the second weekend of June, these private havens open their gates to the general public for London Squares Day – and it's up to you how many you want to cram in, armed with an *A–Z* and the great little directory compiled each year by the London Parks and Gardens Trust, whose largely volunteer staff coordinate and man this event. Almost a hundred squares and gardens support the weekend, many offering homemade cakes, music, plant sales and children's activities to add to the fun. Garden Barge Square (▶ 152), John Lewis Oxford Street Roof Garden, Mecklenburgh Square (▶ 131) and

St George's Fields (▶ 143) are among the gardens that can only be visited through this scheme. For details of the squares and gardens open send an SAE to LPGT, Duck Island Cottage, St James's Park SW1A 2BJ or visit the website (www.londongardenstrust.org).

THE LONDON WILDLIFE TRUST
Harling House, 45–51 Great Suffolk Street SE1 0BS (020 7261 0447/ www.wildlondon.org.uk).
A registered charity that exists 'to fight to sustain and enhance London's wildlife habitats and create a city richer in wildlife', the trust manages fifty-seven nature reserves and wildlife gardens across Greater London, including Camley Street Nature Park in King's Cross (▶ 187), the Gunnersbury Triangle Nature Reserve in W4 (▶ 221), Sydenham Hill Wood (▶ 201) and its flagship garden and advice centre at the Centre for Wildlife Gardening in Peckham (▶ 205). Many of the reserves and gardens have visitor centres and offer information packs, workshops and other events for adults and children alike. Membership of the LWT costs from £15 (individuals)/£10 (unwaged) and £25 for families, which includes free membership for up to four children in the children's 'Wildlife Watch' scheme with its own magazines and activities. Members receive the informative newsletter *Wild in London* and the thrice-yearly *Going Wild in London*, detailing walks, workshops and events.

METROPOLITAN PUBLIC GARDENS ASSOCIATION
The Bury Farm, Chesham, Buckinghamshire HP5 2JU (01494 775878).

Works for the 'protection, preservation, safeguarding and acquiring for public use, of gardens and open spaces' in the capital. Also offers free advice on tree pruning and planting and encourages public interest in the 'beautification of London'.

THE NATIONAL GARDENS SCHEME (LONDON)

Hatchlands Park, East Clandon, Guildford, Surrey GU4 7RT (01483 211535/www.ngs.org.uk).
Visiting gardens open to the public under the National Gardens Scheme offers a fantastic opportunity to see private gardens and many others that are part of non-public organizations – and the money raised goes to a wide range of deserving charities. The 'Yellow Book' listing all the gardens open throughout the country, with addresses, opening times and short descriptions, is published every year at around £8; a shorter guide to London gardens is also available. Londoners can visit private gardens of all styles and sizes and in every corner of the capital and can also gain access to otherwise elusive places such as Lambeth Palace (▶ 245), London Lighthouse (▶ 214), Trinity Hospice (▶ 199) and the Hurlingham Club. Many of the larger gardens offer tea, cakes and plant sales – great for unusual bargains – and there are also some evening openings with wine in summer. The London organizers are always on the lookout for new gardens. If you think your garden offers enough horticultural and design interest to be included in the scheme, contact Mrs Penny Snell, Moleshill House, The Fairmile, Cobham, Surrey KT11 1BG,

or one of the local London organizers listed in the book under your area.

ORIGINAL LONDON WALKS

PO Box 1708 NW6 4LW (020 7624 3978).
Programme of more than two hundred walks in London (and some further afield) exploring little-known corners of the capital such as Old Kensington (including tours of Kensington Gardens and the Roof Gardens), Old Marylebone (featuring many lesser-known garden squares), Little Venice (with its famous canal boat gardens) and the Regent's Canal. The guides are notoriously well-informed and entertaining, boasting retired actors, authors of books on the capital and 'a legendary BBC broadcaster' among them. Send for a quarterly brochure or pick one up in tourist offices and newsagents.

THRIVE

Beech Hill, Berkshire RG7 2AT (0118 988 5688/www.thrive.org.uk).
National charity that works through gardening to change the lives of disabled, disadvantaged and older people is now in partnership with the RHS and has two bases in London, at Battersea Park (020 7720 2212) and Altab Ali Park in Hackney (020 7739 2965). The charity carries out research into the benefits of gardening and has found through its twenty-five years of working with people that gardening can be a force for the good in helping all sorts of people learn or re-learn basic skills, maintain or improve quality of life, build up self-esteem and confidence and also gain qualifications for a move into employment in gardening. Thrive is

also a source of information on easier gardening aimed at older or disabled people, and there is also a special service for blind gardeners. If you would like more information, or to get involved as a participant or volunteer, ring the main number above or either of the London numbers given.

TREES FOR LONDON
Prince Consort Lodge, Kennington Park, Kennington Park Place SE11 4AS (020 7587 1320/ www.treesforlondon.org.uk).
Fantastic organization founded with the aim of providing more trees on London's streets, public spaces and housing estates, particularly in deprived areas (see history on pages 11–12). Lots of opportunities for interested Londoners to help, from sponsoring a tree (from £15 a year), dedicating a tree or small grove for a christening, wedding or to remember a loved one (from £175) or getting their hands dirty on the regular planting days. The original founders were dedicated nightclubbers, and early funds were raised from specially organized 'raves' – even though everyone has grown up now, and the organization become a registered charity with its own director, the urban roots remain and planting days often feature a barbecue and live music from a top club DJ.

URBAN GARDENS SHOW
(020 7288 6464/ www.urban-gardens.com)
Relatively new show at the Grand Hall, Olympia, usually in May, featuring the best in contemporary urban garden design, furniture and accessories, plus a host of celebrity appearances and demonstrations.

LOCAL SOCIETIES

The Royal Horticultural Society has details of the many local horticultural societies throughout the capital that are affiliated to the RHS – most hold regular meetings and an annual flower show and some organize local open garden schemes. The societies are too many to list here in full but include active groups in Blackheath, Camberwell, the City of London, De Beauvoir Town, Dulwich, Finchley, Fulham, Harrow, Hampstead, Highgate, Islington, Kennington, Lambeth, Lewisham, Muswell Hill, Pinner, Streatham, Wandsworth and Wimbledon. Most are run by private individuals who do not want their details published. However, if you contact the RHS Regional Development Department on 020 7821 3069 and explain where you live they will put you in touch with your nearest local society.

BRIGHTER KENSINGTON AND CHELSEA
27 Palace Gate W8 5LS (020 7584 1234).
Annual competition for the best private gardens, balconies, window boxes, communal, school and church gardens, and gardens in front of shops, restaurants and hotels.

FAIRBRIDGE GARDEN SOCIETY
*c/o Fulham Palace Garden Centre,
Bishop's Avenue SW6 6EE (020 7736
7854 or 020 7736 3210/
www.fulhamgardencentre.com).*
Fulham-based society that raises funds
for the Fairbridge charity for
underprivileged inner city youth.
Organizes an excellent series of
outings, lectures and practical
demonstrations, and hosts a great
annual May garden party and
Christmas party at the Fulham Palace
Garden Centre. For more information
about the Fairbridge Charity, ring 020
7928 1704.

LAMBETH LOCAL
HISTORY FORUM
*Minet Library, 52 Knatchbull Road SE5
9QY (020 7926 6076).*
Programme of year-round walks around
different areas of Lambeth, including
many of south London's gardens,
cemeteries and other open spaces.
Some walks venture further afield, to
the South Bank and the City.

NATIONAL SOCIETIES

BRITISH TRUST FOR
CONSERVATION VOLUNTEERS
(BTCV)
*Conservation Centre, Balby Road,
Doncaster DN4 ORH
(01302 572200).*
Lots of conservation projects to get
involved with throughout the country,
including many in London. Also one of
the principal organizations to offer help
with creating community gardens (*see*
pages 13–15).

THE CAMPAIGN FOR DARK SKIES
(www.dark-skies.org).
Campaigns to keep our skies as free of
light pollution as possible.

CENTRE FOR ALTERNATIVE
TECHNOLOGY (CAT)
*Machynlleth, Powys SY20 9AZ
(01654 705950).*
Wonderful eco-resource centre founded
in the 1970s in the hills of north
Wales. A must to visit for anyone even
vaguely interested in ecological design
and/or organic gardening. There are
demonstration houses, eco-loos and
wildlife-gardening and compost-
making displays – plus an excellent
café and a shop selling all sorts of
equipment and books to help make
your life that little bit greener. An
organic vegetable garden and
polytunnels usually offer inspiration, in
spite of the often inclement climate,
while the hydraulic water lifts and
mock-up tunnel providing a 'mole's eye'
view of the soil make it a trip that is
fun for all the family. Residential
courses in everything from organic
gardening to serious eco-building are
held throughout the year, with
accommodation in eco-lodges on site.
For Londoners unable to make a visit,
CAT is still an invaluable resource
centre, with patient and up-to-date
advice, plus a series of excellent cheap
leaflets on all aspects of eco-gardening
and design, available over the
telephone. They also run a mail order
service, Buy Green By Mail (▶ 256).

COMMISSION FOR
ARCHITECTURE AND THE BUILT
ENVIRONMENT (CABE)
*The Tower Building, 11 York Road SE1
7NX (020 7960 2400/www.cabe.org.uk).*
Non-departmental government body
responsible for the built environment.
A new section called 'CABE Space' is
particularly concerned with reclaiming
urban green spaces. They also (with the
Civic Trust) oversee the 'Green Flag'
awards for community gardens and
public green spaces.

COMMON GROUND
*Gold Hill House, 21 High Street,
Shaftesbury, Dorset SP7 8JE
(01747 850820/
www.england-in-particular.info).*
This innovative arts and environment
charity has a range of projects aimed at
involving local people in appreciating
and recording their environment, often
working with artists, poets and
musicians. Many of their projects are
based in the countryside, but their 'local
distinctiveness' campaign has a lot to
say to Londoners.

ENGLISH HERITAGE
*23 Savile Row W1F 2ET
(020 7973 3000).*
English Heritage takes care of the
gardens at Kenwood House, Marble
Hill and Eltham Palace. There are also
small restoration grants available to
owners of Grade I or II listed
properties.

GARDEN HISTORY SOCIETY
*70 Cowcross Street EC1 (020 7608
2409/www.gardenhistorysociety.org).*
Series of informative lectures on all
aspects of garden history, right up to

the present day – plus other events and
an annual newsletter.

HDRA (HENRY DOUBLEDAY
RESEARCH ASSOCIATION)
*The Organic Association, Ryton Organic
Gardens, near Coventry, Warwickshire
CV8 3LG (02476 303517/
www.hdra.org.uk).*
The gardening arm of the Soil
Association (see opposite), geared to
smaller-scale gardeners. Its show
gardens demonstrating the latest
organic growing methods are a must to
visit, while the Heritage Seed Library
offers members a chance to grow and
help keep alive rare and often ancient
varieties of fruit and vegetable seeds.
Free enquiry service for members.

THE HERB SOCIETY
*Sulgrave Manor, Sulgrave, Banbury,
Oxfordshire OX17 2SD (01295 768899/
www.herbsociety.co.uk).*
The national association for herb
lovers; members can attend special
lectures, outings and other events and
receive a quarterly magazine.

LIVING SPACES
*(0845 600 3190/
www.living-spaces.org.uk).*
Relatively new government-launched
scheme that aims to help local people
clean up and make good use of
neglected urban green spaces. The
scheme was set up in 2003 in the light
of a report by the government's green
spaces task force, which shows that
reviving urban green spaces does more
for quality of life than almost anything
else and acts as a catalyst for further
community initiatives. Grants of
£1000–£100,000 are available, and a

trained 'enabler' will be appointed to draw up an action plan and advise the start-up group.

THE MAUSOLEA AND MONUMENTS TRUST
24 Hanbury Street E1 6QR (020 7608 1441/www.mausolea-monuments.org.uk).
Excellent and somewhat eccentric charity striving to preserve tombs and other monuments throughout the country. Life membership is free but donations are always welcome.

NATIONAL GREENSPACE
Caversham Court, Church Road, Reading RG4 7AD (0118 946 9060/ www.greenspace.org.uk).
Formerly the Urban Parks Forum. The organization to contact with concerns about your local park or green space. There is a London branch (▶ 261), but this office is more likely to be manned.

THE NATIONAL PLANT COLLECTIONS
The Stable Courtyard, RHS Garden Wisley, Woking, Surrey GU23 6QP (01483 211465/www.nccpg.org.uk).
Charity that works to preserve the country's plant heritage by building up collections – or 'living libraries' – of different types of plants, many varieties of which are already lost, or in danger of being lost. The National Council for the Conservation of Plants and Gardens (NCCPG) runs the scheme, through which ordinary gardeners can apply to become 'holders' of a collection. Many collections are held in and around London, and some may be visited by appointment. Plant sales, talks, garden outings and information exchange are other benefits to members.

NATIONAL SOCIETY OF ALLOTMENT AND LEISURE GARDENERS
Odell House, Hunters Road, Corby, Northants NN17 5JE (01536 266576/www.nsalg.demon.co.uk).
Champions of our remaining allotment sites and the people to contact to find out about the nearest allotment sites in your area.

THE SOIL ASSOCIATION
Bristol House, 40–56 Victoria Street, Bristol BS1 6BY (0117 929 0661/ www.soilassociation.org).
Any committed organic gardener should be a member of this worthy society, whose name goes back to the main principle behind organic gardening: feed the soil, not the plant. Members receive the three-times-yearly *Living Earth* magazine and a *Truth About Food* booklet.

SOUTHERN WATER
(0845 278 0845/ www.southernwater.co.uk).
Offers advice on saving water in the garden, with an online list of 'water-efficient' plants . They will also fit you with a water meter if you use a sprinkler.

THE TREE COUNCIL
71 Newcomen Street SE1 1YT (020 7407 9992).
Umbrella organization promoting the importance and care of trees in the environment with annual campaigns and the national tree warden scheme run with local authorities. Can pass enquirers on to the right member organization to help with specific tree queries or problems.

GARDEN DESIGNERS
AND SERVICE PEOPLE

Garden Designers

The best way to find a garden designer is on the recommendation of someone whose sense of style you share and whose opinion you respect. Failing that, you can ring the Society of Garden Designers on 01989 566695 (www.sgd.org.uk) for a free list of qualified garden designers (too many London members to list here), or ask in your local garden centre, where many locally based designers may advertise their services. Try to see at least one example of their work first-hand; photographs may not show the standard of finish, which is crucial, particularly in minimalist contemporary designs. The following list of mainly London-based designers, though by no means exhaustive, embraces a huge variety of styles, approaches and budgets. Most will come out for an initial consultancy (some with a standard charge). Though their quotes will probably sound enormous, you do (as with interior design) make some savings through employing a designer, as they can often obtain materials and services at a reduced charge. Plus they take over the hassle of dealing with contractors. If you cannot afford to employ a designer for the entire project, you can still benefit from booking a consultation and commissioning a scale drawing of the scheme that most appeals to you. This can then be given to your own contractor, or you can use it to carry out the work yourself.

AVANT GARDENER
16 Winders Road SW11 3HE
(020 7978 4253).
James Fraser left his native New Zealand more than twenty years ago and set up Avant Gardener, which is fast building a reputation for its exciting use of sub-tropical plants and reclaimed wood. His own garden, which is open under the NGS (▶ 263) is a unique place, combining the hardier exotics, ornamental grasses and some of his favourite plants from his homeland with chunky wooden boardwalks and fences like abstract artworks. Key to Avant Gardener's approach is the fact that Fraser imports and propagates his own plants at his private nursery in Battersea.

B+B UK
1 Prince of Wales Passage, 117 Hampstead Road NW1 3EF
(020 7387 9214).
This modern-minded landscape design practice tackles everything from small London gardens to large-scale town-planning projects. Partner Jonathan Bell has extended his own London home beautifully to include a conservatory-style kitchen and a covetably simple 'glass box' shed, which he uses as a study.

JILL BILLINGTON
100 Fox Lane N13 4AX
(020 8886 0898).
A background in fine art and sculpture comes through in Jill Billington's imaginative garden designs, and she is particularly innovative when it comes to small gardens, as showcased in her book *Really Small Gardens* (RHS/ Quadrille). The depth of her plant knowledge is also impressive.

JINNY BLOM
LANDSCAPE DESIGN
43 Clerkenwell Road EC1M 5RS
(020 7253 2100).
Since her profile was raised by the collaboration with Prince Charles at the Chelsea Flower Show a few years ago, much of Jinny Blom's time is now taken up with the sort of project involving confidentiality agreements and large estates in Gloucestershire. However, she will still turn her hand to London gardens if the ideas and budget are right, and her trademark fusion of contemporary design with wild-looking, often aromatic planting makes for some very exciting spaces.

BLOSSOM
43 Casewick Road SE27 (020 8670 8065 or 07939 153703/
blossomgarden@hotmail.com).
Sarah Walsh and Katherine Kearns were once fellow plot-holders on my allotment site and now have a thriving design business that aims to blend a practical approach with a passion for plants and contemporary design. Their 'Garden for Modern Lovers' at the 2003 Hampton Court Palace Flower Show was well-received and gained them a fair bit of media

attention. Sensitivity to wildlife is another key concern.

CHRISTOPHER BRADLEY-HOLE
55 Southwark Street SE1 1RU
(020 7357 7666).
Well known for his award-winning contemporary gardens at the Chelsea Flower Show and elsewhere and for his stylish use of pared-down modern materials with atmospheric plantings, including ornamental grasses and bearded iris. His book *The Minimalist Garden* (Mitchell Beazley) shows the range of his designs, which include town gardens and roof terraces.

DECLAN BUCKLEY DESIGN
5 Laycock Street N1 1SN
(020 7226 3697/
www.buckleydesignassociates.com).
Declan Buckley's former career as a graphic designer comes over in the strong lines and pleasing proportions underpinning his garden designs. Exotic-looking plants are a passion: his own garden in Islington – sometimes open through the NGS (▶ 263) – looks more like the tropics than north London, with Buddha heads and a Sri Lankan monk's parasol hidden among the swishing bamboos, unusual palms and pseudopanax from New Zealand. He can transform a long narrow garden into a series of intriguing interlinked spaces, but has also designed roof terraces, balconies and even an outdoor bed (see page 50).

DEL BUONO GAZERWITZ
1 Leinster Square W2 4PL
(020 7243 6006)
Tommaso del Buono and Paul Gazerwitz have gained a reputation for

their striking designs, which manage to be contemporary while still respecting period settings. Their work in London has ranged from a 2½-acre garden in Hampstead to transforming a tiny south London back garden into a magical space with softly swishing grasses and a shimmering silver-leaf wall.

MAUREEN BUSBY
8 The Common W5 3TR
(020 8567 9060).
Award-winning gardens in traditional and contemporary styles, but with a particular interest in Japanese gardens. A Gold Medal and Best Small Garden winner at Hampton Court Palace Flower Show 2002, Ms Busby has been asked to create a Japanese show garden at the Chelsea Flower Show in 2004.

GEORGE CARTER
(01362 668130).
Lives in Norfolk not London, but has designed many London gardens in his distinctive, formal-with-a-twist style. He now designs a lot of large country gardens, but his theatrical approach translates well into smart, stylish, low-maintenance gardens or courtyards, with or without his trademark clever two-dimensional urns and other ornaments.

MYLES CHALLIS
(020 8556 8962).
One of the first garden designers to capitalize on the London microclimate by championing the use of hardy and semi-hardy exotic plants. Now works mainly outside London (as curator of the excellent Living Rainforest Centre near Newbury), but could be tempted back to town by the right project.

PAUL COOPER
(01544 230374).
Avant-garde designer who cooks up some really kooky designs, using glass, plastic, metal and fibre optics to create truly modern gardens that sometimes shock as much as they delight: he even created a football-lover's garden, complete with shed striped in the team's colours, for a gardener in Battersea.

LAARA COPLEY-SMITH
(020 8933 1344).
Creative and professional practice that has carried out some stunning projects, mainly in west London. Classical formal schemes with a modern, sometimes minimalist twist, using contemporary materials such as brushed sheet steel for sculptural water features and subtly coloured lighting.

COUTURE GARDENS
Islington (020 7254 9462/
www.couturegardens.com,
couturegardens@amserve.com).
Ruth Collier's portfolio for Couture Gardens is as stylish as it sounds, and her background in film and theatre design means she enjoys working in a wide range of styles. She has transformed a dingy basement area in King's Cross with mirrors, tree ferns and a stunning mural of an arum lily, and brought the breezy charm of the seaside to a Hampstead roof terrace with swishing grasses planted in old wooden packing cases. She also runs courses in urban gardening (▶ 277).

JASON DE GRELLIER PAYNE
(020 8444 3964/www.jdgp.com).
Over the past sixteen years, this young designer has built up quite a

reputation for creating magical gardens using some of the more unusual exotic-looking plants (many coming from Chile and New Zealand) that thrive in the London microclimate. His gardens are by no means just a collection of exotica, however – he likes to make a journey around the garden a real voyage of exploration, with hidden surprises that cannot be glimpsed from the house. A large evergreen component ensures that his designs look good all the year round.

JOANNA HERALD AT HORTUS
(020 8297 0555).
The creator of the wonderful Hortus shop (▶ 244) is a designer of contemporary and classic town gardens with a touch of romance and originality. Designs for 'outdoor living' a speciality.

GAVIN JONES
(rochelle@macmail.com).
The inspired artist who helped create the Cameron Community Gardens in Bow (▶ 178) also works as a consultant in community garden design and alternative streetscapes.

LANDSCAPE DESIGN LTD
71 Egerton Gardens SW3 2BY
(020 7584 7583).
When not on TV (as the BBC's *Curious Gardeners*), writing wonderful books, such as *Gardens for the Future* (Conran Octopus) or working in America and Japan, Guy Cooper and Gordon Taylor might be tempted by a London garden project – adventurous, modern-minded clients only!

ARABELLA LENNOX-BOYD
45 Moreton Street SW1V 2NY
(020 7931 9995).
One of the *grandes dames* of British garden design, Lady Lennox-Boyd is much in demand among the aristocracy both here and on the Continent, and also numbers rock stars such as Sting among her clients. Though much of her work is on huge country estates, her elegant, classical style translates well to smaller sites, and she will turn her hand to a Knightsbridge courtyard – for a price, of course. Her beautiful book *Designing Gardens* (Frances Lincoln) is a good showcase for her style.

TODD LONGSTAFFE-GOWAN LANDSCAPE DESIGN
43 Clerkenwell Road EC1M 5RS
(020 7253 2100).
A respected historian of London gardens – his *The London Town Garden 1700–1840* (Yale), is superbly knowledgable and he is also Gardens Advisor at Hampton Court Palace – Todd Longstaffe-Gowan has turned his hand to latterday London gardens of all sizes, from the newly redesigned grounds of Aubrey House (the largest private garden in London after Buckingham Palace) to a beautiful fernery in the dark narrow back yard of his own east London house.

ARNE MAYNARD GARDEN DESIGN
Clerkenwell House, 125 Golden Lane EC1Y OTJ (020 7689 8100/ www.arne-maynard.com).
Sense of place is everything to this sensitive contemporary designer, whether he is working in the depths of the countryside or in a classic long

London garden; he is not afraid to refer to the 'soul' of the garden, which he seeks in a balance between the house, landscape or surroundings, carefully chosen plants and the dreams and identity of the owner. His sought-after designs fuse a traditional sense of order with a contemporary aesthetic and sensibility. His beautiful book, *Gardens with Atmosphere* (Conran Octopus) features some case histories to illustrate his style and approach.

HARRIETTE MARSHALL
South London (020 7274 3760 or 07903 369960).
Although she is still relatively new to the garden design scene, Ms Marshall's 'Inside Out' garden won a silver-gilt medal in the City Gardens category at the 2003 Chelsea Flower Show. She enjoys working in different styles, from the modern, almost minimalist aesthetic of her Chelsea garden to more traditional designs around period houses using York stone and formal planting. Gardens for families are becoming a speciality.

ANN MOLLO
Notting Hill (020 7603 3762).
On the strength of her own award-winning garden – a romantic tangle of roses, lilies and gothic arbours – Ann Mollo has become a designer of gardens in a similar 'one hundred per cent romantic' style. Her previous career as the art director for films such as *The French Lieutenant's Woman* makes for a theatrical style, with trellis, arches, obelisks and arbours to give the gardens structure over the winter.

LAURA MORLAND
61 Brixton Water Lane SW2 1PH (020 7733 9681/ www.lmgardens.com).
Garden designs that look good all year round, even in the depths of winter, are Laura Morland's special passion. In a framework of green and interesting winter shapes, she combines unusual and well-tried plants to create summer beauty – her sensitivity to colour and texture will appeal to those who care deeply about such subtleties. She also understands the time demands on busy Londoners and endeavours to make her designs easy to care for.

ANTHONY NOEL
(020 7736 2907).
The man who pioneered the painting of pots and sheds in blue and white stripes has now moved on to grander things, but his background in the theatre is still in evidence in the light-hearted elegance of his designs. Having transformed two tiny London gardens of his own, he knows the challenges of city spaces first-hand, and his quirky sense of style and humour is refreshing.

DAN PEARSON
80C Battersea Rise SW11 1EH (020 7924 2518).
One of the most sensitive plantsmen in the business, with a feeling for place that works whether rolling hills or tower blocks are the backdrop. Designs fewer London gardens now, and prefers to work with architects from the beginning of a project. His community garden at Bonnington Square (▶ 157) – created with James Fraser (▶ 268) – is a good place to get an impression of his use of plants and (often) reclaimed materials, and his gardens around the

Millennium Dome were one of the few good things about it.

CHRISTOPHER PICKARD
11 Tanners Yard, 239 Long Lane SE1 4PY (020 7378 7537).
An established professional consultancy priding itself on creative, innovative and elegant results. Mr Pickard is also Principal of the Pickard School of Garden Design (▶ 278).

RHIZOME
(020 8677 5394).
Designers and builders of town gardens, with specialist skills in lighting, irrigation and water features.

HARRIET SCOTT AND TEAM AT R. K. ALLISTON
173 New King's Road SW6 4SW (0845 130 5577).
The classic yet contemporary style of the shop and its products is reflected in the sort of design work carried out by the owner, Harriet Scott, and her team. Though she also designs large country estates, her style translates well to the small London gardens and courtyards owned by many of the drop-in clients. The company prides itself on a quick efficient service – most London projects are completed in two or three weeks.

JANE SEABROOK
(020 7229 5657).
More than forty years designing gardens in the capital mean that Ms Seabrook really knows what she is doing with even the most seemingly unprepossessing of sites: tiny back yards and windswept roof terraces are a speciality. Now semi-retired, she is still willing to take on commissions, and to assist with planting plans and consultancy on an hourly basis.

ROBERTO SILVA
9 Kelross Road N5 2QS (www.silvalandscapes.com).
Some truly stunning contemporary designs including a much-photographed London garden featuring a curving drystone wall that snakes, Andy Goldsworthy-like, through the middle of the garden. Will make your garden into a living, ever-changing, contemporary artwork.

LUCY SOMMERS
(020 8802 1662).
Based in north London, Lucy Sommers really enjoys getting to grips with her clients' personalities and reflecting them in the garden. This means that her designs can range from swathes of naturalistic planting in gravel to highly theatrical creations using sculpture, murals and figurative topiary.

JOE SWIFT AT THE PLANT ROOM
47 Barnsbury Street N1 1TP (020 7700 6766/www.plantroom.co.uk).
The shop front has now closed, but this address, with its stylish little garden out the back, is still the base for Joe Swift's garden design business. You might think of him as a TV star, but his garden designs are clever and contemporary, with lots of bright colour and an emphasis on integrating family life within a strong design. There are lots of examples in his book *The Plant Room* (BBC).

TOM STUART-SMITH
LANDSCAPE DESIGN
*43 Clerkenwell Road EC1M 5RS
(020 7253 2100).*
Tom Stuart-Smith will be known to
many for his award-winning Chelsea
Flower Show gardens – his 2003
garden was quite rightly judged Best
in Show, and illustrated his distinctive
juxtaposition of exquisite modern
meadow planting with simple,
almost minimalistic hard landscaping
and water.

HELEN TINDALE
Basement Flat, 32 Chalcot Square NW1.
With her erstwhile business partner
Karena Batstone (now based in
Bristol), Helen Tindale was
responsible for some fantastic
contemporary London gardens
featuring decking platforms, rendered
and coloured concrete, innovative
planting in the 'new perennial' style,
funky lighting and thoughtful features
for children. A style that perfectly
complements the cool, uncluttered
contemporary interior.

CLEVE WEST
*Navigator House, 60 High Street,
Hampton Wick, Surrey KT1 4DB
(020 8977 3522).*
An imaginative contemporary
approach, as shown in his work
featured frequently in magazines and
on television. Guaranteed quirkiness
and stylishness whether for a large-
scale project – such as his contribution
to the London Wetlands Centre
(▶ 216) – or just a few pots on a
balcony. Creates harmonious planting
schemes that are sensitive to the site.

STEPHEN WOODHAMS
*378 Brixton Road SW9 7AW (020 7346
5656/www.woodhams.co.uk).*
For a while Woodhams was unrivalled
as *the* young contemporary garden
designer and is still much sought after
by pop stars and design-conscious
bankers, etc. Trendy hard landscaping
is his thing – he can transform even the
tiniest roof terrace with galvanized
metal, glass and neon, but his planting
is becoming more skilful and
innovative, too. Definitely not
for traditionalists.

PAMELA WOODS AT
SACRED GARDENS
*(01453 885903/
www.sacredgardens.u-net.com).*
The only garden designer whose work is
almost exclusively geared to the sacred
and spiritual, Pamela Woods is the
woman to approach if you fancy
transforming your garden into a
spiritual haven or leafy sanctuary for
meditation, contemplation or relaxation.
Based in Gloucestershire, she does a
good deal of work in London, and her
style is showcased in her award-winning
book *Gardens for the Soul* (Conran
Octopus). Workshops in sacred garden
design are also available (▶ 279).

DIANA YAKELEY
(020 7609 9846).
Understated elegance is Diana Yakeley's
style, as showcased in her own
Islington garden – a symphony in
shades of green and white, with discreet
changes in levels and an innovative use
of hard materials such as blue-grey
engineering blocks. She is an interior
designer also, and her book *Indoor
Gardening* (Arum) is full of clever ideas.

GARDEN CONSTRUCTION AND MAINTENANCE

Again, the best recommendations are by word of mouth – or check in your local garden centre where companies and individuals may put up cards. Services range from upmarket maintenance companies with large teams of liveried staff to locally based individuals, and charges will vary accordingly. The British Association of Landscape Industries (BALI) (02476 690333/www.bali.co.uk) has a directory of certified companies, to be on the safe side. The following is just a small selection based on my own contacts and research.

CAPITAL GARDENS LANDSCAPES
(0800 7834010).
Businesslike service offered by Capital Gardens, who own several large garden centres in and around London.

FLOWER POWER
(07887 704404).
Two-woman team filling the gap between a major redesign service and pure maintenance: they may take on a clearance job and end up perking up a shrub border or making a wildlife area. 'Local, friendly and reasonable.'

HEWITT LANDSCAPES
(020 7622 9525/
www.hewittlandscapes.co.uk).
General hard landscape construction and garden maintenance.

KITESCAPES (ROBERT KITE)
(020 7738 6512 or 07931 899178).
General construction and hard landscaping (not decking).

THE LONDON POND DOCTOR
(NICHOLAS MEADE)
(01986 873733)
For upkeep and maintenance of urban wildlife ponds.

PATHFINDER
(01784 482677).
Mike Taylor, who heads the Pathfinder team, has worked on award-winning Chelsea gardens with the likes of Arabella Lennox-Boyd and comes well recommended.

SILCHRIS
(07946 221532).
All gardening jobs undertaken by green-minded professional qualified gardeners: clear-ups and maintenance, turfing, planting, brickwork, terraces, window boxes etc. 'No job too small.'

WWW.
THEWINDOWBOXCOMPANY.COM
For custom-made window boxes and other unusual horticultural gifts.

TREE SURGEONS

Ring the Arboricultural Association (01794 368717) for a free list of reputable tree surgeons and registered consultants in your area. Or download information from their website www.trees.org.uk, and click on tree surgeons. Prices vary widely depending on the scale of the work needed. The Association can also offer advice over the telephone and career packs and advice on courses in arboriculture. Your local council will have a tree department and tree officers, who may be able to offer advice, but they will be concerned mainly with street trees. The following tree surgeons will undertake work throughout the capital:

BOB YOUNG
SE27 (020 8761 5187).
Small-scale tree surgery, all aspects of pruning, hedge-laying, coppicing and woodland skills.

CITY SUBURBAN
SE14 (020 7277 9999).

JAY VENN
NW10 (020 8968 3265).
Aboricultural consultant and garden design.

ROOTS TREE SURGERY
N19 (020 7281 3802).

TOMLINSON TREE SURGEONS
N6 (020 8342 8679).

COMMUNITY GARDEN ASSISTANCE

BTCV (▶ 265)

GROUNDWORK TRUST
1 Kennington Road SE1 7QP (020 7922 1230/www.groundwork.org.uk).
Environmental regeneration charity that works in partnership with local people, local authorities and businesses. There are fifty local trusts; the London one can put you in touch with community projects in your area and give advice on grants and aid with your own community idea.

GAVIN JONES (▶ 271)

LIVING SPACES (▶ 266)
(0845 600 3190).
New £30 million government scheme set up to help local residents improve green spaces in their area with the aid of grants and a trained 'enabler'.

LEARNING ABOUT GARDENING

Gardening Courses

The organizations listed below offer a wide range of courses in all aspects of gardening from history and conservation to garden design, practical horticulture and horticultural therapy. Another approach would be to buy a copy of *Floodlight* (the directory of London-based evening and part-time classes), which lists a huge number of classes in all aspects of gardening in colleges and other centres all over the capital. City & Guilds modules and courses in general gardening and garden design (at various levels) are offered, along with more specialized classes in everything from garden history to allotment and organic gardening, propagation, topiary and water. Browse through and highlight the courses of interest in places that are accessible to you. Your local garden centre may also be able to advise on locally available courses.

THE ARCHITECTURAL ASSOCIATION
36 Bedford Square WC1B 3ES (020 7887 4067/www.aaschool.ac.uk/clg).
Europe's leading programme in Landscape and Garden Conservation taught as a Diploma (two years day release) or an MA (one year full time). Includes surveying, researching, analysing, evaluating, protecting and managing designed landscapes.

CAPEL MANOR COLLEGE
Bullsmoor Lane, Enfield, Middlesex EN1 4RQ (020 8366 4442/www.capel.ac.uk).
Full and part-time courses leading to nationally recognized qualifications in horticulture, groundsmanship, garden design and history, arboriculture and environmental studies – based in the beautiful gardens (▶ 197) or at other centres throughout London. Advice sessions, activity days and open mornings are held several times a year when prospective students can come and discuss courses with staff and enjoy a tour of the gardens.

RUTH COLLIER OF COUTURE GARDENS
Islington (020 7254 9462/ www.couturegardens.com/ couturegardens@amserve.com).
Garden designer renowned for her innovative approach to problem areas often encountered by city gardeners offers short courses in all aspects of urban garden design from her studio in Islington. There is usually a course of six days to Design Your Own Garden – see the website for current details.

ENGLISH GARDENING SCHOOL
66 Royal Hospital Road, SW3 4HS (020 7352 4347/ www.englishgardeningschool.co.uk).
The crème de la crème of London gardening courses, held at the beautiful Chelsea Physic Garden (▶ 150). Part-time one-year diploma courses in garden design, practical horticulture, plants and plantsmanship and botanical illustration; short courses in a variety of aspects of garden design – all taught by tip-top nationally known names. Distance learning courses also available.

INCHBALD SCHOOL OF DESIGN
32 Eccleston Square SW1V 1PB (020 7730 5508/www.inchbald.co.uk).
Principally an interior design school, but now offering a respected MA and Postgraduate diploma in garden design, certificates in garden design and short courses in garden design drawing techniques.

KLC SCHOOL OF DESIGN
The Chambers, Chelsea Harbour SW10 0XF (020 7376 3377/ www.klc.co.uk).
Offers a one-year diploma in garden design, plus shorter certificate courses, CAD technical drawing classes and a one-week full-time introductory course in garden design, plus several open learning courses in aspects of garden design and horticulture.

PICKARD SCHOOL OF
GARDEN DESIGN
(01785 859179).
Part-time London-based diploma course in garden design, affiliated to the RHS. One day a week over one academic year or one evening a week over two years, structured to provide a thorough training in the science and art of garden design for those who wish to design at a professional level. The philosophy of garden design as a problem-solving process is key to the approach here.

ROYAL BOTANIC GARDENS, KEW
(020 8332 5000).
Kew's three-year diploma in horticulture is renowned around the world and competition is fierce for places – two years' practical experience with a recognized gardening organization is a prerequisite for candidates. Other training opportunities include the Rotational Training Programme, a three-month unpaid internship and a new volunteer pilot scheme starting up in 2004.

THRIVE
(0118 988 5688/www.thrive.org.uk).
The opportunities for training here are in two kinds (see longer entry on page 263. People with learning difficulties or other mental or physical disabilities can attend a Thrive project and learn gardening and other skills (sometimes leading to a qualification). Others wishing to gain experience of working with gardening and horticulture as a means of therapy can attend as volunteers – people with either gardening, teaching or therapeutic experience are preferred.

PAMELA WOODS AT SACRED
GARDENS DESIGN
(01453 885903/ www.sacredgardens.u-net.co.uk).
For gardeners interested in turning their urban garden into an outdoor sanctuary, workshops are offered by the only designer specializing in sacred gardens. Courses are usually based in Gloucestershire.

Author's note

While every effort has been made to check and double-check all the details and opening hours, etc., at the time of going to press, such information is, of course, subject to sudden change. To avoid disappointment, it is advisable to ring and check, where possible, before setting off on a visit. If you should spot any changes, mistakes or omissions, please send details to the publishers, to help us keep future editions of the book up to date.

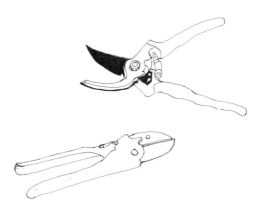

INDEX

Page numbers in **bold** indicate the main entry in Part Two.
Page numbers in *italic* indicate 'Places to go for inspiration' in Part One.